ALLOCATION
OF INCOME
WITHIN THE
HOUSEHOLD

Edward P. Lazear and
Robert T. Michael

The University of Chicago Press
Chicago and London

EDWARD P. LAZEAR is Isidore and Gladys J. Brown Professor of Urban and Labor Economics
in the Graduate School of Business at the University of Chicago and editor of the *Journal of
Labor Economics*. ROBERT T. MICHAEL is professor in the Department of Education and the
College at the University of Chicago and director of the National Opinion Research Center.

The University of Chicago Press, Chicago 60637
The University of Chicago Press, Ltd., London
© 1988 by The University of Chicago
All rights reserved. Published 1988
Printed in the United States of America

97 96 95 94 93 92 91 90 89 88   54321

Library of Congress Cataloging in Publication Data

Lazear, Edward P.
  Allocation of income within the household.

  Bibliography: p.
  Includes index.
  1. Income distribution. 2. Child support.
3. Households—Economic aspects. I. Michael, Robert T.
II. Title.
HB523.L39   1988   339.2′2   87-35837
ISBN 0-226-46966-2

Contents

Acknowledgments

This project has been supported by grant no. P50 HD14256 from the National Institute of Child Health and Human Development (NICHD). We wish to thank V. Jeffery Evans of NICHD for his encouragement throughout this project. Our research assistant on this project, Elizabeth Peters, contributed substantially to its quality by her many hours of careful and thoughtful work. Her effort is gratefully acknowledged. We also thank William Chan for additional research assistance. Reuben Gronau, Gary Becker, Sherwin Rosen, and James P. Smith provided useful suggestions on the manuscript, and James D. Smith gave valuable comments on chapter 7.

One

Introduction

Surprisingly, the allocation of the household's income among its members is not a major topic of study in economics. In fact, it is common practice in many contexts to assume an equal or uniform distribution of income within the family or household. That assumption is too seldom challenged. While the distribution of income across households or the distribution of earnings across earners is studied meticulously, the within-family distribution is seemingly of little interest and often ignored. But from casual and personal observation, one knows that the household does not always distribute income or other resources evenly among its members. While one might expect the distribution to be efficient and, one hopes, equitable, there is no rationale (as well as no evidence) for assuming that it is in fact distributed evenly. Yet the myth persists in economic modeling of well-being and in many social policy contexts that once we know the level of resources available to the household, that is all we need to know.

We stress in this book that it may be important to know about the allocation of resources within the household, and we argue that the first step in learning about this allocation is to admit that we do not know very much about it. We have taken a small second step in this monograph by providing some evidence about the allocation of money resources between adults and children in the household. There are many subsequent steps to be taken. There are enough other recent efforts like our own to offer encouragement that this subject will receive the attention we think it deserves.

Chapter 2 details how several major strands of economic literature have ignored the within-household distribution of income and notes as well a few studies that have addressed this issue. There are admittedly big difficulties in ascertaining how households divide up their income among members. We think these difficulties, rather than any convincing theoreti-

1

cal demonstration of the lack of importance of the issue, explain why so little attention is devoted to this topic. We discuss five of these difficulties: (1) measurement over the life cycle (because some spending is lumpy and age related); (2) measurement of apportionment of private goods (not easily observed; Who used the bar of soap?); (3) measurement of the appropriate allocation of public goods in the household (which family member got what amount of the expenditure on the electricity or on the newspaper or on the apartment's doorkeeper?); (4) measurement of the allocation of nonpecuniary resources (such as leisure time or use of the extra room in the house); and (5) measurement of family externalities (i.e., measurement of the joy or satisfaction to one member from the consumption or gain in well-being of another family member; since family members care about each other, what one member gains is not a total loss to the others). Our study addresses the first three of these difficulties, but unfortunately we have not dealt with the final two.

In chapter 3 we use the 1972–73 Consumer Expenditure Survey (CES) descriptively and find that among large composite goods, such as clothing and housing, many characteristics of the family affect spending patterns. The family's level of income, the education of the head, location of residence, and race influence the broad outlines of spending. As income and education increase, total spending rises. The size of the total expenditure is bigger in cities than in rural areas, highest in the West region and lowest in the North Central region, and substantially lower for blacks than for whites. We find that the more educated spend proportionately more on services and housing and much less, proportionately, on durable goods, while other family characteristics also shift the composition of the consumption bundle (see table 3.4).

The employment status of the husband and wife also shift the spending pattern—more employment is associated with proportionately more spending on services and less on food (see table 3.5). The characteristics of the child appear to affect spending as well—more is spent in total as the child grows older and if the child is employed; more is spent proportionately on food and less proportionately on services if the child is male and as the child grows older (see tables 3.2 and 3.3).

These shifts tell us nothing per se about the allocation of expenditures within the household itself. They do tell us, however, that both the characteristics of the household (e.g., its location) and the characteristics of household members (e.g., age, education, and employment status of the adults; gender, age, and employment status of the children) affect the composition of the consumption bundle. These general facts are not new. One can cite numerous studies of various data sets that show analogous patterns of spending related to household characteristics. These facts imply a more fluid, dynamic environment in the household than would be expected if an automatic uniform distribution of income among the household members were maintained.

On the one hand, experience convinces us that spending is not uniform or equal across household members, so the kind of evidence just cited (and found as well in systems of demand equations in which household members' characteristics are included) is far from surprising—it is indeed rather mundane. But on the other hand, economists in their models and policy pronouncements frequently act as if all household members are in the same boat economically. If all household members are treated equally, how can we explain that households with employed children spend more on durable and nondurable goods, or that those with male rather than female children spend less on services? Whatever explanation we offer, it implies that the household is allocating its resources among members in some nonrandom and not-necessarily-equal manner. Knowing more about that within-household allocation may be important for understanding all kinds of mechanisms that affect behavior. (For example, does the allocation of space for quiet privacy within the home help explain the differences in school or homework performance, as has been suggested by Land 1977?)

Chapter 3 also investigates in more detail the clothing expenditures on behalf of specific members of the household. A uniform distribution is certainly not found (see table 3.6, panel B). In a synthetic husband-wife-son-daughter family, for instance, the clothing expenditures are, respectively: $195, $253, $117, and $124 (or, normalized on the husband's expenditure, they are: 100, 130, 60, 64). In a husband-wife-one-child family the expenditures are $197, $251, and $139 (or normalized, 100, 127, 71), respectively. In a single-adult family the allocation is a bit more even: a mother-son-daughter family spends $185, $114, $139 (or, normalized on the mother's expenditure: 100, 62, 75), respectively.

We might point out that the inflation that has occurred since 1972–73 makes the actual dollar expenses in the data seem quite low. To convert the figures into 1986 units, the Consumer Price Index for the periods involved in this study is:

Year	CPI
1960	88.7
1961	89.6
1972	125.3
1973	133.1
1986	328.4

We use 89.2 for the 1960–61 period and 129.2 for the 1972–73 period, thus the 1960–61 dollars should be increased by a factor of 3.7 to convert them to today's (1986) dollars, and the 1972–73 dollars should be increased by a factor of 2.5.

If differences across families of different sizes reflect the changes within a family that accompany a change in size, then the addition of a child lowers the father's clothing expenditure from $209 by about $30 with the first child, lowers it an additional $21 with the second child, and by another $14 with the third child. Similarly, the mother's clothing expenditure is lowered from about $300 by $59 by the first child, by an additional $23 by the second child, and by another $35 by the third child. To complete the picture, the first child's clothing expenditure (assuming all existing children get the same) declines from $194 (with no siblings) by $52 with one sibling and by another $21 with a second sibling (see table 3.8). Another way to put the discrepancy in allocation is to consider the impact of a change in income on the clothing expenditure for each family member; the income elasticities are 0.69, 0.73, 0.30, 0.26, and 0.36 for clothing for husband, wife, baby, boy, and girl, respectively. All do not share equiproportionately in the additional income!

Chapter 4 investigates what can be learned about the distribution of welfare within the household from information about the distribution of expenditures among household members. Two extreme assumptions are contrasted, one in which each person is completely selfish and derives utility only from his own consumption and the other in which each person is completely loving and derives just as much satisfaction from the consumption by another family member as by himself. Regarding the decision about how the household resources are distributed, in the first extreme the power to allocate the household's resources is crucial, and the member with that power or that right gets a disproportionate share of the total resources. In the other extreme the allocation of the resources is quite irrelevant to all concerned. In the first extreme (complete selfishness) the allocation of resources or of expenditures does tell us something about the distribution of welfare. However, only if we assume the members all have the same utility function and that it is linear can we make a simple translation from the distribution of expenditures into the distribution of welfare.

One of the most important points in chapter 4 is that even under very strong restrictive assumptions about the absence of interdependence of preferences and the absence of public goods, strong assumptions are required about the individuals' utility functions to translate the evidence on spending patterns directly into evidence on welfare. Moreover, the fact that families choose to have children, presumably deriving welfare directly from having their children, makes the evidence on the distribution of spending patterns necessarily an incomplete picture of the distribution of welfare. Only under severely restrictive assumptions can we say much about the distribution of welfare among household members based on information about the distribution of expenditures.

A separate problem arises in evaluating the allocation of several goods among family members when the allocations are made in kind. The value to the recipient of a transfer may not be the same as its value to the giver. A piano lesson for the child illustrates the point well. Here too, if we wish to know about the distribution of welfare, we would have to know far more about the individuals' utility functions than we typically know. In some cases, such as baby-sitting, it is not even clear to whom the expenditure should be assigned in an allocative exercise, for one does not know even the direction of effect of the expenditure on the child's utility. Public goods pose similar problems. In general we are left with the conclusion that unless one specifies an individual's utility function, very little can be learned about the distribution of welfare from information about the distribution of expenditures.

Unfortunately, despite the frequency with which they are used in the economics literature, there is very little information available about utility functions to serve as a basis for assuming one functional form or another, one class of function or another. We have chosen to avoid imposing strong, arbitrary assumptions that would allow us to translate expenditures into welfare. Instead, we have assumed only the minimum necessary to partition expenditures into those spent on behalf of adults and those on behalf of children. Without imposing more structure than we feel should be imposed, we must eschew making statements about welfare. We can, however, make statements about the allocation of income among household members.

Even to make those statements it is necessary to partition the spending bundle among household members, and this requires several assumptions. For one thing, we focus on differences between spending on adults and on children without further detailing the allocation among the adults or among the children. We partition the spending bundle between the two groups, adults and children, and assume the adult expenditures are distributed equally among the adults and that the children each get an equal amount of the expenditures on children. Obviously, if our procedures are valid and our results at this level of disaggregation are of value, then subsequent, further decomposition within the adult group and within the children group could be undertaken.

In particular, our empirical work is derived from the accounting identity:

$$T = AC_A + KC_K,$$

where A and K are the number of adults and children in the household, C_A and C_K are the average expenditures on an adult and on a child in the household, and T is the total expenditure by the household. Two additional relationships are used: $\lambda(Z) = C_A/\tilde{C}_A$, with $\tilde{C}_A$ being the expenditures by the household on a set of observable items consumed exclusively by adults, namely expenditures on adult clothing, alcohol, and tobacco. This ratio is a function of a set of household characteristics, Z, that includes the education of the household head, the household's income, region of residence, race of head, and so forth. The crucial assumption is that the relation between the adult expenditure on clothing, alcohol, and tobacco and the adult expenditure on other items is not affected by the presence or number of children (i.e., the utility function is weakly separable).

The second relationship is $\phi(X) = C_K/C_A$. This is a statement of a behavioral relationship. The ratio of the expenditure per child to the expenditure per adult is expressed as a function of a vector of household characteristics, X, including the characteristics of the children in the household. Given an estimate of the function $\phi(X)$, the effect of various household characteristics on expenditures on children can be calculated.

By simple substitution into the accounting identity, T can be equated to a particular multiplicative relationship of the five elements, A, K, $\tilde{C}_A$, $\lambda(Z)$, and $\phi(X)$. The variables T, A, K, and $\tilde{C}_A$ are observable. Additionally, using households without children provides an estimate of $\lambda(Z)$ as well. This allows us to observe or estimate all of the relevant variables in households with children. The only remaining unknown is the linear relationship of interest, $\phi(X)$, and it is identified. Chapters 5 and 6 employ this procedure and estimate the function ϕ using the data from two separate Consumer Expenditure Surveys (CES) from 1972–73 (in chapter 5) and 1960–61 (in chapter 6).

Chapter 5 uses information on about 5,000 households without children and another 5,000 households with children to study the allocation of the total family expenditures between adults and children. Overall, these households spent on average about $38 per child for every $100 spent per adult. The estimate of $\phi(X)$ implies that a rise in the household income raises the expenditure on the child, as one would expect. It also indicates that the child gets less of any increase in income, both absolutely and relatively, than the adult. At the margin, an extra $1,000 in household income is spent as follows: about $90 on each child (for a total of about $200 on the 2.2 children in the household), about $260 on each adult (for a total of about $500 on the 1.93 adults), and the remaining $300 on taxes and savings (which may be allocated in a similar manner).

A rise in the education level of the head of the household raises the relative and absolute expenditure on the child, even when total income is held constant. When the income and the number of adults and children are permitted to vary as they do with education level, a household head with a high school education spends $40 per child for every $100 spent per adult, compared to a head with postcollege schooling who spends about $45 per child for every $100 spent per adult. The high school educated head spends about $1,280 per child compared to the more educated head who spends about $1,840 per child, or over 40 percent more absolutely. (Recall, that to find 1986 dollars one would multiply these dollar figures by 2.5.)

If the household has two employed adults, that also raises both the relative and absolute amounts spent per child. The relative figure is about $35 per child for every $100 per adult with one employed adult and up to $40 per child for every $100 per adult with two employed adults. In dollars, by one calculation reported in chapter 5, the household with one employed adult spends about $1,160 per child and the household with two spends about $1,400 per child.

Black households, holding other things constant, spend less per child relative to the adult, but blacks also tend to have lower incomes, fewer adults, and more children. When these characteristics are taken into account, the black household spends a little less per child than per adult, compared to the white household—about $36.50 per $100 per adult for blacks and $38.70 per $100 per adult for whites. Blacks spend less absolutely on each child—$1,020 per child for blacks and $1,300 per child for whites. However, because blacks have more children, a larger proportion of household expenditure goes to children in black households: about 33 percent in black households compared to about 30 percent on children in white households.

Rural households also spend less on children than on adults—only $31.70 on the child per $100 per adult for rural households compared to $39.70 per child per $100 per adult for nonrural households. They spend less absolutely as well—$914 per child for rural households compared to $1,340 per child for nonrural households.

There is evidence of substantial substitution between "quantity and quality," that is, between more expenditure per child in smaller households and less expenditure per child in larger households. An additional child reduces the average expenditure per child by about $215, but reduces the average expenditure per adult by $414 as well. The total expenditure on children does rise as the number of children increases.

A change in the number of adults in the household has a dramatic effect on the expenditure per child. Our estimate suggests that an additional adult added to an average household with 1.93 adults lowers the expenditure per child by about $881, when the household's income is held constant. Of course, the additional adult reduces the average expenditure per adult as well—by $709—but that is a much smaller percentage effect for an adult. This finding has important implications when one considers what happens to a family's expenditures upon the removal of an adult, say because of a marital dissolution. The reduction in the number of adults implies a sizeable increase in the proportion of the smaller family's income that goes to the children. If the smaller family also has a much lower level of income, the absolute amount going to the children may actually decline, but the parent left in that household suffers a far more dramatic relative (and absolute) decline in expenditure.

Chapter 5 also estimates the spending on a child from birth through high school age. At an annual household income of $15,000 (again recall that these figures are in 1972–73 level dollars and for 1986 levels you would multiply these figures by 2.5), a two-parent family spends about $25,700 (discounted at 10 percent) on a single child, about $41,900 on two children, and about $52,400 on three children. So the average expenditure falls from $25,700 to $21,000 to $17,500 per child as the number of children increases. Put differently, the incremental expenditure for each of the first three children is $25,700, $16,200, and $10,500, respectively, reflecting the fact that the marginal out-of-pocket expenses decline considerably. As household income rises, of course, the expenditure on children rises as well. For a two-adult, two-child household, the 18-year expenditure of $42,000 on the child at an income level of $15,000 rises to $104,000 at an income level of $50,000, but as stressed above, the expenditure on children does not keep pace proportionately with the change in income. As income in the example just given rises by 230 percent (from $15,000 to $50,000), the expenditure on the children rises by 150 percent.

Chapter 6 uses data from the 1960–61 survey on about 3,400 households without children and about 4,900 households with children. The same relationships are estimated for these data as for the data from 1972–73 used in chapter 5. The estimated average ratio of expenditures per child to the expenditure per adult is $40 per child for every $100 per adult. That figure is remarkably close to the $38 estimate in chapter 5. Although the expenditure per child rose by about 5 percent over the twelve years, the expenditure per adult rose by about 12 percent, so there was a slight decline over time in the relative spending per child. That is what we should expect, since real income rose markedly between the two surveys and the results in chapter 5 indicate that as income rises the share spent per child falls relative to the share per adult. That is just what transpired, apparently, on a small scale between 1960 and 1972.

In terms of the estimated effects of household characteristics, the income elasticity estimated on the 1960–61 data was 0.94, almost the same as the 0.90 estimated in the later data. The effect of the education of household head was again positive but weaker in the 1960 data. This was also true of the effect of a rural residence. The black household again appears to spend less per child than the nonblack household. The black household spends $30.40 per child for every $100 per adult, while the nonblack household spends $41.50; or, in absolute dollars the black household spends $506 per child while the white, with more than 50 percent more income, spends $864, about 70 percent more. (That $506 is $1,872 in 1986 terms.) While geographic region had no appreciable effect in the 1972–73 data, households in the South in the 1960–61 data spend less on children relatively ($32.20 per child for every $100 per adult, compared to $43.80 for a non-South household), and absolutely ($621 per child compared to $918 per child in the non-South).

An additional child again lowers the per child expenditure by $184 (about 22 percent) and lowers the per adult expenditure by $282. These figures are also rather similar to the percentage effects of an additional child in the 1972–73 data. An additional adult had a much smaller negative effect on spending on a child in the earlier year, lowering the per child expenditure by $265 or by 32 percent (compared to an effect of $881 or 69 percent in the 1972–73 data).

Chapter 7 uses the equations estimated in chapter 5 to compute the implied personal distribution of income based on Current Population Surveys (CPS) for 1970 and 1979. Given the chapter 5 equations that relate household characteristics to the apportionment of the household's income between adults and children, we use the large CPS surveys that have information on household income and household structure and characteristics to calculate the income of each household member.

One fact emphasized by this effort is that while the average household may spend about $38 per child for every $100 spent per adult, one-in-ten households have characteristics that imply they allocate less than $20 per child for every $100 spent per adult. Another 1-in-10 households allocate more than $55 per child for every $100 spent per adult (see table 7.2). So there is substantial dispersion in the relative treatment of children.

If one uses a conventional per capita income notion applied to the 1979 CPS data and asks about the characteristics of the lowest 10 percent of the income distribution, approximately 52 percent of those are children. If instead one uses our estimate of how income is allocated within the household and asks about the characteristics of the lowest 10 percent of the income distribution, approximately 82 percent of these are children. Similarly, if one looks at the top 10 percent of these two distributions, about 6 percent of this top decile are children using conventional per capita income measures, but less than 0.5 percent of the top decile are children using our estimation procedure (see table 7.6). We hasten to add a caveat: Remember that we said one cannot interpret these figures as reflecting welfare. Children are small and in many respects have small needs relative to adults. It is unclear to us that a comparison like the one we just reported is even useful to know—that is, that among the bottom 10 percent of the income distributed in the United States, 8.2 of every 10 people is a child. But then, if that is not useful, why is the more conventional measure of children in poverty any more so?

Chapter 8 is a detailed exploration of the implications of our study for child support payments in households that dissolve. It is argued that there is no use trying to disentangle alimony from child support. Unless the court or the payer can explicitly monitor how every dollar is spent in the receiving household, the fungibility of money prevents this distinction from being a useful one.

Given that it is the total level of expenditures that is important, chapter 8 presents a series of tables that suggest the appropriate payment from one parent to another according to a particular criterion. These payments depend on family size and structure, as well as on each family's income. Of course, most important is the criterion used to distribute income among family members. We discuss several possible criteria.

Initially, we examine what would happen if transfers were set to insure that the child consumed the same proportion of his parents' combined income after the divorce as before. This leads to two problems. First, by necessity, this criterion implies that although the child's consumption is maintained, the custodial parent loses relative to the noncustodial parent. Our investigation in chapter 5 indicates that a parent allocates a larger proportion of income to children in a one-adult household. This implies that the household income needed for the child to get to the target income leaves very little income for the custodial parent. With this criterion, the custodial parent almost certainly does not achieve a predivorce level of consumption. Additionally, with joint custody, there may be no feasible level of transfers that places the child back at his previous level of consumption.

This leads to the conclusion that the household unit, rather than the child, should be the relevant unit of analysis for the determination of transfers. The rule that we suggest and use extensively in chapter 7 is that the ratio of resources in the two households should be equal to the ratio of the weighted number of members, adjusted for age of members. This easily handles issues of joint custody. Since joint custody may involve fixed costs (e.g., a full-time bedroom may be maintained for a child who resides there only part-time), the formula is adjusted to take such costs into account.

The treatment of household income is a problem for a number of reasons. First, the tax rate implicit in the transfer scheme creates adverse incentives. Also, luck matters in the determination of income and should not be ignored. We propose a rule that amounts to assuming that variation in income near some predicted level is more likely to involve effort than luck, while big discrepancies in income level are likely to reflect luck not effort. This permits a mapping of observed income into income-for-transfer purposes that reduces adverse incentives on effort but permits both households to share the risks that are related to luck. This mapping requires a predicted income, which is a function of the individual's observable characteristics and earnings history over the years preceding the divorce.

Other family members who were not part of the original household may also contribute income to the new households. We discuss how their income might be treated. Because of fungibility, we suggest treating total income in the household as the relevant concept. This also avoids adverse incentive effects that would result if one member's income was taxed while the other's was not. Of course, our algorithm is sufficiently general so that any proportion of the other member's income (zero included) could be used to compute the income level on which transfers are based.

The appropriate way to deal with children with special needs, the timing of transfer payments (accelerated or constant), and other issues are also raised. The final product in chapter 8 is a series of tables that indicate the appropriate size of a transfer from a noncustodial parent to the custodial parent (or vice versa!) under various circumstances. A more generalized computer program to perform these calculations is also available from the authors.

Chapter 9 discusses the implications of our work for two long-standing topics—household size equivalence scales and estimates of the cost of a child—as well as the need for future research in a number of key areas.

Two

The Limitations of Existing Economic Literature

It has been taken for granted that some members of a family cannot
be rich while others are poor.

—Michael Young

There is an honored tradition in economics of ignoring the distribution of
income within the household. Attention is typically focused on the distribution of resources among families, households, earners, or consumer
units. In this chapter we argue that this tradition, although firmly established, is neither necessary nor wise.

We begin by noting some of the practical issues that are, or would be,
affected by knowing more about the within-family distribution of income.
We document how consistent the economic literature is in sidestepping this
topic and note a few important exceptions to this general approach. We
then discuss the nature of the difficulties in the empirical study of this
issue, which helps explain why it has received so little attention.

The Practical Issues

Questions about the distribution of income and well-being have been central to mainstream developments in economics. There is little need to justify an intellectual interest in the question of for whom the productive
capacity of the economy is engaged. The individualistic ethic that underlies the assumptions of modern economics implies an interest in the person, not simply in the family or household unit. Yet, in a number of matters of social policy, economists and others have acted as if the family unit,
not the individual, is at the heart of an issue, thereby conveniently skirting
the problem of what happens *within* the family.

We do not intend to argue for or against government regulations pertaining to what is private and thus to be left to the family's discretion and what
is not private and thus to be regulated, supervised, or controlled by the
state. But there are times when the state does intervene in intrafamily de-

12

cisions, justifiably or not, just as there are times when family members call upon the state to intervene, wisely or not. When this occurs, the state frequently must take a position on how resources within the family should be distributed. Such an intervention frequently takes place in a circumstance involving some pathology, but the state seems to act as if it is desirable to impose on the pathological case whatever is true in the more conventional, nonpathological family. Here is where our investigation may be useful. We suggest that the assumptions used by the agents of the state—the legislators, the social workers, the judges—about that conventional, normal, modal family are based on ignorance not fact, on convenience not evidence. They may be quite incorrect. Consider the following examples.

Much social concern is expressed for those in poverty. Because of our lack of information on the within-family distribution of income, poverty concepts overwhelmingly pertain to family or household units. For practical purposes the assumption is implicitly made that income is distributed uniformly within the household (or uniformly after adjustment for nutritional needs). There is essentially no information about, and apparently almost no concern about, the incidence of impoverishment among *individuals* within family units. A family unit is designated as either "in poverty" or "not in poverty" based on a family-conditioned concept of the poverty level. Once the number of households in poverty is measured, then, to estimate the number of *persons* in poverty, all members of those households in poverty are assumed to be in poverty, and no one else. How accurate or inaccurate is this estimate of the number of individuals who experience impoverished lives? We currently have no way of knowing.

Family law issues are another example of an arena where knowledge about the allocation of resources within the family would be useful. The new legal area of children's rights addresses the issue of the parents' right to choose the distribution of income or well-being within the family. The equitable disposition of the family's tangible resources upon dissolution of a marriage should, one would think, depend in some way upon the actual distribution of resources within the marriage. The practice of community property, or equal ownership of tangible assets, assumes that the property rights within a marriage are shared equally between the adults. Were that found not to be the norm, would that be the appropriate practice at the time of marital dissolution? Similarly, when estate taxes are levied at the time of the death of one family member, the practice in effect assumes a certain (usually uniform if not known to be otherwise) distribution of family assets, but with relatively little evidence on the actual nature of that distribution.

Government policies dealing with issues of both poverty and family law assume the equal distribution of family resources among its members (or at least its adult members). But is this assumption based on a justifiable norm? Here we must distinguish between two very different connotations of the term "norm." A norm is a standard that might be based on an ethical or moral judgment, or it might be based on modal or typical behavior. This book has nothing special to contribute to ethical or moral considerations, but it does provide evidence on what is typical behavior. To that extent it should help clarify issues of public social policy, such as taxation, transfer payments, and the regulation of property rights at the time of divorce. Aside from these specific applications, the information we provide has important implications for other social science research that may in turn affect social policy.

For example, knowing how resources are allocated within the family will help analysts judge economic trends over time. Suppose income allocation is systematically different in families of different sizes, or in families with two adults compared to families with one adult, or in families headed by a person of one age, education, ethnic, or religious group compared to another, or in wealthy families compared to poor families. Then, over time, changes in the distribution of the population by family size, by family structure, or by demographic or economic condition will affect the distribution of income or well-being among individuals. These changes will go undetected as long as intrafamily distribution is treated as an unknown variable about which social scientists have no interest.

In addition, if these allocation differences exist and are ignored, then causal or structural relationships in social science research will inevitably be incorrectly estimated. To illustrate, suppose that families systematically devote more resources to male children: if ignored, this practice could lead to incorrect inferences about sex discrimination in the labor market.

The common practice, in the face of so little evidence about the way resources are distributed within the family, is to assume a uniform distribution of resources among family members. Yet there is indisputable evidence that this assumption is not correct. At one extreme is the evidence of child abuse, deprived children, and battered spouses. By one estimate in 1973, about 0.5 percent of all American families physically abused a child. The American Medical Association has suggested that the battered child syndrome is likely to be "a more frequent cause of death than such well-recognized . . . diseases like leukemia, cystic fibrosis, and muscular dystrophy, and it may well rank with automobile accidents and the toxic and infectious encephalitides as causes of acquired disturbances of the central nervous system" (Light 1973, 199, 207).

Among the British working class between the wars, Young (1952) documents that housewives and children seemed to get a low percentage of the husband's income for their own and household expenses: the "housewives often did not know either what their husbands earned or how they spent their money" (1952, 308). It appeared "customary in working class families for husbands to give their wives a more or less fixed allowance, whatever the size of the family and whatever the change in their earnings" (1952, 314). Young concludes, caustically, "The bread-winners are often the meat-eaters" (1952, 305). These conclusions were not greatly modified by Young when he published *The Symmetrical Family* two decades later (Young and Willmott 1973). Land (1977) reviews British data on spending for food, clothing, and housekeeping and concludes, "The standard of living of individual members of the family may differ quite markedly and it cannot be assumed that all earning members pool their wages for the purchase of goods and services for the family as a whole" (1977, 173). Pahl (1980) surveys the evidence again and finds recent confirmation that many British wives do not know what their husbands earn and share in their family's income only through a housekeeping allowance set, by fiat, by the husband.

At the other extreme are examples of great sacrifice by parents for the education or health care of their child, or by family members for a goal (such as a career) of great importance to one family member or another. For example, Leopold Mozart did not allocate his family's resources evenly between his daughter, Nannerl, and her younger brother, Wolfgang (much to our pleasure). Differences in resource allocations exist at the extremes; there is no reason to suppose that they do not also differ along a continuum.

In short, casual but clear evidence indicates that incomes within families are not distributed uniformly. Indeed, the distribution of income among persons may in fact look quite different from the per capita income distribution constructed on the assumption of a uniform distribution of income within families.

The Economic Literature's Consistency

There is no lack of economic research explaining or describing the distribution of income. With remarkable consistency, however, that research focuses on the distribution of money income among recipients of income or among families or households and does not address the issue of distribution of income *within* families. The models of income distribution based on stochastic shocks, such as the theories of Champernowne (1973), Lydall (1968), Mandelbrot (1960), Aitchison and Brown (1957), and Roy (1950), address the positive skew in the distribution of income. All these studies take the conventional distribution of income as their object of focus, relying on proportionate or multiplicative random shocks to generate the observed skew. The human capital explanation for the distribution of income relies on wealth-maximizing investment behavior by individuals, but again, Becker (1975), Mincer (1970, 1974), Taubman (1975), and others are explaining the distribution of earnings among adults (usually men) in the labor force. A few recent studies look at the impact of a second earner on the distribution of family earnings (e.g., Smith 1979; Layard and Zabalza 1979; Gronau 1982), but here too no interest is expressed in the intrafamily distribution.

In study after study measuring the distribution of income, the phenomenon is drawn from data that preclude evidence on the distribution of income within households. The major data sources used to calculate the size distribution of income for the United States only provide information on family income or on individual earnings. Studies typically use Census or Current Population Survey (CPS) data (e.g., Mincer 1974; Chiswick and Mincer 1972; Schultz 1969; Miller 1966; Budd 1970; Paglin 1975; Kuznets 1975; Soltow 1960; Metcalf 1969), or Department of Commerce Bureau of Economic Analysis (BEA) data (e.g., Solow 1967; Schultz 1964; Goldsmith 1958; Budd 1970), or Internal Revenue Service (IRS) income statistics (e.g., Lydall 1959, for the U.K.; Lampman 1962; Smith and Franklin 1974). Indeed, the nature of the data has shaped the empirically oriented theories—both stochastic process models and human capital investment—toward the family income phenomena.

In theoretical contexts further removed from the data, the analysis does address the distribution of individual income, but these papers are of very little help in understanding the observed distributions (see, e.g., the public finance literature on optimal tax policies and general welfare economics, such as Stiglitz 1969 and Mirrlees 1971).

Another indicator of the consistency with which the empirically oriented literature focuses upon family income or earnings among earners is the treatment of this issue in treatises and texts. For example, in his treatise *The Economics of Inequality,* Atkinson (1975) devotes only one page to the issue, noting that "we know very little about just how *equally* income is divided among different (family) members," and concluding that "calculations of intra-family transfers are not likely to be possible" (1975, 41). In texts such as Johnson's *The Theory of Income Distribution* (1973, chap. 17), Taubman's *Income Distribution and Redistribution* (1978), or Kakwani's *Income Inequality and Poverty* (1980), there is practically no discussion about the unit of analysis by which the size distribution of income is defined.

Not only are studies that seek to describe or explain the distribution of income consistent in their choice of the unit of analysis, the studies that use income distribution as an exogenous variable, or as a simultaneously determined variable, follow suit. Consider the literature on economic development and income distribution: Kuznets (1955) uses annual income of families and unrelated individuals and is followed by Kravis (1960) and Schultz (1969); Adelman and Morris (1973) use a family income concept, as do Paukert (1973) and Chenery et al. (1974); Papanek (1978) uses a measure of wages among earners. Likewise in the study of income distribution in socialist countries, family income (see Slama 1978) or earnings among earners (see Kyn 1978, for Czechoslovakia; Wiles 1975, for the USSR) is the measure used.

In looking at the relationship of the business cycle and income distribution, CPS data for families and unrelated individuals are used by Schultz (1969), Metcalf (1969, who decomposes results by family structure), Mirer (1973), and Budd and Whiteman (1978), while Beach (1976) looks at individuals with income. In considering the effects of inflation on different segments of the income distribution, family or consumer unit income is taken as the measure (see, e.g., Hollister and Palmer 1972, or Michael 1979). In adjusting income distributions to reflect permanent, as distinct from transitory, income, Carlton and Hall (1978), for example, use Panel Study of Income Dynamics (PSID) family income; others who adjust for life-cycle fluctuations, such as Paglin (1975) or Lillard (1977), use the earnings of earners (see also Hall and Mishkin 1982). In discussing taxes and their impact on income distribution, once again the emphasis is on the family unit, as seen in work by Pfaff and Asam (1978), Pechman and Okner (1974), Gillespie (1965), and others. As mentioned above, the vast literature on the incidence of poverty also focuses on the family or household as the unit of study; see, for example, Mahoney (1976), Plotnick and Skidmore (1975), and Reynolds and Smolensky (1977). (An exception, using British tax data, is Fiegehen and Lansley 1976, which is discussed in chapter 7.)

In short, the empirically oriented literature has overwhelmingly taken the family or household or the earner as the appropriate unit of analysis in studies of income distribution.

Why This Consistency?

The explanation for this consistent pattern in the literature is not that this is the theoretically appropriate unit. Indeed, practically none of these studies offers any discussion of the unit of analysis, and most only mention it in passing. As mentioned above, papers sufficiently far removed from empirical analyses typically use "the individual" as their unit of analysis. We know of few clear statements that defend the use of the family or household as the appropriate, rather than the convenient, unit of analysis. One clear, if not convincing, statement was made years ago by H. Tout in the context of the definition of poverty: "Poverty is a characteristic of a family, not of an individual, who is said to be in poverty only because he happens to be a member of a family which is in poverty" (Tout 1938, 24). More recently, Simon Kuznets argues that the family is "the unit that makes most decisions relating to employment, other sources of income, and the disposition of income received—and is therefore the relevant unit in the analysis of the size distribution of income" (Kuznets 1975, 223). When the issue is addressed in empirical studies, however, the rationale is clearly data availability (see, e.g., Budd and Whiteman 1978, 15 or Benus and Morgan 1975, 209).

Were one to argue that the family is the correct as well as the convenient unit, then the boundaries of that unit should be specified. Is a family defined by living arrangements, by marital and blood ties, or by the pooling of resources? Is it defined narrowly as the primary group, or is membership extended to more distant relatives or part-time members as well? Given the fluid structure of households today, how is the unit to be redefined when someone moves into the household, or when the family splits up at the time of a separation or divorce, or when a child moves away from home? How should one treat children who are part-year residents with each of their formerly married parents? The problems in understanding income distributions using the family or household as the unit of analysis may be nearly as intractable analytically as the measurement problems that arise when we use the individual as the unit of analysis.

The strongest critics of the tradition of using the family as the basic unit of analysis are in England. Some years ago Michael Young complained, "It is painfully obvious to the student of social policy that growing knowledge about the distribution of the national income between families has not so far been matched by a growth of knowledge about the distribution of the family income between members" (Young 1952, 305). The 1980 edition of the United Kingdom's Central Statistical Office *Social Trends* states, "We have no data about the flows of income between people within households" (United Kingdom CSO 1979, 133); but at least they sound concerned! It is not likely that we can convince the reader that the focus of the research efforts on income distribution over the past decades has been ill-conceived, nor would we wish to. We do wish to raise doubts about the wisdom of accepting, as consistently and casually as the literature has, the family or household as the appropriate and viable basic unit of analysis in the study of income distribution.

One compelling reason for using the household as the unit of analysis is that many consumption decisions are made in a household context. Some aspects of consumption are not chosen at the level of the individual, so there is much commonality in the standard of living within the household. For example, even if they wished to, parents cannot choose to live in a wealthy suburb and force their children to live in a poor neighborhood. In fact, in chapter 8 we will revert to the household as the unit of analysis for the purposes of alimony and child-support calculations because outsiders can at best dictate how much goes to a household but cannot go beyond to prescribe how resources are allocated within that household. All this being said, the purpose of this book is to examine intrahousehold consumption decisions so that the invariance of the standard of living within the household can be analyzed.

Another explanation for the consistency of using the family as the basic unit of analysis is simple: convenience. This is the form in which data are collected, reported, and made available. It is the natural unit of analysis not necessarily from the theoretical perspective but from the perspective of the market economy. Incomes are earned in the marketplace by employees and wealthholders and are expended by consumer units or families. The data are available in the form they are because of the difficulties of measuring the income consumed by individual family members. These difficulties occur at several levels.

First, over the life cycle there are periods or events in which particularly large expenditures are typically made: birth expenses, higher education expenses, special events such as weddings and household formation expenditures, medical expenses during illness, and long-term care expenses during old age are representative. It seems inappropriate, therefore, to use for analytical purposes a cross-sectional snapshot of expenditures in one particular week or even in one year. The exceptional expenditure on college tuition in some particular year would not imply that the college student of the family routinely received a relatively large share of the family income. But the same logic implies that if a preschooler receives a relatively small share of the apportionment of family income in some year, we should not conclude that that person routinely gets less than average. So here as with any other measure of income, a point-in-time distribution need not reflect a longer-run distribution. For many if not most policy and theoretical issues, it is the distribution over some longer horizon that is of greater interest, therefore this problem is one of data use rather than data generation.

The second difficulty is that the apportionment of some private goods among family members is not easily observed. The allocation of a gallon of milk, a bag of sugar, a bar of soap, or the telephone local message units is not typically known, even though in principle this allocation could be made. There are, as well, a host of expenditures that essentially disguise the consumable and make it difficult to apportion expenditures appropriately. The disguised consumption of private goods such as public schools, public libraries, and public recreational facilities hidden in taxes illustrate this measurement problem.

A third difficulty is that "family goods" or public goods within the family abound. These goods, whose consumption by one member of the family does not reduce their availability to other family members, are a part of the explanation for the economic advantages of family or household formation. They involve fixed costs with little or no marginal cost of provision, hence, as family size increases the per person costs decline. The purely public goods in a household include the security, heat, and light of the home, its location, and a wide array of other items; the quasi-public goods include the fixed-cost components of many other household items, such as shared durables (e.g., the automobile, kitchen equipment), nondurables (e.g., the newspaper), and services (e.g., laundry or health care). Aside from the problem of data generation here, the aspect of these public goods that causes analytic difficulty is that while they may be consumed equally by all family members, they may not be valued equally. In a study of the intrafamily resource allocation, it is, of course, necessary to distinguish the allocation of dollars or time from the resulting distribution of utility. How one allocates the public goods will depend on the purpose of the exercise.

Fourth, many nonpecuniary resources are allocated within a family that affect the true distributions of resources and well-being but are not reflected in typical expenditure data. If, for example, one family member's bedroom is on a noisy street while another's is not, that fact would not usually be known. Or, one family member may receive more goods, another more leisure. This problem of allocating nonpecuniary resources is analogous to the problem of measuring a worker's remuneration rate by the dollar wage alone instead of by that wage plus the value of the fringe benefits, the positive and negative workplace amenities, and the training attributes of a job. So this problem isn't unique, but that doesn't make it more manageable.

Fifth, the family festers with externalities. Interdependence of preferences and caring for the welfare of other family members may make the discrepancy even wider between the distribution of expenditures among family members and the resulting distribution of well-being. The former we may hope to observe, at least in large part; that is the data generation issue. The latter we may never observe directly; it may forever be finessed by arbitrary assumptions of functional forms.

So we have suggested five difficulties in identifying the distribution of income within a family: life-cycle measurement, apportionment of private goods, apportionment of public goods, measurement of nonpecuniary items, and externalities. The first two can be handled in a straightforward manner by greater survey detail in the apportionment of private goods in the household and perhaps by using panel data. Similarly, the fourth problem in principle can be addressed in the family as adequately as in the firm. The difficulties of public goods and externalities seem to us to be far more difficult to overcome.

But surely—as there is no theoretical justification for persistently using the family as the unit of analysis, and as there appears to be some nontrivial progress that might be made in data collection—some effort in the direction of measuring the allocation of income within households seems warranted. The rationale of data limitations is itself endogenous. There is so little data in part because there is so little apparent concern about the currently accepted measures.

Throughout our discussion of the difficulties of measuring the income consumed by separate family members, we did not specify what concept of income we have in mind. There are four distinct concepts of family income in the literature that we think are useful and should be identified. All four could be measured as a flow per unit of time (e.g., per year) or averaged in some appropriate way to yield a measure of the family's "permanent" income (i.e., a constant flow over time from its stock of wealth). The four concepts are:

1. *Money income:* the flow of dollars into the household from all sources including wage earnings, transfer payments, return on financial capital in the form of interest, dividends, capital gains, etc.

2. *Monetized income:* money income plus the money value of the household's own stock of durables (such as its home, automobile, and clothing), the money value of the household's use of the social stock of durables (such as public roads and sewers), and perhaps even less tangible assets like the money value of the laws governing social behavior.

3. *Full income:* monetized income plus the money value of the household member's nonmarket time. [This time is frequently evaluated at its labor market value, so that (ignoring for the moment the difference be-

tween money income and monetized income) full income reflects money income as it would be if all household members devoted all possible time to earning wages.]

4. *Real, Full income:* As the technology (or knowledge and skills) differs by which households transfer money resources into desirable, consumable products, the differences in technology or efficiency reflect differences in achievable levels of nonmarket commodities. When full income is adjusted by the household's relative level of technology, the income is expressed as real, full income. Differences in economies of scale between, say, a household of two people and one with five people affect the real, full income of the two households just as surely as do differences in their wage earnings.

Most studies of income distribution focus on money income, although a few attempt to measure one or another of the broader concepts of income. Unfortunately, we also focus on money income in this study, and we do not overcome the difficulties of measuring nonpecuniary resources or externalities. The latter are uniquely associated with knowing the utility function or preferences of the household members. As we show in chapter 4, without knowing about these preferences one cannot speak to these externalities, and hence one cannot speak to the distribution of well-being or welfare. By their nature the nonpecuniary resources do not pertain to money income or monetized income. Considering the four concepts of income just defined, together with the five difficulties of measurement discussed above, table 2.1 expresses the full range of researchable problems. The cells with X's indicate those areas to which our efforts in this volume are directed. Needless to say, even if we adequately deal with the issues we address here, much remains to be done.

Table 2.1   Research Problems of Allocation of Income within the Household (XXX indicates problems addressed in this volume)

Income Concept	Life Cycle	Private Goods	Public Goods	Nonpecuniary Resources	Externalities
Money	XXX	XXX	XXX		
Monetized					
Full					
Real, Full					

Exceptions

There are several strands of research, mostly theoretical, that are exceptions to the above generalizations about the existing literature on the allocation of income. The first concerns decisions on allocation of goods within the household. Two types of decision rules have been modeled, one is based on fiat and one is based on game-theoretic bargaining strategies. The first has been explored extensively by Becker (1974, 1981a, 1981b). He defines a household head as the individual who makes net transfers to other members of the family because of altruistic preferences. The head fully internalizes all externalities within the family. The presence of an altruistic head induces all family members to behave efficiently, even if other members are not altruistic. While the construct of a head does not automatically imply *what* the distribution of family resources among members will be, it does (in the absence of strategic behavior) provide a theoretical justification for treating the family as having a single, well-behaved utility function.

In the bargaining model, the family members engage in a gaming strategy that results in an equilibrium distribution of the objects of choice. This scheme, as explored in a series of papers by Manser and Brown (1979, 1980) and by Horney and McElroy (1980), essentially involves competitiveness prior to marriage, where each partner has a threat point below which he or she refuses to pair with the potential spouse. Several objective functions for the distribution of the marital rent have been explored, including dictatorial behavior as well as standard Nash-bargaining that maximizes the product of the members' gains. Manser and Brown (1979, 1980) and McElroy and Horney (1981) apply this empirically by examining labor supply decisions of husbands and wives.

A similar model, in spirit, is discussed by Becker (1974, 322–26) in his theory of marriage as the division of output between mates. The gaming is not stressed by Becker as it is in the Nash-bargaining models, but he relies on the competitive nature of the marriage market to provide the impetus for a distribution of the gains from marriage on the basis of the relative clout of the two spouses. This yields information about asymmetry in the distribution of resources between the mates. The competitive edge that one spouse has over the other comes from that spouse's marketability.

All of these models, however, are mute on the issues of how, in fact, conflict is resolved and resources allocated *after* the marriage; how the homogeneous composite good is decomposed into elements satisfactory to both partners; or how children, who are not a party to the initial bargaining or contract and who would seem to have no (or little) competitive clout, are subsequently brought into the allocation decisions.

Recently the decisions about allocation of resources at the time of divorce or separation and the flow of money between the noncustodial and custodial parent have been addressed. Mnookin and Kornhauser (1979) consider the question of how divorce laws affect these private decisions. Peters (1983) investigates the effects of divorce laws on the alimony, child support, and property settlement at the time of separation. Weitzman (1981a, b) details the different economic circumstances of the husband and wife after a divorce. Weiss and Willis (1985) address questions of motivation and causation in the apparent reluctance of noncustodial parents to continue to contribute to their children.

A different descriptive strand of literature that inquires into the decision rules by which families allocate resources is the empirical literature in the consumer product and marketing area. Here attention is focused on which family member is directly involved in decisions about gross apportionment of income (e.g., clothing, durables, food), and who is involved in decisions about fine distinctions in consumption (e.g., brand of product, size of package, frequency of purchase). For a review of some of this literature, see Davis (1976).

These various studies of decision rules within the family do not investigate directly the nature of the distribution of resources within the family. One area in which this has been done to some degree is the research on the cost of children. Several studies over the past decade have attempted to measure what the total expenditure is in dollars and time value in raising a child from birth to, say, age 18. Cain (1971) provided an early estimate of this cost, and Reed and McIntosh (1972) made a more detailed study, while Espenshade (1977, 1984) and Turchi (1983, 1984) have provided more current estimates. Historical estimates have also been made by Lindert (1978), while the well-known work of Henderson (1949, 1950) offers a more indirect, intriguing alternative method of measurement. See Espenshade (1972) for a thorough literature review of this subject and Turchi (1984) for a useful review of methodology. The recent studies are specific to birth order and family income or socioeconomic status and provide a rough estimate of annual expenditures of money (and sometimes time) on child-related items. As we discuss in chapter 4, these estimates reflect the value of the income transferred from the parents but do not necessarily reflect the value of the income received by the individual child.

Deaton and Muellbauer (1986) estimate the costs of children, using something close to what they refer to as the Rothbarth (1943) method. They estimate that parents in Sri Lanka and Indonesia spend on their children between 30 and 40 percent of what they spend on themselves. The Rothbarth method, as used by Henderson (1949, 1950), is similar to the approach we take and defines some subset of goods as "adult goods." The Deaton and Muellbauer results are about the same as those we obtain using American data.

Another field of research discusses differential investments in children. One set of studies investigates the influence of family investments in the subsequent success of children (e.g., see Leibowitz 1974; Taubman 1976; Griliches 1979; Behrman et al. 1980; Bound, Griliches, and Hall 1984). Another analyzes the influence of different attributes and capacities of children on the investments by families (see, e.g., Behrman, Pollak, and Taubman 1982, 1986; Rosensweig and Schultz 1982; Behrman 1985). A related, less empirical literature focuses on the intergenerational income distribution (see Becker and Tomes 1976, 1979; Willis 1981) or the quantity-quality substitution in childbearing and rearing (Becker and Lewis 1974). Similarly, the oft-cited essay by Reder (1969, 211–14) speculates explicitly about the relationship between the extent of dispersion in intrafamily income in one generation and the long-run inequality of wealth.

Summary

1. Although there are exceptions, the income distribution literature rather consistently uses the family or the earner as its unit of analysis and makes no effort to look at the intrafamily income distribution as well.

2. That practice is justified on grounds of data limitation and convenience rather than on any theoretical basis. Correspondingly, the lack of data on intrafamily distribution of resources is in part the result of this complacency.

3. The scant data that exist suggest that incomes are not uniformly distributed within families, even though that is the implicit assumption on which much social policy is based.

4. Over the past two decades, the changing nature of family size, structure, and labor force participation patterns increases the importance for social science research addressing the intrafamily income distribution.

In short, the presumption that underlies the focus of much of the empirical research and policy debate on income distribution seems born of ignorance and is supported by neither theory nor fact. This situation can be improved.

Three

Descriptive Evidence from Spending Patterns

Periodically over the past hundred years, the Bureau of Labor Statistics, U.S. Department of Labor, has surveyed households about their income and expenditures. The primary purpose of the survey is to ascertain an appropriate bundle of goods and services to use as the consumption basket that is priced each month in computing the U.S. Consumer Price Index (CPI). Such a survey was conducted in the two-year period 1960–61 and again in 1972–73. We have used these two data sets in our study.

The 1960–61 Consumer Expenditure Survey (CES) was a one-time interview with information on annual expenditures on most goods and services and a supplemental one-week expenditure schedule for food and a few other purchases. The survey was conducted by the U.S. Bureau of the Census. A general-purpose tape with the survey results was made available for analysis; it reports the income and expenditures of 13,728 households. (This sample is used in chapter 6, where, for example, subsets of households with no children and households with children under age 17 are selected for study for reasons described in chapter 4.)

The 1972–73 survey was more complex, with a quarterly panel interview in which the household was visited by an interviewer every three months over a fifteen-month period, and with two one-week recordkeeping diaries of spending on certain items also collected from the households. The data from the various interviews and diaries were tabulated by the U.S. Bureau of the Census and a general-purpose tape was made available with annual expenditures and income information on 19,975 households of whom 9,869 were interviewed in 1972 and the remaining 10,106 in 1973.

The households are representative of all regions of the country, all levels of income, education, household size, and so forth. For example, there are about 4,600 one-person households and about 1,800 with more than five household members; about 4,300 heads of household have no more than 8 years of schooling while another 3,000 have at least 16 years of schooling; about 13,600 of the heads of household are married; about 2,000 are black; about 11,700 own their own home (or have a mortgage). While 400 of the heads are under 20 years of age, each 10-year age interval from 20 to 60 has almost 3,000 household heads, and another 2,300 are over age 70. We have selected subsets of households from the 1972–73 survey for our analysis, as described below. These data are used in the remainder of this chapter for descriptive purposes and are used more intensively in chapter 5 with the methods suggested in chapter 4.

Data are now available from the 1980–81 Consumer Expenditure Survey. Although this survey has much in common with the 1960–61 and 1972–73 surveys, its basic structure is quite different. It is no simple task to convert the data from the 1980–81 format to the earlier format. Still, in principle, this can be done. Subsequent research using the new data may be informative for at least two reasons: First, it will provide one more data set with which to validate results. Second, it will permit an examination of trends over a longer period of time by comparing the 1960–61 results with those from 1980–81. This book does not include any material from the 1980–81 survey because the analysis that the new data alone deserve would be an effort as large as the one contained herein for 1960–61 and 1972–73.

Spending Patterns by Characteristics of Children and Parents

We begin by selecting four samples of husband-wife families with zero, one, two, and three children. Table 3.1 describes these four samples; one notes very few interesting differences in their demographic descriptions. (The glossary of definitions of all variables is found in the appendix at the end of this chapter.) The income and expenditure levels do rise somewhat with family size, although the average proportion of before-tax income spent on total consumption remains relatively stable: 68 percent, 76 percent, 69 percent, and 70 percent, respectively. Likewise the spending pattern, as reflected in the proportion of total consumption spent on each of seven major components, changes very little on average from families of one size to families of another size. The variation within a family size dominates the between-group differences. For example, the variation in the proportion spent on food between groups is about 5 percentage points while the variation within a group is 8 or 9 percentage points.

Since these gross indicators reflect little variation by family size in

Table 3.1   Husband-Wife Families of Size 2 through 5,* Characteristics and Spending Patterns

| | Husband-Wife Families of Size: | | | |
Characteristic	2	3	4	5
	Panel A: Demographic Characteristics			
EDUC: Husband	11.9 (3.3)	12.1 (3.1)	12.6 (3.1)	12.4 (3.0)
Wife	12.0 (2.0)	12.2 (1.8)	12.3 (1.7)	12.1 (1.8)
AGE: Husband	46.4 (15.0)	40.5 (13.6)	38.3 (9.5)	39.4 (7.9)
Wife	44.4 (15.2)	37.9 (13.3)	35.5 (9.0)	36.6 (7.4)
REGION: NE	0.18	0.21	0.23	0.21
NC	0.30	0.28	0.28	0.31
S	0.32	0.31	0.28	0.29
W	0.20	0.20	0.21	0.19
RESIDENCE: SMSA1M	0.40	0.43	0.43	0.41
Town	0.42	0.42	0.40	0.40
Rural	0.18	0.15	0.17	0.19
RACE: BLACK	0.05	0.07	0.05	0.06
SURVEY YEAR 1973	0.50	0.50	0.53	0.52
RENTER	0.31	0.32	0.22	0.18
	Panel B: Income and Consumption			
INCOME (BT)	14,163 (9,412)	14,026 (10,865)	16,910 (9,638)	17,443 (11,450)
INCOME (AT)	11,160 (7,005)	11,107 (8,165)	13,544 (7,553)	14,096 (9,289)
TOTAL CONSUMPTION	9,666 (4,478)	10,611 (4,923)	11,737 (4,893)	12,151 (5,734)

Panel C: The Spending Pattern

FOOD (%)	0.19	(0.08)	0.19	(0.09)	0.21	(0.08)	0.23	(0.09)
HOUSE (%)	0.29	(0.10)	0.27	(0.10)	0.26	(0.09)	0.24	(0.08)
CLOTHING (%)	0.05	(0.04)	0.06	(0.04)	0.06	(0.04)	0.07	(0.03)
NONDURABLES (%)	0.07	(0.04)	0.07	(0.04)	0.07	(0.04)	0.07	(0.04)
DURABLES (%)	0.16	(0.14)	0.18	(0.13)	0.17	(0.12)	0.17	(0.12)
TRANSPORTATION (%)	0.06	(0.04)	0.06	(0.04)	0.05	(0.03)	0.05	(0.03)
SERVICES (%)	0.18	(0.10)	0.17	(0.09)	0.17	(0.08)	0.18	(0.09)
(N)	(2,461)		(2,196)		(1,851)		(1,078)	

*Families of size 3, 4, and 5 have 1, 2, and 3 children of any age, respectively, and no other family members.

NOTE: Standard deviations are in parentheses.

spending patterns, we turn immediately to the within-family-size variation. For descriptive purposes we have run ordinary least-squares (OLS)
regressions on the proportion spent on each of seven expenditure items for
each family size separately. The regression is of the form:

$$P_{ij} = X_{1j}\beta_1 + X_{2j}\beta_2 + X_{3j}\beta_3 + X_{4j}\beta_4 + u_{ij}, \qquad (3.1)$$

where P_{ij} is the jth family's expenditures on item i expressed as a proportion of the family's total consumption; X_1 is a vector of 10 demographic
characteristics (education of head, age of head, and dummies for three
regions, two city sizes, race, year of survey and renter status); X_2 is a
vector of eight dummy variables reflecting employment status of the husband and wife (not employed, part-time employed, full-time employed for
each spouse separately); X_3 is a vector describing the child (for family size
3) or the children (for family sizes 4 or 5) in seven dummy variables reflecting sex, age 6–11, age 12–17, age 18–24, age 25 +, and whether the
child is employed part-time or full-time; X_4 is total consumption.[1]

Notice that with X_4 included in the regression,

$$\left.\frac{\partial P_i}{\partial X_3}\right|_{X_4} = \beta_3 = \frac{\partial s_i}{\partial X_3}\frac{1}{X_4},$$

where s_i is the spending on item i, hence $P_i = s_i/X_4$ and $X_4 = \sum_{i=1}^{7} s_i$. So
the partial relationship between a characteristic (X_3) and spending on item
i is:

$$\beta_3 X_4 = \frac{\partial s_i}{\partial X_3}. \qquad (3.2)$$

Also, from a side regression on total expenditure,

$$X_{4j} = X_{1j}\gamma_1 + X_{2j}\gamma_2 + X_{3j}\gamma_3 + e_j, \qquad (3.3)$$

the total effect of a family characteristic (e.g., X_3) on the spending on item
i is:

---

1. For the seven items—food, housing, clothing, durables, nondurables, transportation,
and services—the series of seven regressions using the identical block of explanatory variables (X_1, X_2, X_3, X_4) form a seemingly unrelated system of equations. The adding-up constraints on the partial derivatives across the seven items, for example,

$$\sum_{i=1}^{7} \frac{\partial P_i}{\partial X_k} = \sum_i \beta_{ik} = 0,$$

are not imposed, but as seen in the tables that follow, they are very closely approximated.

$$\frac{dP_i}{dX_3} = \frac{\partial P_i}{\partial X_3} + \frac{\partial P_i}{\partial X_4}\frac{dX_4}{dX_3},$$

or[2]

$$\frac{ds_i}{dX_3} = \beta_3 X_4 + (\beta_4 X_4 + P_i)\gamma_3. \qquad (3.4)$$

Table 3.2 shows these estimated magnitudes for family size 3. Panel A indicates that, holding total consumption constant, if the child is a boy, spending shifts toward food and nondurables and away from clothing and services. Columns 2 and 3 indicate that if the child is employed, spending shifts toward durable and nondurable goods and away from services and perhaps housing. The final four columns indicate that if the child is over age 5, the family spending shifts toward food and away from housing and perhaps services. Panel A of table 3.2 holds total consumption fixed while the final row of that panel comes from a regression estimating equation (3.3) and tells us that the magnitude of *total* spending is higher if the child is employed and if the child is older. (There are few observations in the oldest age group, which probably explains the statistically insignificant −$96.) The dramatically larger expenditure for the age group 18–24 probably reflects the expenditure on college. Panel B of table 3.2 uses equation (3.4) to calculate the full effect of the child's characteristic on the expenditure on each item.

Table 3.2 tells us that both the magnitude and the composition of the family's spending pattern is altered by the age, sex, and employment status of the child—the magnitude is higher for older, employed, and male children. The table cannot, of course, suggest anything about the degree of equality in spending on the child relative to the parents, the subject of later chapters. It does establish that there are statistically significant and sizable

2.

$$\left[\frac{dP_i}{dX_3}\right] = \beta_3 + \beta_4\left[\frac{dX_4}{dX_3}\right], \qquad (1)$$

and

$$\frac{dP_i}{dX_3} = \frac{ds_i}{dX_3}\frac{1}{X_4} - \frac{P_i}{X_4}\frac{dX_4}{dX_3}. \qquad (2)$$

So substituting equation (2) into (1) and rearranging terms:

$$\frac{ds_i}{dX_3} = X_4\beta_3 + (\beta_4 X_4 + P_i)\frac{dX_4}{dX_3}. \qquad (3)$$

Notice that the term $\beta_4 X_4$, if divided by P_i equals η_i, the income elasticity of s_i, minus unity: or $\eta_i = (\beta_4 X_4/P_i) + 1.0$. The income elasticities for the seven items shown in table 3.2 are, for food through services: 0.78, 0.56, 1.19, 0.73, 1.83, 0.87, and 1.19, respectively.

Table 3.2   The Relation of Family Spending Patterns to Child's Characteristics, Husband-Wife Families with *One* Child

Expenditure Item	Employment			Age			
	Male	Part-Time	Full-Time	6–11	12–17	18–24	25+
			Panel A: Partial Effect (see equation 3.2)				
FOOD	$ 95.*	$ –104.	$ –20.	$ 577.*	$ 567.*	$ 291.*	$ 338.*
HOUSING	10.	–53.	–178.	–232.*	–401.*	–269.	–331.*
CLOTHING	–44.*	–44.	–12.	–24.	49.	–4.	–50.
NONDURABLES	53.*	62.*	100.*	105.*	52.	36.	–21.
DURABLES	–53.	39.	289.*	–165.	–32.	–136.	46.
TRANSPORT	30.	21.	51.	–39.	–23.	125.*	51.
SERVICES	–91.*	78.	–231.*	–222.*	–211.*	–42.	–34.
$\frac{\partial \text{ TOTAL CONSUMPTION}}{\partial \text{ Child's Characteristics}}$	182.	979.*	882.*	558.	484.	1505.*	–96.
			Panel B: Total Effect (see equation 3.4)				
FOOD	$122.	$ 43.	$ 112.	$ 660.	$ 639.	$ 516.	$ 324.
HOUSING	38.	98.	–42.	–146.	–326.	–37.	–346.
CLOTHING	–32.	24.	50.	15.	82.	101.	–56.
NONDURABLES	63.	114.	147.	135.	77.	115.	–26.
DURABLES	5.	352.	571.	13.	123.	345.	15.
TRANSPORT	39.	71.	96.	–11.	1.	200.	47.
SERVICES	–53.	278.	–52.	–108.	–112.	265.	–53.

*$t \geq 2.0$.

differences in the family's consumption bundle depending on the characteristics of the child.

Table 3.3 shows the partial effects on spending patterns (comparable to panel A of table 3.2) of the older and younger child in families of size four.[3] A full set of seven dummy variables was used for *each* of the two children in the regression analysis. The shifts in spending patterns on the older child mirror rather well the patterns seen in table 3.2 for the single child. This suggests that the pattern seen in table 3.2 is not an arbitrary one. When we compare this pattern with that of the younger child in the two-child family, the similarity by age categories erodes substantially.

The final row in each panel of table 3.3 shows the effect of that child characteristic on total consumption. Here the different effects of the first and second child's characteristics are of interest. While the older child exhibits effects somewhat similar to the single child, the characteristics of the second child in a family of four has no significant effect except during the college-age period. One must recall that these derivatives do not reflect the influence of the presence of a first or second child on total consumption: all families in the analysis that underlies table 3.3 have two children. It is only the influence of the different age, sex, and employment status of each of these two children that is investigated here. The table shows that, as with the single child, total expenditures are somewhat higher if the children are male, older, and employed.

Table 3.4 indicates the effects of other family characteristics on the spending pattern of families with one child (panel A) and families with two children (panel B). Families living in large cities (in SMSA's of one million or more) spend relatively less on durables and more on food; black families spend relatively less on food and nondurables and more on clothing and transportation; a higher education level of the husband is associated with a relatively smaller share of the budget on nondurable and durable goods and a larger share spent on services and housing; families with an older head appear to spend relatively more on services and food and less on durables. (Recall that the average age of the head of these families is about 40, so "older" means 45 or 50 compared to 30 or 35.) The sum of the partial effects for each characteristic in table 3.4 is approx-

---

3. The regressions for family size 4 use the same set of variables in s_i but use only three dummies reflecting employment status instead of eight: 95 percent of the families have a full-time employed husband, so the three dummies reflect the employment status of the wife (not employed, part-time, full-time) with a full-time employed husband. The income elasticities for the seven items, when estimated for the four-person families, are quite similar (except for transportation) to the estimates for the three-person families: 0.79, 0.52, 1.16, 0.71, 1.94, 1.05, and 1.12, respectively.

Table 3.3   The Relation of Family Spending Patterns to Child's Characteristics, Husband-Wife Families with Two Children

Expenditure Item	Employment			Age			
	Male	Part-Time	Full-Time	6–11	12–17	18–24	25+
			Panel A: Partial Effect—Older Child				
FOOD	$ 81.*	$ −181.*	$ −179.	$ 382.*	$ 405.*	$ 363.*	$ 567.*
HOUSING	−51.	4.	−286.*	−339.*	−501.*	−441.*	−374.*
CLOTHING	−60.*	−29.	43.	−18.	66.	−11.	−100.
NONDURABLES	18.	27.	−9.	89.*	59.	127.*	−123.
DURABLES	78.	110.	591.*	−164.	19.	−67.	−318.
TRANSPORT	28.	−9.	36.	68.*	67.	179.*	95.
SERVICES	−94.*	79.	−195.*	−19.*	−115.*	−150.	7.
$\frac{\partial \text{ TOTAL CONSUMPTION}}{\partial \text{ Child's Characteristics}}$	53.	871.*	−224.	630.*	1044.*	1505.*	2597.*
			Panel B: Partial Effect—Younger Child				
FOOD	$ 29.	$ −109.	$ −207.	$ 179.*	$ 238.*	$ −45.	$ 990.*
HOUSING	1.	−39.	−184.	1.	−68.	163.	217.
CLOTHING	−42.	4.	−48.	44.	102.*	49.	−115.
NONDURABLES	5.	13.	227.*	−19.	−55.	14.	27.
DURABLES	112.	−36.	502.	−162.	−263.	−474.*	−1483.*
TRANSPORT	2.	68.	58.	−35.	1.	71.	−19.
SERVICES	−107.	100.	−348.	−8.	45.	222.	383.
$\frac{\partial \text{ TOTAL CONSUMPTION}}{\partial \text{ Child's Characteristic}}$	5.	876.	1225.	621.	9.	2053.*	−45.

*$t \geq 2.0$.

Table 3.4   The Relation of Family Spending Patterns to Family Demographic Characteristics, for Families with *One* and *Two* Children

Expenditure Item	Age (per year)	Residence		Region			Color	Education of Head (per year)
		Rural	SMSA1M	NE	NC	S	Black	
Panel A: Family Size Three								
FOOD	11.*	-78.	124.*	165.*	41.	22.	-185.*	-11.
HOUSING	2.	-105.	33.	86.	-47.	-57.	-116.	26.*
CLOTHING	-1.	-60.*	19.	80.*	28.	42.	186.*	5.*
NONDURABLES	-2.	66.*	-30.	43.	68.*	94.*	-80.*	-15.*
DURABLES	-34.*	158.	-239.*	-373.*	-85.	-110.	125.	-60.*
TRANSPORT	2.	-16.	80.*	25.	-49.*	-87.*	135.*	7.*
SERVICES	21.*	34.	13.	-26.	45.	95.	-66.	47.*
(Sum)	(-1)	(-1)	(0)	(0)	(1.)	(-1.)	(-1.)	(-1.)
∂ TOTAL CONSUMPTION / ∂ X_1	66.*	-985.*	622.*	-436.	-776.*	-278.	-997.*	422.*
Panel B: Family Size Four								
FOOD	13.*	-82.	89.	72.	-92.	-203.*	-150.	-25.*
HOUSING	-1.	-67.	29.	54.	9.	27.	45.	23.*
CLOTHING	-3.	-44.	-7.	48.	6.	11.	205.*	13.*
NONDURABLES	-2.	91.*	-31.	16.	43.	83.*	-156.*	-21.*
DURABLES	-31.*	52.	-178.*	-131.	74.	-38.	-6.	-70.*
TRANSPORT	3.*	19.	56.*	24.	-52.*	-89.*	142.*	12.*
SERVICES	20.*	31.	42.	-83.	11.	207.*	-80.	68.*
(Sum)	(-1.)	(0)	(0)	(0)	(-1.)	(-2.)	(0)	(0)
∂ TOTAL CONSUMPTION / ∂ X_1	27.	-951.*	1126.*	-192.	-205.	3344.	-1017.*	423.*

*$t \geq 2.0$.

imately zero, since the total expenditure, among other things, is held constant. The final row of each panel shows that total consumption is higher, other things held constant, for families living in nonrural areas and higher still for families in large cities; higher for families with a higher level of schooling of the husband; and higher for families with a nonblack husband. Some of these differences will become important in the estimation procedure used in later chapters.

Let us consolidate the message of tables 3.1 through 3.4. Although the family spending pattern, as measured by the proportions of total consumption spent on several broad items like food, clothing, and durables, does not seem to vary dramatically with family size, there is a large amount of variation in the spending pattern for families of any given size. This variation is closely associated with different family income levels (as we've known since Engel's study in 1895) and with other family characteristics, such as age, race, education of the family head, and location of residence. These patterns too have been documented previously (for a very partial list of studies, see Prais and Houthakker 1955, Deaton and Muellbauer 1980, and Michael 1972). We have also found that characteristics of the children in the family—age, sex, birth order, employment status—affect both the family's spending pattern and the magnitude of the family's total consumption bundle.

As discussed, another set of variables in regression (3.1) were eight dummies reflecting the employment status of the husband and the wife. First, we asked if all this information about the employment status of both spouses has any discernible statistical effect on the proportions spent on the several composite consumption items. Using the families with one child (2,196 observations), the answer is *yes*, judged by an *F*-test on the set of eight dummy variables (see table 3.5, panel A, column 1). However, the sex of the two earners seems not to matter statistically. We can look at the employment status of the two parents without regard to who has which status using five dummy variables and further identify the gender of the two using the three additional dummies. Columns 2 and 3 of panel A in table 3.5 show that the employment status of the two spouses, but not the information about the gender-specific employment of the two, appears to affect the spending pattern.

Turning to the magnitude of the effects of employment status on spending, panel B of table 3.5 makes comparisons between the three most common employment statuses: (1) husband full-time and wife not employed (38 percent of the sample); (2) husband full-time and wife part-time (22 percent); and (3) husband full-time and wife full-time (26 percent). Panel B shows the effect of the wife employed part-time or full-time compared in each case to the wife not employed. The results in columns 1 and 2 suggest that the part-time employment of the wife has an appreciable effect, lowering expenditures on food and housing and raising expenditures on durables and services. By contrast, the full-time employment has a much smaller impact.

To check on the sensitivity of these results, the equations were re-estimated in ordinary double-log form; again the part-time status is of much more influence than the full-time employment of the wife (results not shown). These double-log regressions were also run on the subset of families with husband full-time employed ($n = 1,905$). The other results hold husband's employment constant by regression coefficient. The runs on the smaller subset (shown in columns 3 and 4 of panel B, table 3.5) confirm again the much larger impact of the part-time employment of the wife. The magnitude of the negative effect on housing and the positive effect on durables is again evident, but the double-log form reduces considerably the effect on the food expenditure and yields a large negative effect of full-time employment on durables. (The adding-up constraint is also not satisfied in the double-log regressions, one might note.)

Panel C of table 3.5 shows the implied effects of having at least one full-time employed family member; here the effects are quite substantial. The proportion of the consumption bundle spent on housing and services rises considerably, and the proportion spent on food, in particular, falls. (Recall that by the form of the regression the total is held constant here, so the sum of these changes will necessarily be approximately zero.)

Described in broad terms, the results in table 3.5 suggest: (1) the employment patterns of the husband and wife do affect the pattern as well as the level of the family's spending; (2) the gender of the employed spouse seems not to affect the pattern of spending; (3) the part-time employment of the second earner seems to have a bigger effect than the full-time employment of that earner, especially so on durables (positively) and on housing and food (negatively); (4) the full-time employment of at least one spouse is associated with a sizeable shift in spending toward housing, services, and transport and away from food and durables.

In short, then, these tables tell us that family spending patterns are not only affected by characteristics that influence the family's real income and hence its command over resources (e.g., its nominal income, the age and education of the head, and perhaps race and location), it is also affected by the behavior (employment status) and characteristics (sex, age, etc.) of the family members. That is not surprising, perhaps, but is it consistent with the common implicit assumption that resources are divided equally among family members? We turn to more direct, but less global, evidence in the following two sections.

Table 3.5   The Influence of the Employment Status of the Parents on Spending Patterns of Families with One Child

Panel A
F-Tests of the Significance of the Employment Dummy Variables

Item	F-Test, Eight Dummies	F-Test, Five Employment Status Dummies	F-Test, Three Gender-Specific Dummies
FOOD	5.55*	7.96*	1.54
HOUSING	5.22*	7.17*	1.94
CLOTHING	2.02	1.49	2.90
TRANSPORT	1.45	2.07	0.41
NONDURABLES	2.74*	3.34*	1.72
DURABLES	1.46	1.28	1.75
SERVICES	2.21	3.39*	0.24

*Significant at .01.

Panel B
Implied Effect on Dollar Expenditure of Wife's Employment
(in families with full-time employed husband, expenditure compared to family with wife not employed)

Item	Wife Part-Time (all families, $n = 2,196$)	Wife Full-Time (all families, $n = 2,196$)	Wife Part-Time (husand FT only families, $n = 1,905$)	Wife Full-Time (husand FT only families, $n = 1,905$)
FOOD	$ -138.	$ -32.	$ -5.	$ 46.
HOUSING	-180.	-5.	-175.	62.
CLOTHING	6.	16.	24.	33.
TRANSPORT	15.	40.	19.	26.
NONDURABLES	13.	1.	32.	34.
DURABLES	211.	2.	152.	-111.
SERVICES	66.	-22.	52.	-4.
(Sum)	(-7)	(0)	(99)	(86)

Panel C

Expenditure Effects of Full-Time Employment

Item	Husband Full-Time Compared To Not Employed, Given Wife Not Employed	Wife Full-Time Compared To Not Employed, Given Husband Not Employed	Both Full-Time Compared To Both Not Employed
FOOD	$-650.	$-742.	$-682.
HOUSING	446.	164.	441.
CLOTHING	29.	85.	46.
TRANSPORT	84.	175.	123.
NONDURABLES	-90.	58.	-89.
DURABLES	-169.	-111.	-167.
SERVICES	350.	371.	328.

Expenditures on Clothing

One of the few items in the CES that can be identified as spent on a young child (a boy or a girl, separately) or an adult man or adult woman is the clothing expenditure. In this section we look at the clothing expenditure for boys, girls, men, and women in the combined sample of families with zero, one, two, and three children. Here, unlike the previous section, we look *across* family types instead of *within*. In this manner we can investigate how the husband's clothing expenditure is affected, for example, by the presence of a child (to anticipate: we find it declines by $30 from an average of $182), by the presence of a second child (it declines an additional $21), or by the presence of a third child (it declines another $14). Under various assumptions we also can estimate how one child's presence affects the clothing expenditure on the other child.

It is tempting to call the change in total expenditure on an item that is associated with the addition of a member of the family the amount that is consumed by that member. For example, one could regress total expenditure on clothing within the household on characteristics of that household, including number of children. If the addition of one child raised expenditure on clothing, say, $50, one might infer that the additional child received $50 worth of clothing. That inference is obviously incorrect. It is possible that substitution away from expenditure on the adult and toward expenditure on the child might leave the total expenditure on clothing unchanged, even though the child receives adequate clothing. Appropriately defined, all consumption by the new member is substitution away from other members. The substitution either takes the form of fewer goods consumed or of less leisure enjoyed by others so that family income can be increased.

The data on clothing in our data set allow us to calculate the magnitude of this mistake in inference. Since information is present on the breakdown of clothing expenditures by family members, as well as on the total amount of clothing expenditure, it is possible to determine how much of a new family member's consumption of a particular good represents a substitution from consumption of that same good by others as compared to a substitution of consumption of another good or leisure by others.

For this analysis we used the husband-wife families with zero, one, two, or three children *plus* the female-headed families with one, two, or three children. Because the detailed clothing expenditure is reported for babies, for boys and girls aged 2–15 separately, and for men and women aged 16 and over separately, we could not identify the separate expenditures on children over age 16 from the expenditures on their parents. So we have excluded families with children age 16 and over in this section. Table 3.6

Table 3.6 Summary Statistics on Sample of 7,106 Families with Zero, One, Two, or Three Children, and by Family Type

Variable	Mean*
Panel A: All 7,106 Families	
EDUC: Head	12.3 (3.0)
AGE: Head	38.2 (13.2)
INCOME (BT) (000)	13.4 (9.0)
SOUTH	0.31
RURAL	0.16
BLACK	0.08
ADULTS EMPLOYED	0.73
CHILD MALE	0.30
CHILD 0–5	0.34
CHILD 12–15	0.10
Family Type: MF	0.40
Family Type: MF 1 Child	0.20
Family Type: MF 2 Children	0.22
Family Type: MF 3 Children	0.12
Family Type: F 1 Child	0.03
Family Type: F 2 Children	0.02
Family Type: F 3 Children	0.01
Clothing: Baby	$ 23.19 (76.78)
Clothing: Boy	52.98 (107.00)
Clothing: Girl	59.72 (129.23)
Clothing: Children Total	135.90 (193.91)
Clothing: Man	181.79 (216.35)
Clothing: Woman	262.98 (310.07)
Clothing: Total	580.67 (541.53)

Panel B

		Family Type						
		Husband-Wife				Female-Headed		
Clothing	All	Children				Children		
Expenditure	Families	0	1	2	3	1	2	3
Baby	$ 23.	$ 4.	$ 47.	$ 34.	$ 27.	$ 19.	$ 21.	$ 28.
Boy	53.	0.	41.	100.	149.	61.	104.	145.
Girl	60.	0.	52.	107.	165.	78.	128.	148.
Children								
Total	136.	5.	139.	241.	340.	158.	254.	320.
Man	182.	196.	197.	195.	179.	0.	0.	0.
Woman	263.	295.	251.	253.	220.	243.	185.	172.
Total	581.	495.	588.	689.	739.	402.	438.	492.
(N)	(7,106)	(2,864)	(1,414)	(1,561)	(827)	(203)	(164)	(73)

*Standard deviations in parentheses.

shows the summary statistics for this sample of 7,106 families. Several of the variables are the same as in the previous section. South, Rural, and Black are dummy variables defined to be 1 if the family lived in the Southern region of the United States, in a rural area, and if the family head is black, respectively, and defined to be zero otherwise. The variable Adults Employed shows the proportion of adults who are employed (thus takes the values 0.0, 0.5, or 1.0); Child Male indicates the proportion of the children who are males; while Child 0–5 and Child 12–15 indicate the proportion of the children within these age ranges. The family-type variables are defined as 1 for the appropriate category and zero otherwise, where the categories are male-female (MF) with no children (or more precisely husband and wife since only married couples or females with young children are included); male-female-one-child, etc.; and female-one-child, etc. The clothing expenditures are in dollars spent in the survey year on the respective categories.

The mean clothing expenditures in table 3.6 are not the averages per capita but rather the averages per family. The average per capita clothing expenditures are:

Adult	$229
Man	194
Woman	263
Child	124
Boy	117
Girl	132

Clothing expenditures per woman are 35 percent higher than clothing expenditures per man; the gender-specific difference is also found among children's clothing, where expenditures for girl's clothing are 12 percent higher than for boy's clothing. The expenditure for the child is a little more than half the expenditure for the adult. The total clothing expenditure for a family of four with these average expenditures would be $706. Assuming equal sharing of expenditure ($176/person) would overstate the expenditure on the boy and the girl by $59 and $44 (or by 50 percent and 33 percent), respectively, and would understate the expenditure on the father and mother by $18 and $87 (or by 9 percent and 33 percent), respectively.

At least with respect to this one item, a uniform distribution of spending among family members is clearly not observed. Two points are relevant here: First, the result does not imply that the whole spending bundle is apportioned unequally, because it could be that the differences seen in clothing expenditures are offset by expenditures on other items. But on this one item, there are substantial differences among all four family members, with greater differences between children and adults than between the sexes. It is this adult-child difference that is emphasized in later chapters. Second, expenditure may not be a good proxy for welfare in the case of certain commodities. Clothing is an obvious example, because children's clothing is less expensive than adult clothing of a given quality.

The spending on each clothing category is regressed on the family-size variables alone and separately on the family-size variables plus the set of demographic and economic variables listed in table 3.6. The results from both regressions are shown in table 3.7; panel A, of course, closely mirrors panel B of table 3.6.

The income elasticities implied by these regressions yield an interesting pattern. Evaluated at the sample means, the elasticities for clothing for baby, boy, girl, and total children, respectively, are 0.30, 0.26, 0.36, and 0.31; while for adult man and woman, they are more than twice as high: 0.69 and 0.73. The elasticities are higher for females in both age groups. When income rises, females apparently get proportionately more of an increment than males in terms of clothing, and adults get substantially more of an increment than children. (Recall that the income measure here is before tax income, so the relatively low level of all these elasticities is not especially interesting.)

Next, notice that the spending patterns do not differ by region, but that rural families spend less and black families spend more on almost every category of clothing. The clothing expenditure on women rises substantially when more family adults are employed, surely reflecting the fact that employed women spend considerably more on their clothing than do women who are not employed in the labor market (see Lazear and Michael 1980). The sex of the child has the already observed effect—less is spent on boys (an average of $30 less according to the regression). The ages of the children appear to have an intuitively reasonable effect—less is spent on preschool-aged children and more on older (12–15) children. It is interesting to notice that the ages of the children seem to have no effect on the clothing expenditures of the parents.

We summarize some results from panel B of table 3.7 regarding the effect of an additional child on the clothing expenditures in table 3.8. The addition of each child lowers each parent's clothing expenditure by 10 to 20 percent, with a smaller dollar effect for second and third children. The net increment to the family's clothing expenditure and the gross expenditure on children's clothing declines dramatically with each additional child. If the children's clothing expenditure were distributed evenly among the children, the figures suggest that the impact of a second or third child on the previous child's (or children's) clothing allotment is larger (both

Table 3.7 Clothing Expenditure Regressions, for Subtotals of Clothing Expenditure (insignificant coefficients in parentheses)

| | Clothing Expenditure | | | | | | |
| | | | | Children | | | |
Family Type	Baby (0–2)	Boy (2–15)	Girl (2–15)	Total (0–15)	Man (16+)	Woman (16+)	Total (all ages)
				Panel A			
MF	5.	(0)	(0)	(5.)	196.	295.	495.
MF 1 Child	42.	41.	52.	135.	(2.)	−43.	93.
MF 2 Children	29.	100.	106.	236.	(−1.)	−41.	193.
MF 3 Children	22.	148.	165.	335.	−17.	−75.	244.
F 1 Child	14.	62.	78.	153.	−196.	−51.	−94.
F 2 Children	16.	104.	128.	249.	−196.	−110.	(−57.)
F 3 Children	23.	145.	148.	315.	−196.	−122.	(−3.)
(R^2)	(0.05)	(0.25)	(0.20)	(0.40)	(0.05)	(0.01)	(0.03)

Panel B

	(−4.)	−36.	−55.	−95.	65.	(−30.)	(−60.)
Intercept							
Family Type:							
MF 1 Child	(−2.)	15.	181.	194.	−30.	−59.	105.
MF 2 Children	(−10.)	64.	231.	285.	−51.	−82.	152.
MF 3 Children	(−8.)	100.	269.	362.	−65.	−117.	180.
F 1 Child	−21.	42.	201.	222.	−155.	(42.)	110.
F 2 Children	−14.	70.	249.	304.	−163.	(−18.)	123.
F 3 Children	(1.)	102.	268.	370.	−166.	(−36.)	168.
EDUC: Head	0.	0.	1.	3.	7.	10.	21.
AGE: Head	(−0.)	(0.)	0.	0.	−2.	−1.	−2.
INCOME (BT) (000)	0.	1.	2.	0.	9.	14.	27.
SOUTH	(0.)	(−0.)	(1.)	(1.)	(7.)	(10.)	(18.)
RURAL	(1.)	−5.	−7.	−12.	−23.	−37.	−72.
BLACK	(6.)	(6.)	13.	25.	41.	67.	134.
ADULTS EMPLOYED	−9.	8.	(7.)	(6.)	(−14.)	57.	49.
CHILD MALE	(2.)	139.	−170.	−30.	19.	(3.)	(−7.)
CHILD 0–5	61.	−68.	−80.	−86.	(4.)	(3.)	−80.
CHILD 12–15	(8.)	34.	68.	110.	(2.)	(22.)	134.
(R^2)	(0.11)	(0.51)	(0.49)	(0.51)	(0.23)	(0.22)	(0.29)

Table 3.8   Impact on the Family's Clothing Expenditure of One, Two, or
                 Three Children

	Increment Spent on Clothing of:			
	Children	Father	Mother	Total
(Reference level—no children)*	($3.)	($209.)	($300.)	$504.)
1 Child	+194.	−30.	−59.	+105.
2 Children	+91.	−21.	−23.	+47.
3 Children	+77.	−14.	−35.	+28.

	If Children's Clothing Expenditure Is Spent on Children Equally:	
	Amount Spent Per Child	"Cost" to Child of Another Sibling
1 Child	$194.	
2 Children	142.	−$52.
3 Children	121.	−21.

*Estimated from regression, with sample mean values of EDUC, AGE, INCOME
(BT), SOUTH, RURAL, BLACK and ADULTS EMPLOYED.

absolutely and proportionately) than the impact on the parents' clothing
allotments. That is, the first child gives up more ($52) than both parents
combined ($21 and $23) for the second child.

Table 3.9 is useful in answering the question of how misleading it is to
infer the allocations of spending from regressions on a composite expenditure. As already mentioned, some studies of spending patterns use inappropriate logic: If one knows the total household spending on, say, food
for a family of size two and a family of size three, one defines the impact
of the third family member on per capita consumption of food as the total
spending in the size three family, divided by three, minus the total spending in the size two family, divided by two. But this logic assumes a particular pattern of substitution that may not be warranted.

We have applied that logic to the regression on the total clothing expenditure (shown in col. 7, panel B, table 3.7). But one can also do much
better by using the regression run specifically on clothing expenditures of
girls, boys, women, and men to estimate the spending for clothing on each
family member. Then one can infer the impact of an additional family
member on the clothing expenditure for other family members. Comparisons can be made that permit us to see how well the first procedure works,
since we know more accurately in this one instance what the truth is.

Table 3.9 uses regressions as indicated and calculates values for a husband-wife family with the sample mean value for the adult-related explanatory variables—Education, Age, Income, South, Rural, Black, and

Adults Employed. Panel A shows the "truth"—in this example the couple with no children spend $209.15 on the man's clothing, $299.57 on the woman's clothing. Panel B shows what one would infer each spent if total clothing expenditure were used. The total would be correct ($504.20, which is quite close to $508.72), but of course we would attribute a spending of $252.10 to each adult, overstating the spending on him and understating the spending on her.

Table 3.9   Comparison of Estimates of Clothing Expenditure by Detailed Expenditure Regressions and from Total Expenditure Regression

Family Type	Clothing Expenditure for Whole Family and Family Members				
	Total	Man	Woman	Boy	Girl
Panel A: Level Expended, Estimated from Separate Regressions (cols. 2, 3, 5, 6; table 3.7)*					
Husband-Wife:	($508.72)	$209.15	$299.57	—	—
Husband-Wife, Boy 14:	(652.63)	200.99	265.14	$186.50	—
Husband-Wife, Boy 14, Girl 9:	(726.50)	168.48	229.74	149.26	$179.02
Panel B: Level Expended, Estimated from Composite Regression (col. 7, table 3.7)*					
Husband-Wife:	504.20	(252.10)	(252.10)	—	—
Husband-Wife, Boy 14:	735.50	(245.17)	(245.17)	(245.17)	—
Husband-Wife, Boy 14, Girl 9:	719.05	(179.76)	(179.76)	(179.76)	(179.76)
Panel C: Implied Change in Expenditure, Derived by Subtraction Using Panel A					
Adding First Child, Boy 14:	+143.91	−8.16	−34.43	+186.50	—
Adding Second Child, Girl 9:	+73.87	−32.51	−35.40	−37.24	+179.02
Panel D: Implied Change in Expenditure, Derived by Subtraction Using Panel B					
Adding First Child, Boy 14:	+231.30	−6.93	−6.93	+245.17	—
Adding Second Child, Girl 9:	−16.45	−65.41	−65.41	−65.41	+179.76

*Numbers in parentheses in panels A and B are inferred, the other numbers are from the regressions.

Now add to this hypothetical family a 14-year-old boy. Row two of panel A shows what the spending for each of the three family members is in this new circumstance, and panel C shows the impact of the presence of this 14-year-old boy on the man's and the woman's clothing expenditure. It seems the boy's presence has a tiny effect on the man's clothing expenditure and a sizeable ($34.43) effect on the woman's, reducing the discrepancy in clothing expenditure between the man and woman (a discrepancy of about $90 is reduced to a discrepancy of $64). Had we used instead the total clothing expenditure, we would have estimated the numbers in panel B with the implied impact of the presence of the 14-year-old boy on the man's and the woman's clothing expenditure as shown in panel D: a reduction of $6.93 for each. If we had assumed the total was allocated evenly, we would infer the boy got $245.17 in clothing instead of the "actual" $186.50. Finally, the additional total clothing expenditure ($231.30) is itself substantially higher than implied by the estimates in panel A ($143.91).

Briefly, if we now add a second child—a nine-year-old girl—in the calculations, one can again compare the "true" impact with that implied by the regression on total clothing expenditure. One notable discrepancy is the implied effect of the girl's presence on the boy's clothing: a decline of $37.24 in "truth," compared to $65.41 in panel D.

The comparisons of panels A and B suggest to us that if panel A is assumed to represent the truth, the cruder, easier, and more common procedure used in panel B is tolerably accurate and appears to be adequate for many purposes. It masks much inequality, however: whether it is acceptably accurate to describe four expenditures of approximately $170, $230, $150, and $180 (row 3, panel A) as being about $180 for each of the four (row 3, panel B) depends on the purpose of that description. For purposes of estimating the changes in expenditures, as distinct from estimating the levels, the crude procedure is far less adequate.

Expenditures on Schooling

There is also enough detail on schooling expenditures to permit an actual assignment to one family member. Unlike the detail for clothing, we can only assign the expenditure to a child or to an adult; we cannot be gender-specific. Moreover, a few items cannot be assigned. Table 3.10 indicates the assignments of schooling expenditures we made; they result in four categories (children's, adults', miscellaneous, and total); each of these can be further partitioned into public (PB) and private (PR).

Table 3.10   Assignment of Detailed Schooling Expenditures into Categories

Children's Schooling
Nursery or Kindergarten Private School, Tuition (PR)
Private Elementary or High School, Tuition (PR)
School Books or Supplies for Private Nursery School or Kindergarten (PR)
School Books or Supplies for Private Elementary or High School (PR)
Nursery of Kindergarten Public School, Tuition (PB)
Public Elementary or High School, Tuition (PB)
School Books or Supplies for Public Nursery School or Kindergarten (PB)
School Books or Supplies for Public Elementary or High School (PB)

Adults' Schooling
Business or Secretarial Private School, Tuition (PR)
Technical or Trade Private School, Tuition (PR)
Private College or University, Tuition (PR)
School Books or Supplies for Private College or University (PR)
School Books or Supplies for Private Business or Secretarial School (PR)
Private Technical or Trade School, Books (PR)
Business or Secretarial Public School, Tuition (PB)
Technical or Trade Public School, Tuition (PB)
Public College or University, Tuition (PB)
School Books or Supplies for Public College or University (PB)
School Books or Supplies for Public Business or Secretarial School (PB)
Public Technical or Trade School, Books (PB)

Miscellaneous Schooling
Other Private School, Tuition (PR)
Combined Books and Tuition for Private School (PR)
School Books or Supplies for Other Private School (PR)
Combined Expenses for Private School (PR)
Other Living Expenses for Private School (excluding room and board) (PR)
Other Public School, Tuition (PB)
Combined Books and Tuition for Public School, Tuition (PB)
School Books or Supplies for Other Public School (PB)
Combined Expenses for Public School (PB)

Total Schooling
All of the above.

The average annual expenditure on schooling is only about $50; the breakdown into the several expenditure categories and by family type is shown in table 3.11. OLS regressions have been estimated for the Children's, Adults', and Total Schooling expenditures (rows 1, 4, and 10); these are reported in table 3.12. Families with more educated heads of household spend more on schooling; those with higher incomes spend more on their children's schooling but less on current adult schooling. The sex of the child appears to have no influence on the child's schooling ex-

Table 3.11   Schooling Expenditures by Family Structure and Size, for Specified Type of Expenditure

Type of Families Expenditure	All Families	Husband-Wife Families				Female-Headed		
		Number of Children				Number of Children		
		0	1	2	3	1	2	3
Children's	18.	0.	19.	33.	57.	10.	11.	13.
Public	2.	0.	2.	5.	6.	1.	2.	3.
Private	16.	0.	17.	28.	51.	9.	9.	10.
Adults'	25.	31.	27.	19.	21.	7.	9.	10.
Public	14.	18.	13.	11.	9.	2.	5.	10.
Private	11.	13.	14.	8.	12.	5.	4.	0.
Miscellaneous	4.	2.	3.	7.	8.	1.	2.	0.
Public	1.	1.	1.	1.	1.	0.	1.	0.
Private	3.	1.	2.	6.	7.	1.	1.	0.
Total	47.	33.	48.	59.	86.	17.	22.	24.
Public	17.	19.	16.	17.	16.	3.	8.	13.
Private	30.	14.	32.	42.	70.	14.	14.	11.
Proportion spent on child:	0.50	0.05	0.47	0.64	0.71	0.69	0.64	0.54
(N)	(7,106)	(2,864)	(1,414)	(1,561)	(827)	(203)	(164)	(73)

Total Schooling Expenditure for Families Including Those with Children > Age 16.

Total	135.	33.	144.	187.	261.	61.	86.	114.
(N)	(9,837)	(2,864)	(2,231)	(2,423)	(1,498)	(370)	(275)	(176)

penditure nor on the public-private composition of the child's schooling expenditure, judging from results not reported here. The age of the child also has no influence, but recall that for reasons discussed above we have excluded consideration of expenditures on children over age 15, so college expenses for children are not included in this section; we are looking at only families with no children or those with children under age 15.

For the total expenditure on schooling, it does not matter whether we can identify if it is spent on a parent or a child, so we have also selected a separate sample including families with a child over age 16. That sample adds 2,700 additional families to the smaller sample, and the final two rows of table 3.11 show that this augmented sample has an average schooling expenditure of $135, far higher than the $47 average reported above. Here, too, the average expenditure in husband-wife families with one, two, or three children is far greater, presumably reflecting college costs. We have also rerun the two regressions on total schooling expenditures with this augmented sample, and the results are shown in col. 4 of table 3.12. With these older children included, the top panel of the table now shows that schooling expenses rise with the number of children, as one would expect. Regarding the other variables, the education of head and the family income now have much stronger positive effects, and the presence of a child over age 16 raises the schooling expenditure considerably.

Of substantive interest, we note that the regression on children's schooling expenditure implies that while the presence of the first child in a husband-wife family is associated with an incremental expenditure of $27, the

Table 3.12   Regressions on Schooling Expenditures, for Two Subcategories and Total Schooling

Explanatory Variables	Children's Schooling	Adults' Schooling	Total Schooling	Total Schooling (with child 16+)
		Panel A		
Intercept	0.	284.*	305.*	33.*
MF, 1 Child	75.*	− 176.*	− 107.*	110.*
MF, 2 Children	89.*	− 231.*	− 144.*	153.*
MF, 3 Children	138.*	− 234.*	− 96.*	228.*
F, 1 Child	68.	− 236.*	− 183.*	28.
F, 2 Children	52.	− 235.*	− 194.*	53.
F, 3 Children	64.	− 237.*	− 191.	80.*
(R^2)	(0.03)	(0.07)	(0.02)	(0.02)
		Panel B		
Intercept	− 59.*	0.	− 68.*	− 398.*
EDUC: Head	1.*	8.*	10.*	25.*
AGE: Head	0.	− 1.*	− 1.*	1.
INCOME (BT)	2.*	− 1.*	2.*	7.*
SOUTH	14.*	− 8.	8.	16.
RURAL	− 7.	− 8.	− 17.*	− 23.
BLACK	1.	4.	2.	20.
ADULTS EMPLOYED	1.	7.	10.	− 3.
CHILD MALE	1.	− 3.	− 5.	− 18.
CHILD 0–5	− 7.	− 20.*	− 33.*	− 71.*
CHILD 12–15	− 3.	4.	− 3.	− 115.*
MF, 1 Child	27.*	− 9.	24.*	63.*
MF, 2 Children	37.*	− 18.*	27.*	90.*
MF, 3 Children	59.*	− 15.	54.*	140.*
F, 1 Child	36.*	− 31.*	11.	35.
F, 2 Children	36.*	− 29.	14.	78.*
F, 3 Children	37.*	− 33.	9.	54.
CHILD 16+[a]	—	—	—	240.*
(R^2)	(0.07)	(0.04)	(0.05)	(0.15)

*$t \geq 2.0$.
[a]The variable CHILD 16+ used only in regression in col. 4.

presence of the second child is associated with a much smaller increment
($10). A third child, however, is associated with a larger increment ($22).
The results in table 3.11 also imply a reduction in adult schooling expenditure when children are present in the family.

Appendix: Definitions of Variables Used in Chapter 3

Variable	Definition and Values
EDUC	Education level of husband and wife
	= 7 if some grade school completed
	= 10 if some high school completed
	= 12 if high school graduate
	= 14 if some college completed
	= 17 if college graduate or graduate work.
	(For missing value for wife, the value 12 was used; there were no missing values for husband by nature of subsample selection.)
	[general-purpose tape (GPT) variable loc 46 for head and 50 for spouse]
AGE	Age in years of husband and wife.
	[GPT variable loc 71 and 80, and 89 if necessary]
INCOME(BT)	Household annual income before personal taxes.
	[GPT variable loc 775]
INCOME(AT)	Household annual income after personal taxes.
	INCOME(BT) less: federal tax [GPT variable loc 935]; state and local tax [945]; personal property and other personal taxes [955]; social security tax (payroll or self-employed [general-purpose detailed tape (GPDT) var loc 25011 and 25012]; railroad retirement tax [GPDT 25013]; private pensions or retirement [GPDT 25015]; government retirement [GPDT 25014]; self-employment retirement [GPDT 25016]
TOTAL CONSUMPTION	Total consumption expenditure, including gifts and insurance.
	Sum of annual total expenditure [GPT variable loc 124] plus gifts and contributions [loc 764] plus total insurance payments [GPDT variables loc 25001, 25003, 25004, 25006–25010, and 25017]
REGION	Region of the country in which household is located, using Census regions. North East; North Central, South, West.
RESIDENCE	Size of town in which household resides:
	SMSA1M: Dummy is 1.0 if household lives in SMSA with population of 1 million or more, 0 otherwise;
	TOWN: Dummy is 1.0 if household lives in city smaller than 1 million, 0 otherwise;
	RURAL: Dummy is 1.0 if household lives in rural area, 0 otherwise.
BLACK	Household head's race is black.
	Dummy is 1.0 if head is black; 0 otherwise.
	[GPT variable loc 45]
	[GPT variable loc 45]

SURVEY YEAR 1973   Year in which the household was surveyed was 1973. Dummy is 1.0 if household was surveyed in 1973, 0 otherwise. [GPT variable loc 6]

RENTER   Household rented its house (i.e., did not own the house or have a mortgage).

Dummy is 1.0 if household rented housing during the survey year. [GPT variable loc 54 with a value 4]

EMPLOYMENT STATUS   Eight dummy variables indicating the employment status of the husband and wife.

FT is full-time status, defined as "usually worked full-time (35 hours or more per week) when working AND worked more than 26 weeks in the survey year.

PT is part-time status, defined as EITHER "usually worked full-time . . . when working and worked less than or equal to 27 weeks OR "usually worked part-time (less than 35 hours per week), when working.

Not Employed is neither FT nor PT.

With two persons and three categories each, there are nine combinations, one is dropped (the omitted group is Not Emp, Not Emp), leaving eight dummy variables.

Four

Benchmark Models and Their Empirical Application

What can be learned about intrafamily income distribution from existing surveys of detailed spending patterns by households? A number of data sets, including those described in chapter 3, provide extensive information on both the demographic composition of families or households and the consumption pattern of the family. It is tempting to use that information to estimate the distribution of income among family members and to draw inferences about welfare. But those inferences depend crucially upon the nature of the family members' utility functions.

In the first section of this chapter, we explore how conclusions about the distribution of welfare within the family differ under various assumptions about the agents' utility functions. The ability to use expenditure data to infer anything about the distribution of welfare among family members is sensitive to those assumptions. We then propose an empirical strategy that enables us to partition family expenditures into consumption by children and consumption by adults. We use this strategy in the following chapters.

Models of Family Utility

For simplicity, we consider families that have one adult and one child. To begin, assume that there are no public goods.

Case 1: Selfish Adult, Selfish Child

This is the simplest case to analyze, but, fortunately, it lacks realism. We use it as our benchmark. It is characterized by

$$U_A = U_A(C_A), \tag{4.1}$$

$$U_K = U_K(C_K),$$

where U is utility, A refers to adult, K to child, and C is the homogeneous, composite consumption good. Under the assumption that the functional forms of U_A and U_K are identical and linear, the distribution of welfare in the household is measured perfectly by the distribution of the consumption good. The distribution of C between C_A and C_K would reveal the distribution of income and the distribution of welfare within the family.

It is not innocuous to assume that both members have the same utility function. Children may require fewer resources to attain a given level of utility than adults (food is an obvious example). If so, $C_A = C_K$ would result in more utility for the child. Differences in taste represent a less straightforward, but essentially similar, issue. If one person is easy to please while the other is hard to please, equal allocation of dollars, or C, would not mean equal welfare.

If individuals are selfish, then control of the family resources is crucial. In fact, with a purely selfish adult, it is difficult to understand how the child acquires any resources and utility at all. The flow of resources to the child can be rationalized in a bargaining framework. A child can cause the adult disutility by engaging in disruptive behavior, interpreted here as bringing about a reduction in C_A. The adult then "bribes" the child by awarding some C_K to him. How the shares are determined is not essential for this analysis. The fact remains that the distribution of welfare in the household is measured perfectly by the expenditure on each member as long as the utility function and the social welfare function are linear.

Does it matter whether children are endogenous or exogenous? Clearly, it does: if the existence of children is exogenous to the household (i.e., their presence not chosen), then the above reasoning may be correct. But if the presence of the child is endogenous (i.e., found only in households that choose to have a child), then the utility function U_A is not consistent with this choice. In the simplest, purely selfish case of equation (4.1), endogenous children have no place. However, the adult's utility function could be modified to allow for endogenous children. Suppose, for example, that the resources required to raise a child are fixed at $\bar{C}_K$ (because of social pressure or whatever), which may vary with family income and social status. The adult may derive utility from the child in the same way that he derives utility from other possessions, and his choice to have the child and expend resources on the child are simply part of his own utility-maximizing strategy. The adult's maximization problem is the standard one:

$$\text{Max } U_A = U_A (C_A, K), \qquad (4.2)$$
$$\scriptstyle C_A.K$$

subject to

$$\text{Wealth} = C_A + K\bar{C}_K,$$

with

$$U_{K_i} = U_{K_i}(\bar{C}_{K_i}),$$

where $i = 1$ to K, and K is the number of children chosen. The difference between this situation (eq. 4.2) and the exogenous children case (eq. 4.1) is that the distribution of expenditures in the household no longer measures the distribution of welfare. Even in the cleanest case, where U_A is separable so that $U_A = U_A(C_A) + U(K)$ and $U_A(C_A) = U_K(C_K)$ for all $C_A = C_K$, the fact that the child produces utility for the adult introduces a nonpecuniary component so that the adult is willing to trade C_A for additional children. This is easily glossed over, but not necessarily adequately handled, by assuming that the child derives utility from the adult comparable to the utility the parent derives from the child. The endogeneity is not symmetric, however.

Case 2: Complete Externality for Both Adult and Child

At the other extreme is the case where an individual's utility is the sum of the utility that he derives directly from his own consumption plus the utility derived indirectly by the consumption of the other household member:

$$U_A = U(C_A) + U(C_K), \qquad (4.3)$$
$$U_K = U(C_K) + U(C_A).$$

Here, A and K do not care whether they receive utility directly or indirectly by enjoying the other member's satisfaction. This might be called perfect love within the household. Again we ignore differences in utility functions across individuals, that is, $U(C_A) = U(C_K)$ if $C_A = C_K$, or simply $U(\cdot)$ is the same function for both A and K.

Under these circumstances, control of initial resources is irrelevant to the distribution of welfare. If A has all the resources, his problem is to

$$\text{Max } U_A = U(C_A) + U(C_K), \qquad (4.4)$$
$$\scriptstyle C_A.C_K$$

subject to

$$\text{Wealth} = C_A + C_K.$$

Regardless of the distribution of income between C_A and C_K, the welfare is distributed equally with $U_A = U_K$. If $U''(C) < 0$, the household's resources are always shared equally among members. If $U'' > 0$, either member of the household would receive all resources, but neither member would care about the identity of that member. $U'' = 0$ implies total indifference to intrahousehold resource allocation.

Since all household members have the same utility function, there is always complete equality in the distribution of welfare regardless of the distribution of expenditures. The allocation of expenditures bears no relationship to the allocation of utility across household members. All members receive exactly $\bar{U} = U(C_A) + U(C_K)$ utility; the optimal allocation of resources merely insures that $\bar{U}$ is maximized subject to the wealth constraint.

Endogeneity of children is natural with this utility function. If $U'' < 0$, the adult can always increase his utility by producing an offspring and splitting total resources with him. In fact, in this extreme case, the adult produces as many offspring as technologically feasible, sharing resources equally among household members; that is, $U'' < 0$ implies $\bar{U}$ is an increasing function of K! Increasing the size of the household decreases per capita consumption, but increases per capita welfare. The optimal policy in such a world is one where fertility equals fecundity, even without counting the utility of the offspring! Each member's utility rises as his level of consumption is driven to subsistence.

As a corollary, if fecundity varies across individuals, those families that are fortunate enough to have large families have higher utility levels for the same amount of income. This implies that for a given family income, lower per capita income is associated with higher per capita utility. If income varies as well across families, this counterintuitive implication continues to hold as long as income and fecundity are not sufficiently negatively correlated.

These examples are extreme. They do serve to point out, however, how precarious is the jump from data about intrahousehold expenditure allocation to statements about welfare. In the selfish case (eq. 4.1), the distribution of expenditures measures the distribution of welfare perfectly. In the case with complete love (eq. 4.3), the distribution of expenditures bears no relation (or possibly a negative relation) to the distribution of utility. In the selfish case, control of resources is essential; in the perfect love case, it is irrelevant.

Case 3: Less Than Complete Externalities for Adult and Child

This case is a generalization of the previous one. Here the utility of other family members affects an individual's own U_i:

$$U_A = U_A(C_A, C_K), \tag{4.5}$$

and

$$U_K = U_K(C_K, C_A),$$

but not necessarily by the same amount as would be obtained by consuming C oneself, as in:

$$U_A = U_A(C_A + C_K),$$
$$U_K = U_K(C_K + C_A).$$

If symmetry is assumed, so that the child's love for the parent matches the parent's love for the child, then

$$\left. \frac{\partial U_A/\partial C_A}{\partial U_A/\partial C_K} \right|_{\substack{C_A = C_0 \\ C_K = C_1}} = \left. \frac{\partial U_K/\partial C_K}{\partial U_K/\partial C_A} \right|_{\substack{C_K = C_0 \\ C_A = C_1}}. \tag{4.6}$$

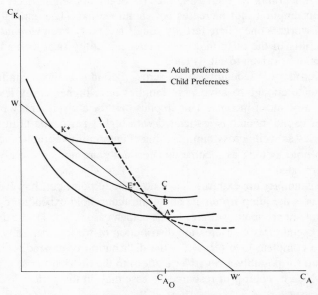

Figure 4.1 Two indifference maps: adult preferences (*dashed curve*) and child preferences (*solid curves*).

Control of resources affects the allocation of expenditures in general. If the assumption of symmetry is dropped so that the adult's love for the child exceeds the child's love for the adult, then

$$\frac{\partial U_A/\partial C_A}{\partial U_A/\partial C_K}\bigg|_{\substack{C_A = C_0 \\ C_K = C_1}} < \frac{\partial U_K/\partial C_K}{\partial U_K/\partial C_A}\bigg|_{\substack{C_K = C_0 \\ C_A = C_1}}, \tag{4.7}$$

for any pair C_0, C_1. Here control of resources affects the allocation of expenditures and the amount of inequality as measured by expenditures or by almost any social welfare function. It also affects the total welfare of the household as measured by almost any social welfare function.

The issues are illustrated by figure 4.1. WW' is the household's budget constraint. It has a slope of -1, implying that transfers between members are costless. E^* represents equal allocation of goods to the adult and child. If the adult controls resources and has the indifference map indicated by the dashed curve, he would choose point A^*, whereas if the child controls resources and has the indifference map indicated by the top solid curve, he would choose point K^*. Note that as drawn, K^* is farther from equality than A^*, reflecting that the adult's love for the child exceeds the child's love for the adult. Asymmetric preferences imply that control of resources affects the allocation of expenditures and the inequality in expenditures.[1] If deviations from equality were viewed negatively and symmetrically (so that C_A, $C_K = C_0$, C_1 yields the same social welfare as C_A, $C_K = C_1$, C_0), then giving control of resources to the "least selfish" individual maximizes social welfare.[2] But no general statements are made about the desirability of awarding control of resources to the adult rather than the child since this depends fundamentally upon the nature of the social welfare function, an unaddressed issue. The point is that, since the chosen expenditure allocation depends upon the identity of the controller, inequality and the level of social welfare depends upon this identity as well, except under very rare circumstances (such as symmetry in both the utility functions and the social welfare functions).

Notice that a move from A^* to E^* raises the child's welfare by *less* than it would be if he were totally selfish. A selfish child's indifference curves

---

1. If preferences are asymmetric but the child's selfishness is matched by the parent's love (or vice versa), then the two would both choose the same point along WW' because the indifference maps appear identical.

2. If the adult is less selfish and chooses C_A, C_K, while the child is more selfish and would choose $\check{C}_A$, $\check{C}_K$, then we know the inequality is greater when the child chooses, that is, $|C_A - C_K| < |\check{C}_A - \check{C}_K|$. So, if the social welfare function exhibits both symmetry [i.e., $S(C_0, C_1) = S(C_1, C_0)$] and dislike of inequality [i.e., $S(C_0, C_0) > S(C_0 + \sigma, C_0 - \sigma)$ for $\sigma \neq 0$], then $S(C_A, C_K) = S(C_K, C_A) > S(\check{C}_K, \check{C}_A)$.

are horizontal lines, so that a move from A^* to E^* would raise his utility by $C - A^*$ "dollars." The loving child is indifferent between E^* and point B, so if C_A were held constant at C_{A_0}, the child's increase in utility is only $B - A^*$ "dollars" (the value of a dollar of C_K depending of course on C_A and C_K).

A move toward equality in expenditures could even bring about a decrease in the utility of the individual whose level of expenditures increases. Given point A^*, one can imagine a set of preferences by the child that would make E^* lie on a lower indifference curve than A^*. If the child's preferences were the dashed curve rather than the solid ones, such a situation would arise. A necessary condition is that both individuals' utility functions are biased in the same (not symmetric) direction. For example, if the parent loves the child more than himself, the child must love himself more than he loves the parent. Under those circumstances, the change in the level of expenditures does not even have the same sign as the change in welfare. It is also obvious that, except in the case where utility functions are identical (not simply symmetric) across individuals, the distribution of expenditures and welfare depends upon the identity of the resource controller.

One additional case is worth mentioning here. The nature of love can be even more indirect. Utility may depend upon one's own consumption and the total utility of others. This allows the adult to receive utility because his own consumption makes the child happier which in turn makes him happier. This case, a special example of the case described above, is analyzed by Becker (1974) and will be discussed in greater detail below.

To summarize, initial assumptions about the nature of the household member's utility functions dramatically affect implications about the appropriateness of using expenditure data to measure welfare inequality within the household and about the importance of control over resources within the household. In Case 1—complete selfishness—expenditures measure welfare inequality perfectly and the control of resources affects inequality. With symmetry of the utility function and the social welfare function, the total utility of the household is unaffected by the identity of the controller. In Case 2—complete love—there is no relationship between expenditures and welfare inequality. In fact, there is no welfare inequality as all members have the same welfare. Hence control is irrelevant. In Case 3—partial and asymmetric love—expenditures imperfectly reflect the distribution of welfare, and the control of resources affects expenditures and thereby inequality and social welfare. Here a move toward more equality in expenditures necessarily increases the less-well-off member's utility by less than the measured increase in his expenditures; he may even be made worse off.

It appears Case 3 contains the worst of both Cases 1 and 2 in ability to investigate the distribution of utility or real income within the household by studying expenditures. Yet Case 3 also appears more intuitively plausible than either Case 1 or 2. The traditional approach of ignoring intrahousehold allocations could be motivated by assuming Case 2. But full and symmetric love among all household members seems inconsistent with casual experience, with evidence on abused children and battered spouses, with evidence on the use of fertility control, and with much other observed behavior.

Other Complications

To this point, we have dealt with a single, homogeneous good, C, allocated as a private good between the two household members, A and K. Many of the interesting and most difficult problems arise only when there is more than one good. Consider the two goods case, where both X and Y are consumed by adults and children. The most general utility function is:

$$U_A = U_A(X_A, Y_A, X_K, Y_K),$$
$$U_K = U_K(X_K, Y_K, X_A, Y_A).$$

For simplicity, consider the case where utility is separable, then

$$U_A = P_1 U(X_A) + P_2 U(Y_A) + P_3 U(X_K) + P_4 U(Y_K), \qquad (4.8)$$
$$U_K = \bar{P}_1 U(X_K) + \bar{P}_2 U(Y_K) + \bar{P}_3 U(X_A) + \bar{P}_4 U(Y_A),$$

where P_i is a weight with $\Sigma P_i = \Sigma \bar{P}_i = 1$. If A controls resources, then the first-order conditions for utility maximization imply, in general:

$$P_1 U'(X_A) = P_3 U'(X_K),$$
$$P_2 U'(Y_A) = P_4 U'(Y_K), \qquad (4.9)$$
$$P_1 U'(X_A)/\pi_X = P_2 U'(Y_A)/\pi_Y,$$

$$\pi_X(X_A + X_K) + \pi_Y(Y_A + Y_K) = \text{Wealth},$$

where π is the price of X or Y.

If A were allowed to transfer only general resources to K, A must view the value of the transfer as equal to its cost. A dollar transferred to K is worth λ in utility to A, where λ is the marginal utility of income, whether K spends the dollar on X or Y. This follows directly from equation (4.9):

$$\frac{P_3 U'(X_K)}{\pi_X} = \frac{P_4 U'(Y_K)}{\pi_Y} = \lambda. \qquad (4.10)$$

For the child, the value in utility is $\bar{\lambda}$:

$$\frac{\bar{P}_1 U'(X_K)}{\pi_X} = \frac{\bar{P}_2 U'(Y_K)}{\pi_Y} = \bar{\lambda}. \tag{4.11}$$

By substitution,

$$\frac{\lambda}{P_3} = \frac{\bar{\lambda}}{\bar{P}_1} \text{ (and } \frac{\lambda}{P_4} = \frac{\bar{\lambda}}{\bar{P}_2}). \tag{4.12}$$

The marginal utility to A of a dollar spent on X by K, λ/P_3, equals the marginal utility to K of a dollar spent on X by K, $\bar{\lambda}/\bar{P}_1$. On the margin, not only is A indifferent between buying X for himself and buying it for K, but K and A get the same marginal utility from that good.

If utility functions were symmetric so that $P_i = \bar{P}_i$, and if there were less than perfect altruism so that $P_1 > P_3$, $P_2 > P_4$ and similarly for $\bar{P}_i$, then equation (4.12) implies $\lambda < \bar{\lambda}$. Since the utility functions are symmetric and quasi-concave, this implies that A commands more resources than K in order to equate marginal utilities.

It is often the case, however, that the adult is not indifferent to the pattern of consumption by the child. Paternalism often hinges on this concern. There are goods the adult wants the child to consume in quantities greater than the child would choose—lessons, health and dental care, and, more broadly, manners. There are other goods that the adult wants the child to consume in smaller quantities than the child might choose—leisure time, certain foods (candy, alcohol), drugs, tobacco, high-speed automobiles, and so on. In these cases the adult may attempt to earmark transfers, requiring by the nature of the transfer that they be consumed in one form and not another. Here, the value to the adult of the transfer of one dollar is still one dollar, and in utility terms it is still λ. But the constraint on the child that the dollar be spent on one good and not another means that equation (4.11) does not hold: the ratio for the forbidden good exceeds the ratio for the transferred good. The value of the transfer to the giver (A) now exceeds its value to the receiver (K). This implies that it is inappropriate to attribute the dollar spent on K as worth a dollar to K unless the transfer is spent as K would choose to spend it.

This point goes to the heart of the issue of using spending patterns to measure within-family income distribution. Consider an expenditure item like baby-sitting. Should one categorize this expenditure as the child's income or as the parent's income, or both? Notice that this is neither a measurement issue (the actual number of dollars spent on baby-sitting can be observed) nor a standard public goods problem (only the child is baby-sat, not the parent as well). For the parent, a marginal dollar spent on baby-sitting must be worth a dollar, or in utility λ, but for the child its value in utility need not be $\bar{\lambda}$, indeed $U'(Y_K)$ need not even be positive. Without information about the utility function, assumed or adduced, one does not know how to apportion the baby-sitting expenditure.

Consider a similar item that involves a public good: a daughter's wedding. Should this expenditure be viewed as an expenditure on the child's or the parent's behalf? Both daughter and parent must consume the item jointly, but its value to each need not be the same—indeed, its value to each may not even be positive. If the child were neutral about her wedding, but the parent derived utility from it, then the expenditure should be attributed to the parent because only the parent is willing to forego consumption for it.

Compare this to the approach that attributes the expenditure to the child if it would not have been made in the absence of the child. What does this measure? Certainly not welfare, since, by assumption, the child derives no utility from the expenditure. What about the "cost" of a child? "Cost" has meaning whether we think of the cost of an inanimate object or a human being. But what is traded off is the cost to the person making the decision to purchase a commodity against the benefit that *that* person derives from that commodity. It has nothing to do with how the recipient feels about the expenditure, and it is not appropriate to say that the welfare of the child is measured by the "cost" in expenditures on the child. Expenditures on a child may increase the child's utility, but not by the amount of the expenditure, except under special circumstances. The condition under which the "cost of the child" measures the child's welfare is when the adult cares only about the child's utility level and not about the allocation of the child's consumption. Also required is that the child derive no utility from the parent's consumption. Under that circumstance, maximization of the adult's utility is equivalent to first determining the amount of wealth to be allocated to the child and then allowing the child to maximize his own utility subject to the wealth constraint. The adult's problem is:

$$\text{Max } U_A[X_A, Y_A, U_K (X_K, Y_K)], \tag{4.13}$$

by the selection of X_A, X_K, Y_A, and Y_K subject to $\pi_X(X_A + X_K) + \pi_Y(Y_A + Y_K) = \text{Wealth}$. The parent's first-order conditions for X_K and Y_K are

$$\frac{\partial U_A}{\partial U_K} \cdot \frac{\partial U_K}{\partial X_K} - \lambda \pi_X = 0,$$

and

$$\frac{\partial U_A}{\partial U_K} \cdot \frac{\partial U_K}{\partial Y_K} - \lambda \pi_Y = 0,$$

which are the same first-order conditions for the child if we define the child's marginal utility of income $\bar{\lambda}$ to be $(\lambda/\partial U_A/\partial U_K)$. The expenditure on the child, or the "cost of the child," measures the child's utility. It is still true, of course, that adding up expenditures only gives us the sum of marginal values, which, with diminishing marginal rates of substitution, understates total utility. But this is true even in a one-person situation and is not a complication introduced only in the family context.

If a public good were enjoyed by both parent and child, as in the case of a house located in a good suburban school district, then its contribution to the utility of the household has the standard public good attributes. Both derive utility from the commodity, although not necessarily to the same degree.

Savings can be discussed in this context. Define X as consumption today and Y as consumption tomorrow. To the extent that X and Y have some publicness to them, the following issue arises: The child may have a preference for X over Y because the child is less likely to be living in the same household when Y is consumed. On the other hand, the probability that the child will be alive during the next period is higher, so his preference for savings may be higher than that of his parent. This is an important issue because savings is a large expenditure item in most budgets; the question of how to allocate its value between parent and child is central. One straightforward way to deal with this issue is to think of a steady state in which there is as much dissaving taking place as saving. Under the appropriate assumptions, this nets out in a cross section so that proper inferences can be drawn merely from the expenditure data. The easiest strategy regarding savings is merely to assume that it is allocated in the same way as current consumption expenditures. This is the strategy followed throughout the empirical sections that follow.

We have discussed certain intrafamily externalities, but additional problems exist both within the family and beyond its domain. One issue results from the costly enforcement of contracts. Even in a world of completely selfish parents and children, enforcement costs can produce externalities. They may result because the person with control over resources cannot always make an enforceable contract with another party. For example, the child might be willing to pay an amount greater than cost to be given piano lessons, or better nourishment, or more schooling.[3] If his promise to repay the selfish parent when he becomes an adult were enforceable, such a transaction might occur, but in the absence of a cheap enforcement mechanism, efficient exchanges such as these may not take place. A related

3. This is discussed and empirical evidence is provided in Lazear (1983).

issue mentioned only in passing is that of preference revelation. We assume that the utility functions of the parent and child are known. However, one can imagine a situation where the child tries to convince the parent that the child's utility function is different than it actually is, thus causing the parent to allocate resources more to the child's liking than the parent would have chosen. We explore this issue no further here, but this and other complications[4] serve to remind us of the simplifying nature of the models discussed in this section.

Summary

Where does this leave us? What is the answer to the question we used to introduce this chapter: What can be learned about intrafamily income distribution from surveys of spending patterns? Nothing, without first specifying something about the nature of the family members' utility functions. Without some guidance from the utility function, even measurable items such as baby-sitting expenses cannot be allocated. With special utility functions, one can infer everything about the distribution of utility from expenditure data. Making those assumptions, however, is too much like the caricatured economist's response to the problem of how to open a can of food found while stranded on a desert island ("assume we have a can opener"). Instead of assuming the problem away, we propose a compromise: some restrictive assumptions are made that allow the use of existing survey data to estimate something, although not everything, about the distribution of income within families. The next section discusses this strategy.

An Empirical Strategy

In chapter 2 we identified five difficulties in the measurement of individual income in a family-income context: life-cycle measurement; apportionment of private goods (i.e., who consumed the quart of milk?); apportionment of public goods; measurement of nonpecuniary resources that also affect well-being; and externalities or the difficulty of measuring the inter-

---

4. Another externality that might be mentioned is the effect of the family's decision on nonfamily members. For example, "society" may wish all children to attend school or to receive certain preventive health care, even if the individual family would not choose these expenditures. The allocation of resources within the family is not independent of these external pressures.

dependence of preferences, where one person gets satisfaction from another person's consumption. We do not know how to handle the latter two problems. They are, incidentally, problems that plague income distribution studies generally; they are not limited to the intrafamily distribution.[5] Of the remaining three problems, the life cycle is most easily handled by integrating out age-specific effects to obtain lifetime values. This section focuses upon the remaining two problems: the unobserved apportionment of private goods and the apportionment of public goods.

Let us think of the consumption bundle of the family as having three kinds of items: (1) those easily assignable to a particular person or at least to an adult or a child (examples might be expenditures on a tricycle, children's books, tobacco or alcohol, or clothing for female adults, etc.); (2) those items that are private goods but whose consumption is usually masked in expenditure survey data (e.g., groceries); and (3) those items that are public goods within the family (e.g., electricity, artwork, perhaps TV).

Measurement of Private Goods

The apportionment of the assignable private goods is trivial. The question is how to apportion the unassignable private goods (e.g., the groceries) among family members. The task is simplified by assigning the expenditure either to the adults or to the children. We do not address here the assignment of these expenditures between the two adults or among the several children.

One strategy that might appear sensible for allocating the groceries and other essentially private goods between adults and children is this: Assume the shares of groceries consumed by adults and by children are the same shares as we see among the allocable private goods. That is, let $\tilde{C}_K$ and $\tilde{C}_A$ be the identifiable items (in dollars) consumed by children and by adults, respectively. Then calculate:

$$\frac{\tilde{C}_K}{\tilde{C}_K + \tilde{C}_A} = \lambda, \tag{4.14}$$

and assume that λ percent of the groceries are consumed by the children and $(1 - \lambda)$ percent consumed by the adults. The flaw in this strategy is

5. The distribution of nonpecuniary resources includes the distribution of leisure time and all the issues related to the limitations of GNP measurement or the illusion that only market exchanges have value. Regarding interdependence of preferences, the problem is greater in the intrafamily comparisons than in cross-family comparisons because the interdependence of preferences itself is presumably far greater within the family.

that λ depends not only on the family's behavior but also on the detail with which the survey happened to collect expenditure information. If the survey probed for information about child-related expenses, λ will be relatively high; if it probed on, say, adult clothing or adult sports consumption, λ will be relatively low. In short, λ tells us as much about the survey design as about behavior. It is arbitrary from the point of view of behavior and thus unacceptable as a strategy for allocating the other private goods.

A related strategy appears more useful, however. If public goods are ignored, then total expenditure in the family, T, is apportioned as

$$T = AC_A + KC_K, \tag{4.15}$$

where A is the number of adults, K the number of children, and C_A and C_K the average consumption by an adult and by a child in the family. The ratio C_K/C_A is of interest. Suppose that that behavioral ratio is affected by a set of demographic and economic characteristics, X; that is,

$$\frac{C_K}{C_A} = \phi(X). \tag{4.16}$$

The vector X can include all characteristics of the household including family size, the ages and number of children, among other things. The value of $\phi(X)$ is a measure of neutrality: if $\phi(X) = 1$, then on average the household treats adult and child members identically with respect to expenditure. If $\phi(X) < 1$, then the household "favors" adults relative to children. If $\phi(X) > 1$, then the household "favors" children relative to adults.[6]

Define λ_A as the proportion of total expenditures on the adults in the family to observed expenditures on the adults, and likewise λ_K as the ratio of total expenditures on children to observed expenditures on children:

6. The interpretation of $\phi(X)$ depends upon the nature of the decision maker's utility function. Consider the following specific example in which $\phi(X)$ has straightforward implications. Consider all monotonic transformations of a Cobb-Douglas utility function. Specifically,

$$U = f[C_A C_K^{\phi(x)}],$$

where $f' > 0$. Then the first-order conditions insure that

$$C_K = \phi(X)C_A,$$

so that $\phi(X)$ can be interpreted as the weight given to consumption by the child relative to consumption by the adult in contributing utility to the decision maker. It is also true, of course, that $\phi(X)/[1 + \phi(X)]$ always reflects the share of household income that goes to the child even if prices of child consumption relative to adult consumption were to change (say, through an enforceable government subsidy to expenditures on children). This Cobb-Douglas case illustrates that, if a specific utility function is assumed, it may be possible to make definite statements about the relationship between expenditures and welfare.

$$\lambda_A \equiv \frac{C_A}{\tilde{C}_A}; \; \lambda_K \equiv \frac{C_K}{\tilde{C}_K}. \tag{4.17}$$

Those ratios are merely statements of the relationship between true and observed expenditures; they reflect survey design as well as behavior.

The basic strategy for estimating C_K/C_A is to substitute suitably parameterized versions of equations (4.16) and (4.17) into (4.15). By substitution we have:

$$T = \lambda_A A \tilde{C}_A + \phi(X)\lambda_A A \tilde{C}_A (K/A). \tag{4.18}$$

In a typical cross-sectional expenditure survey, the total expenditure, T, the number of adults, A, and number of children, K, in the family are known for each household. Selection of observable adult expenditure items defines $A\tilde{C}_A$. The only two terms in equation (4.18) that are not observable are λ_A and $\phi(X)$.

There are several specific ways to proceed at this point. The first approach eliminates λ_A and estimates a multiplicative form of $\phi(X)$. First, substitute for T using equation (4.15) and then substitute for C_K using equation (4.17). Assume that

$$\phi(X) = \phi_0 X_1^{\phi_1} X_2^{\phi_2} \ldots X_N^{\phi_N}. \tag{4.19}$$

After rearranging terms and taking logs, one obtains

$$\ln\left(\frac{K\tilde{C}_K}{A\tilde{C}_A}\right) - \ln\left(\frac{K}{A}\right) = \ln\left(\frac{\lambda_A}{\lambda_K}\right) + \ln \phi_0$$
$$+ \phi_1 \ln X_1 + \ldots + \phi_N \ln X_N. \tag{4.20}$$

The intercept of the right-hand side of equation (4.20) is $\ln(\lambda_A/\lambda_K) + \ln \phi_0$, and all terms on both sides are observable. The first item on the left-hand side is the ratio of observed expenditures on children to observed expenditures on adults; the second item is simply the ratio of the number of children to the number of adults; the X's are demographic and economic characteristics of the family.

This first approach does not permit us to identify C_K/C_A completely, although it allows us to get a clear estimate of how that ratio varies with household demographic characteristics. The nature of our inability to completely identify C_K/C_A is made clear by equation (4.20). The constant term contains two components: The first is the contribution of measurement factors to the true relationship between adult and child expenditures, and the second is a behavioral contribution, ϕ_0. Without an estimate of ϕ_0, the level of $\phi(X)$ cannot be measured, hence C_A/C_K is not identified. In fact, there is no way to identify ϕ_0 without somehow measuring λ_A and λ_K. But this approach does provide useful information on ϕ_1 thorough ϕ_N, the way that expenditures on children relative to adults vary by demographic and economic characteristics of the family.

Another unattractive feature of this approach is the implicit assumption that the X's do not affect the relationship between the true and the measured expenditures differently for adults and for children, that is, the X's do not affect the ratio λ_A/λ_K. But since age, education, and income affect the consumption bundle, it is likely that they will affect λ_A/λ_K.

A second estimation approach permits us to avoid this difficulty and to identify ϕ_0 as well, thus yielding full estimates of the ratio of the true expenditures on children to the true expenditures on adults, not simply estimates of the way this ratio varies with the X's. The price we pay for the advantages of this second approach is additional assumptions, in particular the assumption of the separability of the utility function.[7]

The necessary separability assumption for the second approach is:

$$U_A = U_1(\tilde{C}_A, \bar{C}_A) + U_2(\tilde{C}_K, \bar{C}_K; K), \tag{4.21}$$

with

$$U_2(\, , \, ; 0) = 0.$$

Recall that $\tilde{C}$ is, as above, the observable expenditure and define $\bar{C}$ as the remainder: $\bar{C} \equiv C - \tilde{C}$. This assumption implies that the ratio $\tilde{C}_A/C_A$ is independent of the number of children and their consumption. It is this assumption that allows identification of λ_A. The reason is that in a childless family AC_A is equal to the family's total expenditures, T. Thus:

$$\lambda_A = \frac{AC_A}{A\tilde{C}_A} = \frac{T}{A\tilde{C}_A}, \tag{4.22}$$

which is directly observable for the childless family. Moreover, λ_A can vary with Z, a set of characteristics of the family that excludes characteristics of children in the family. Write λ_A as

$$\lambda_A = \lambda_A(Z) = \lambda_0 + \lambda_1 Z_1 + \lambda_2 Z_2 + \ldots + \lambda_m Z_m, \tag{4.23}$$

parameterized here as a linear function of the Z's. Since λ_A can be observed for each childless family (calculated from eq. 4.22), a regression of observed λ_A on the set of $Z_1, Z_2, Z_3, \ldots, Z_m$ yields estimates of the parameters $\lambda_0, \lambda_1, \ldots, \lambda_m$. It is crucial here that the set of Z's be independent of children. This condition holds so long as the utility function is homothetic and separable as in equation (4.21). With the parameters λ_0,

---

7. This approach was first used in Lazear (1978).

$\lambda_1, \ldots, \lambda_m$ estimated from childless couples, an estimate of λ_A can be computed for each family with children. Given λ_A, it is straightforward to estimate λ_K for each family with children by substituting $\lambda_A(X)$ and the definitions of λ_K and λ_A into equation (4.15), yielding:

$$\lambda_K(Z) = \frac{T - \lambda_A(Z)A\tilde{C}_A}{KC\tilde{}_K}. \tag{4.24}$$

With λ_A and λ_K estimated, the relevant values for each family can be substituted into equation (4.20), leaving only $\ln\phi_0$ as the intercept. Thus, with ϕ_0 as well as $\phi_1 \ldots \phi_N$ estimable, we can obtain $\phi(X)$, which, by equation (4.16), is the ratio of interest, C_K/C_A.

Notice that this second approach uses two new pieces of information: the calculated λ_A from childless couples and a measure of both $A\tilde{C}_A$ and $K\tilde{C}_K$ for the family with children. The items in $A\tilde{C}_A$ are the same as those used to calculate λ_A from childless couples, but the remaining term $K\tilde{C}_K$ requires identification of a few expenditure items unambiguously consumed by the children. That may or may not be possible. Moreover, there is an unattractive feature of equation (4.20), even though it can now be estimated. The distribution of the dependent variable (and also presumably the equation's error term) is the ratio of two random variables. The error has a Cauchy distribution for which moments do not exist. It is known that estimates obtained under these circumstances may be badly behaved and have undesirable finite sample properties.

But fortunately there is a third approach that circumvents many of these problems. This approach estimates equation (4.18) directly. As before, the estimated $\hat{\lambda}_A$ from equation (4.23) is used, but instead of using equation (4.19), $\phi(X)$ is parameterized as a simple linear function:

$$\phi(X) = \phi_0 + \phi_1 X_1 + \phi_2 X_2 + \ldots + \phi_N X_N. \tag{4.25}$$

Substituting equation (4.25) into equation (4.18) directly leaves

$$T = (\hat{\lambda}_A A\tilde{C}_A) + \phi_0(\hat{\lambda}_A A\tilde{C}_A K/A) + \phi_1(\hat{\lambda}_A A\tilde{C}_A K/A)(X_1) + \ldots + \phi_N(\hat{\lambda}_A A\tilde{C}_A K/A)(X_N),$$

or simplifying the notation with $D_0 \equiv \hat{\lambda}_A A\tilde{C}_A$ and $D_1 \equiv D_0(K/A)$, write:

$$T = (D_0) + \phi_0(D_1) + \phi_1(D_1 X_1) + \phi_2(D_1 X_2) + \ldots + \phi_N(D_1 X_N). \tag{4.26}$$

All that is required in addition to the demographic and economic variables in the sets Z (for estimating $\hat{\lambda}_A$) and X (used in eq. 4.26) is: T, K, A, and $A\tilde{C}_A$ for families with children. All are generally available. Thus, the linear equation (4.26) can be estimated. The notable aspects of this equation are that it implies that the coefficient on D_0 is 1 and that the equation should be estimated without an intercept. Both are testable and provide some gauge on the reasonableness of equation (4.26).

It would be desirable to obtain some indication of the reasonableness of the separability assumption (eq. 4.21) as well. As that is our identifying assumption, we have not been able to think of a way of checking its validity—any scheme that permitted us to check it would permit us to do without it. In households with no children we can measure λ, but we cannot investigate directly the effect children might have on it; in households with children there is no way we have thought of to measure λ directly. If we knew of a way, we would not need to use the separability assumption. Introspection or conjecture are all we have to rely on at this point. This assumption is crucial for the analysis that follows, but we cannot determine its accuracy.

The crucial separability assumption is that the ratio of the marginal utilities of $\tilde{C}_A$ to C_A is unaffected by the presence or number of children. A change in the number of children in the household can be expected to alter the relative prices of various nonmarket commodities and might alter the relative price of the composite good $\tilde{C}_A$ relative to the price of the larger composite good C_A. But our equation (4.23) estimates the ratio C_A to $\tilde{C}_A$ in childless households by using, in the vector Z, many of the exogenous covariates that affect fertility, including age, gender, and education of the household head, family income, location, race, and number of adults in the household. Consequently, to the extent that these covariates capture the changes in prices that accompany changes in number of children, equation (4.23) has already taken those possible price effects into account.

Our point can be made with respect to homotheticity of the utility function. Since expenditures devoted to children are assumed to be separable in the utility function, the remaining choice between C_A and $\tilde{C}_A$ must be independent of income. Removing the expenditures on children's goods is analogous to a pure income effect on adult goods. But the form then requires that the ratio of adult observed goods to adult unobserved goods be independent of income. In chapter 5, we present some evidence that indirectly bears on this issue. When adult-only households are examined, the ratio $\tilde{C}_A$ to C_A can be estimated. It is permitted to depend on income: the effect of income on the ratio is not statistically significant. That the effect is insignificant suggests that an assumption of homotheticity is not rejected by the data. While this informal check on our assumption is no more than suggestive, it is not contradictory.

With equation (4.26) estimated, $\phi_0, \phi_1, \ldots, \phi_N$ are used in equation

(4.25) to calculate the ratio of interest, C_K/C_A (see eg. 4.16). The degree of preference for children or for adults in the family's spending pattern is reflected by the deviation from unity in C_K/C_A. In the next two chapters, equations (4.23), (4.26), and (4.16) are used to calculate that ratio for various family types.

Measurement of Public Goods

Valuation of public goods always presents difficulties, and these difficulties are no less pronounced in the family context. In this section several approaches are suggested that might be used to assess the value of public goods within the family.

A straightforward and theoretically reasonable approach is to split goods into those that are public and those that are private. The private goods are allocated as before, and the public goods are divided up evenly among all individuals. For example, if the household has four members and $1,000 of a public good is purchased, then each member is assumed to receive $250 of that public good. Note that even though the good is public and all consume it fully, it is not the case that each receives $1,000 of value. The reason is that consumption of the public good is pushed until the sum of marginal utilities across all consumers equals the marginal utility of a private good. Thus, the marginal utility of the public good in our example is one-fourth the marginal utility of the private good if the decision maker treats all four individuals in the family symmetrically.

Formally, if the decision maker's utility function were

$$U = f(X_1, Y) + f(X_2, Y) + f(X_3, Y) + f(X_4, Y), \qquad (4.27)$$

where X_i is the private good consumed by individual i, and Y is the public good, then

$$\frac{\partial U/\partial X_i}{\partial U/\partial Y} = \frac{\partial f/\partial X_i}{4\partial f/\partial Y}. \qquad (4.28)$$

Thus, the marginal utility of the private good is four times as large as the marginal utility of the public good to any one of the four individuals in the household.

But there is no reason to assume such neutral preferences. An alternative approach assumes that the ratio of utility derived by a child from public goods to the ratio derived by an adult from those same public goods is equal to the ratio of private expenditures on children to private expenditures on adults. In this formulation one argues that the adult allocates expenditures in the family on public goods with the same concern for the child as reflected in the expenditures on private goods. This, essentially, is the formulation we use in the subsequent empirical effort. We will now elaborate on its attributes.

Formally, if the decision rule is to maximize:

$$U = f(X_1, Y) + f(X_2, Y) + \phi f(X_3, Y) + \phi f(X_4, Y), \qquad (4.29)$$

where individuals 1 and 2 are adults and individuals 3 and 4 are children, then optimization requires that

$$\frac{\partial f}{\partial X_i} = 2(1 + \phi) \frac{\partial f}{\partial Y} \text{ for } i = 1, 2, \qquad (4.30)$$

and

$$\phi \frac{\partial f}{\partial X_i} = 2(1 + \phi) \frac{\partial f}{\partial Y} \text{ for } i = 3, 4.$$

Thus, the marginal utility from the public good, Y, relative to the marginal utility from the private good, X, as seen by the adult and by the child, respectively, is:

$$\frac{2f/2Y}{2f/2X_i} = \frac{1}{2(1 + \phi)} \text{ for } i = 1, 2,$$

$$= \frac{\phi}{2(1 + \phi)} \text{ for } i = 3, 4, \qquad (4.31)$$

or, more generally, with A adults instead of two, and K children instead of 2, equation (4.31) becomes:

$$\frac{MU_Y}{MU_i} = \frac{1}{A + \phi K} \text{ for adults,}$$

$$= \frac{\phi}{A + \phi K} \text{ for children.} \qquad (4.32)$$

Or, put differently, the total consumption by the adult, C_A, and by the child, C_K, can be expressed as:

$$C_A = X_A + \left(\frac{1}{A + \phi K}\right) Y,$$

$$C_K = X_K + \left(\frac{\phi}{A + \phi K}\right) Y. \qquad (4.33)$$

Expressing (4.33) as a ratio:

$$\frac{C_K}{C_A} = \frac{X_K + \left(\dfrac{\phi}{A + \phi K}\right) Y}{X_A + \left(\dfrac{1}{A + \phi K}\right) Y}, \tag{4.34}$$

and since $\phi = C_K/C_A$, equation (4.34) implies:

$$\frac{C_K}{C_A} = \frac{X_K}{X_A}. \tag{4.35}$$

Equation (4.35) implies that when we know the ratio of the private goods, X_K/X_A, we also know the ratio of the total of the private and the public goods, C_K/C_A. The assumption that yields this result is embedded in equation (4.29): that is, the adult weighs equally (at the weight ϕ) the utility to the child of either the private good, X_i, or the public good, Y. The adult is not more or less disposed toward spending on the child relative to the adult in either private goods or public goods. That assumption, of course, cannot be tested here, so it is a maintained assumption. It seems intuitively sensible to us.

Let us explore briefly what this assumption means and how it might be understood. Put aside for the moment the common utility function, f, and the homogeneous nature of the public good, Y. Some public goods are surely valued more highly by adults—say, living near a golf course—while others are valued more highly by children—say, living near a playground. Now, our assumption suggests that the bundle of public goods purchased by the household's decision maker has the same relative attractiveness to the adults and the children, as does the bundle of private goods purchased. That is, each adult's consumption of the public good Y^A is $\left(\dfrac{1}{A + \phi K}\right) Y$, and each child's consumption of the public good Y^K is $\left(\dfrac{\phi}{A + \phi K}\right) Y$, so the ratio of the public goods consumed by each child to public goods consumed by each adult is $\left(\dfrac{\phi}{A + \phi K}\right) Y \Big/ \left(\dfrac{1}{A + \phi K}\right) Y$, which simply equals ϕ. Or, expressed in a form that will be useful immediately below, the proportion of the household's whole public goods consumption that is consumed by the adults, Y_A/Y, is $(A/A + \phi K)$.

When $K = 0$, the proportion consumed by the adults is, of course, 100 percent. If $A = 2$ and $K = 2$ and, say, $\phi = 0.5$, then the proportion of Y

consumed by the adults is $(A/A + \phi K) = 2/3 = 67$ percent, and that is the same percentage of the bundle of private goods consumed by the adults.

Consider, then, how the estimation of ϕ proceeds. In a household with no children but with public goods:

$$T = AX_A + Y^A, \tag{4.36}$$

and defining the observable adult private goods, $A\tilde{X}_A$, as we did earlier, we can write $\lambda = T/A\tilde{X}_A$, and we can estimate λ as a function of a set of household characteristics that exclude children. Then going to the equation for households with children:

$$T = AX_A + KX_K + Y, \tag{4.37}$$

we substitute λ and ϕ and derive:

$$T = \hat{\lambda}A\tilde{X}_A + \phi\hat{\lambda}A\tilde{X}_A\left(\frac{K}{A}\right) + Y - \left(\frac{A + \phi K}{A}\right)Y^A. \tag{4.38}$$

Notice that the first two terms in equation (4.38) are equivalent to equation (4.18). Recall that we established that the proportion of the household's public good Y that is consumed by the A adults in the household is $(A/A + \phi K)$, or:

$$\frac{Y^A}{Y} = \frac{A}{A + \phi K}.$$

So the last two terms in equation (4.38) drop out, leaving equation (4.38) equivalent to equation (4.18). So we have in effect included the adult's portion of the public goods in our estimate of λ and attributed the additional expenditure on public goods to the children's portion of the total consumption bundle.

A very different approach is to start out by ignoring the distinction between expenditures on children and adults and to think in terms of total expenditures for the family. Some proportion of those expenditures go for goods that are public or exhibit scale economies in other respects. In previous work, the size of these scale economies and the way in which these scale economies vary across household sizes has been estimated (Lazear and Michael 1980). One could do the same thing here. Income would be blown up by an estimate of the scale economy and then apportioned throughout the household by using one of the methods described above. The difference would be that λ_A and λ_K in equation (4.17) and T in equation (4.15) would then be functions of the scale economies. Explicitly, T in equation (4.15) must be blown up by the size of that scale economy so that λ_A and λ_K change proportionately. This is the approach that was employed by Lazear (1978). At least in those data, the effect of blowing up income by the scale economy factor was to alter dramatically the effects of family size on the proportion of income going to children and adults, as one would expect. But this did not affect the impact of other characteristics on that ratio. In any case, it is another strategy worthy of consideration, but we do not pursue it further in this book.

Summary

This chapter has explored how various assumptions about the family's preferences affect what can be learned about the within-family income and welfare distribution from detailed data on family spending patterns. While assumptions about preferences alternately imply that a uniform distribution of income within the family is probably a good approximation to truth or that observed spending patterns reflect the actual distribution quite well, none of these assumptions about preferences seems very palatable. More appealing assumptions, unfortunately, make inference more difficult.

We have suggested a compromise in which some restrictive assumptions are imposed on both preferences and behavior that permit the use of spending data to estimate the apportionment of the family's expenditures between adults and children. In the next chapter the strategy detailed here is employed to investigate the allocation of family expenditures between adults and children.

Five

The Division of Income between Adults and Children: Evidence from the 1972–73 Consumer Expenditure Survey

In this chapter we estimate the relationship between the relative expenditures on adults and children within the household and the demographic characteristics of the family. Chapter 4 described a method for estimating the allocation of expenditures within the family and discussed some of the pitfalls of more naive approaches as well as the limitations of the approach we adopt. Our method does come to grips with the difficulties encountered when one uses information from a survey that definitionally cannot avoid the classification of goods as part of its design. We pointed out that one naive way to measure the allocation of expenditures would be to eyeball the data (or do the same thing in a more sophisticated fashion), but this suffers from the drawback that the results of such an examination are as much affected by the survey designer's classification scheme as they are by the family's actual behavior. In order to circumvent this difficulty, we have obtained statistical identification by comparing households without children to those with children. This makes it possible to isolate those differences in expenditures that reflect behavior from those that merely reflect measurement.

By using this approach, one can obtain answers to questions that are important in the analysis of income distribution within a family. In particular:

1. Do children receive the same share of family expenditures as adults, or is one group favored over the other, on average?

2. Does the treatment of different family members depend upon family characteristics: e.g., on its size; on the race, level of education, and age of its members; on the number of parents within the family; on the location of the household and whether it is a farm or not; on the work status of the adults and the children?

With the exception of the restriction of separability of the utility function and the assumption that adults weigh public goods available to their children in the same way they weigh private goods for their children, the method employed here does not require any explicit utility function. Consequently, results are insensitive to changes in assumptions about the family utility function. On the other side of that coin, our reluctance to assume some particular utility function prevents us from concluding much about the distribution of welfare in the household.

There are a few other limitations. First, the treatment of savings is superficial. Throughout this chapter, we assume that the allocation of benefits from savings mimics that from consumption, enabling us to ignore the entire issue of savings. As a result, most of the analysis is conducted in terms of expenditure rather than income. Issues related to savings are complicated because the composition of the household may change between the time the savings allocation is made and the time the saved resources are consumed. In order to deal with such issues, it would be necessary to extend the analysis to consider interactions between families as well, for example, between the household of the parent and the newly structured household of the grown child. The problem at hand is sufficiently difficult without these complications.

In the same vein, the value of spillovers to the rest of society—that is, how the consumption of resources by individuals in one family affects the utility of individuals in another family—is lost. For example, the value to society as a whole of having educated or well-fed children is not measured.

The approach followed throughout this chapter is described in chapter 4. As discussed in that chapter, this approach does not require the classification of strictly child-related expenditures. All that is necessary is the classification of those expenditures consumed exclusively by adults. This follows the method traditionally employed in this literature (pioneered by Henderson 1949, 1950) and is therefore useful for purposes of comparison. One limitation is that we are unable to identify the parameter that relates observed expenditure on children to actual expenditure on children, λ_K. But this parameter primarily reflects the survey design and is of little interest.

The data used in this chapter come from the 1972–73 Consumer Expenditure Survey (CES), as described in chapter 3. The same method is employed in chapter 6 to obtain estimates from the 1960–61 CES data. This allows comparisons derived from an examination of the thirteen-year period, 1960–73. Changes may reflect different attitudes toward, or expectations about, family life over this period. In the final section of the chapter, the estimates are examined for robustness against different specifications of the model. The results suggest that many of the basic conclusions are quite invariant with respect to changes in some of the assumptions, but that others are quite sensitive to functional form. This suggests that caution is warranted in making use of our estimates. Nonetheless, we think they are useful.

Methods and Data

To summarize the method, the goal is to apportion the family's total expenditures, T, into two elements: the average per capita expenditure on an Adult, C_A, and that on a child, C_K. One can directly observe T, A, and K but not C_A and C_K.

The budget constraint is

$$T = AC_A + KC_K. \tag{5.1}$$

(We could use the notation in chapter 4 distinguishing private goods (X) from public goods (Y), but for simplicity of presentation we do not distinguish between these two here.) Further, a subset of the adult expenditures in any household can be identified. Expenditures on adult clothing, alcohol, and tobacco are observable. Since it is reasonable to suppose that these three items are consumed exclusively by adults, define the sum of these three items as the observed adult expenditure $A\tilde{C}_A$. (This practice does not originate here; see Henderson 1949, 1950)

It would be preferable to expand the set of commodities consumed exclusively by adults, since one would expect that random measurement error would be less bothersome in larger, aggregated commodity sets. Unfortunately, even in a data set that is most explicit about consumer expenditure patterns, with over 2,000 specific items identified, we could find no other items that could be categorized as consumed by adults exclusively without a substantial amount of guesswork. Nor is it clear that there *are* a large number of commodities of this type, at least when weighted by their shares in the household budgets. Items such as food, housing, utilities, and transportation, which comprise the major part of family expenditures, are clearly not attributable to any one individual directly. Clothing is already categorized, and other expenditure categories are small indeed as compared with this grouping. Thus, it must be admitted that the inability to use a large number of commodities in defining $A\tilde{C}_A$ is as much a defect of our strategy as it is of survey design.

That having been said, rewrite equation (5.1) (also eq. 4.18) as:

$$(T) = \lambda_A (A\tilde{C}_A) + \phi(X)\lambda_A(A\tilde{C}_A K/A), \tag{5.2}$$

where the variables in parentheses are measurable for each family. The estimation procedure is then completed in two steps.[1] First, data from all households with no children are used to estimate a form of equation (4.23) (the 1972–73 CES has 5,032 usable observations).[2] Specifically,

$$T = \lambda_0(A\tilde{C}_A) + \lambda_1(A\tilde{C}_A Z_1) + \lambda_2(A\tilde{C}_A Z_2) + \ldots + \lambda_m(A\tilde{C}_A Z_m). \quad (5.3)$$

With the parameters λ_0 through λ_m estimated, calculate for each of the j families with children:

$$\hat{\lambda}_{Aj} = \hat{\lambda}_0 + \hat{\lambda}_1 Z_{1j} + \ldots + \hat{\lambda}_m Z_{mj}. \quad (5.4)$$

The only remaining unknown in equation (5.2) is the function $\phi(X)$. So, as the second step, run the following regression for the j families with children:

$$(T_j) = (D_{0j}) + \phi_0(D_{1j}) + \phi_1(D_{1j}X_{1j}) + \ldots + \phi_N(D_{1j}X_{Nj}), \quad (5.5)$$

where, as in chapter 4, $D_{0j} = \hat{\lambda}_{Aj}A_j\tilde{C}_{Aj}$, and $D_{1j} = D_{0j}(K_j/A_j)$. This regression yields estimates of ϕ_0 through ϕ_N which permit the estimation of the ratio of interest (eq. 4.16) for each of the j families with children:

$$\frac{C_{Kj}}{C_{Aj}} = \phi(X_j) = \phi_0 + \phi_1(X_{1j}) + \ldots + \phi_N(X_{Nj}). \quad (5.6)$$

A number of demographic variables come to mind as possible regressors for equation (5.3). Since education may affect expenditure patterns,[3] the

---

1. Notice that the nature of equation (5.4) or (5.3) is somewhat unorthodox. We regress total consumption on its components, whereas the more usual form for an expenditure equation is to regress the spending on some component—food or shelter, or husband's clothing or wife's clothing—on total consumption. The latter form flows more naturally from a behavioral model, and its error term would be both interpretable and constrained across all items. The form we use is not behaviorally motivated but comes from an accounting identity (eq. 5.1) and statistical control for background variables (eq. 4.23). The error term that should be appended to equation (5.3) has no convenient interpretation, nor does the equation have an intercept. Gronau (1986a,b) offers an alternative formulation of this model that addresses this issue.

2. The selection of households was made on the following basis:

Total sample of 1972–73 CES	19,975	
Retain only those with:		
no children under 15	13,401	
head under age 65	9,521	
reported income	8,932	
positive total consumption	8,874	
education of head reported	8,304	
employment status reported	7,954	
no children older than 15	5,032	sample

head's education measured in years completed (EDUC) is included as one variable. Similarly, since life-cycle considerations clearly affect expenditure patterns (the purchase of durables is an obvious example), the age of the head (AGE) is included. Since spouse's age and education are highly collinear with the values for the head, those variables are omitted and AGE serves as a proxy for the entire household effect.

The income level of the household affects the relationship between $\tilde{C}_A$ and C_A unless the goods that make up $\tilde{C}_A$ have a composite income elasticity of 1.0. Therefore, the household income *before taxes* is included as a regressor (INCOME). (Note that the dependent variable, T, is the family's total consumption expenditure, not its income.)

The work status of individuals in the household also may affect expenditure patterns. One manifestation of this difference is that working members spend a greater proportion of their earnings on clothing as an input to their work activity. Thus, the proportion of adults in the family who are employed in the survey year (ADULT EMP) is included.

Men may have different expenditure patterns than women, so define a dummy variable (FEMALE) which is equal to 1 if the head of the household is female. This variable is also likely to pick up household size effects, since female-headed households consisting only of adults are likely to be smaller than male-headed ones.

Finally, dummy variables for whether the household was located in the south (SOUTH), was rural (RURAL), or was headed by a black individual (BLACK) were included. The set of nine regressors in equations (5.3) and (5.4) are then: EDUC, AGE, INCOME, ADULT EMP, FEMALE, SOUTH, RURAL, BLACK, and A (the number of adults).

Next consider the X variables for equation (5.5). All of the variables included in equation (5.3) are also present in (5.5), but the X vector also includes variables that are related only to households with children.[4] In

3. Michael (1972) argues that education increases real income and causes individuals to behave as if they are richer, for example.
4. The selection of households was made on the following basis:

Total sample of 1972–73 CES	19,975	
Retain only those with:		
children	6,583	
head under age 65	6,485	
head over age 17	6,472	
reported income	6,177	
positive total consumption	6,159	
education of head reported	5,987	
employment status reported	5,985	
no children older than 15	4,967	sample

particular, K is the number of children in the household, and since it is interesting to examine the way in which expenditures on children vary with age, two child-age variables were included: CHILD YOUNG measures the proportion of children who are under 6 years of age and CHILD OLD measures the proportion of children who are 12–15 years of age. Similarly, CHILD MALE measures the proportion of all the children in the family who are male.

The variable OWNCHILD measures the proportion of the children in the family who are the "own" children of the head of household. (The information comes from a variable indicating the relationship of each household member to the head. If the relationship is "child" of the head, the youth is an "own" child, whereas if the relationship of the youth to the head was "other relative" or "other," we considered the youth not to be an "own" child.) Finally, to determine whether the child's employment activity has an effect on resources spent on the child, CHILD EMP, which measures the proportion of the family's children who are employed, is included. The sample of families with children over 16 years of age is eliminated because their consumption cannot be separated from the consumption of the adults in the family. The vector of variables in X includes the nine variables in Z plus K, CHILD YOUNG, CHILD OLD, CHILD MALE, OWNCHILD, and CHILD EMP.

Table 5.1 shows the means (and standard deviations) of the relevant variables for the two subsets of households from the 1972–73 CES. The two groups are the set of households or families with no children (5,032 observations) and the set of families with one or more children under age 16 living at home (4,967 observations). The samples seem comparable in the sense that variables that are common to both have similar values. For example, the mean value of the education level of the head and the proportions of south, rural, and black households are close to equal across samples. The major exceptions are that the sample of households without children living at home is older, is more likely to have a female head, has slightly fewer adults, and spends less on total current consumption. The households without children have a somewhat lower family income but a higher per capita income than the families with children. Also, a somewhat higher proportion of adults work in the childless households.

Estimation of $\lambda_A(Z)$

The sample of 5,032 households without children is used to estimate equation (5.3). Table 5.2 shows the regression results. It reveals that the data

Table 5.1   Characteristics of Households with and without Children

Variable	Households without Children		Households with Children		Households with Children and Nonblack, Nonrural, and Non-South	
	Mean	(Standard Deviation)	Mean	(Standard Deviation)	Mean	(Standard Deviation)
EDUC	12.11	(3.2)	12.40	(2.87)	12.73	(2.80)
AGE	43.87	(15.4)	33.91	(8.47)	33.89	(8.21)
INCOME (000)	11.36	(16.7)	13.23	(8.97)	14.16	(9.20)
SOUTH	0.31		0.30		0	
RURAL	0.13		0.16		0	
BLACK	0.09		0.11		0	
ADULT EMP	0.78		0.71		0.70	
FEMALE HEAD	0.24		0.11		0.10	
A	1.64	(0.55)	1.93	(0.40)	1.94	(0.39)
K	—		2.20	(1.23)	2.18	(1.18)
OWNCHILD	—		0.98		0.99	
CHILD YOUNG	—		0.54		0.55	
CHILD OLD	—		0.17		0.17	
CHILD MALE	—		0.50		0.50	
CHILD EMP	—		0.02		0.02	
T	6998.	(4054)	9184.	(4498)	9699.	(4468)
$A\hat{C}_A$	652	(627)	631	(531)	673	(547)
(N)	(5,032)		(4,967)		(2,762)	

Table 5.2   Estimation of Equation (5.3) Using Households without Children

Variable	Coefficient	Standard Error
Constant*	4.20	0.61**
EDUC	− 0.024	0.024
AGE	0.027	0.0054**
INCOME	− 0.00470	0.00297
SOUTH	0.316	0.150**
RURAL	1.383	0.258**
BLACK	− 0.708	0.264**
ADULT EMP	0.039	0.272
FEMALE	− 0.387	0.206**
A	1.47	0.147**
(N = 5,032)		

*Note that the constant term is really the coefficient on $A\tilde{C}_A$ and that all other coefficients are the coefficients on the variable times $A\tilde{C}_A$. The regression is run without a true constant.
**$t > 2.0$.

fit the specification reasonably well and that coefficients are estimated with a moderate degree of precision. Recall that the coefficients $\lambda_0, \lambda_1, \ldots, \lambda_9$ are being estimated, and these have the interpretation of the derivative of the ratio $(C_A/\tilde{C}_A)$ with respect to the variable Z (see eqs. 4.17 and 4.23). So, for example, the coefficient on BLACK implies that blacks have a lower ratio of total expenditure to expenditures on adult clothing, alcohol, and tobacco than nonblacks. That is, blacks consume a higher proportion of these three items (alcohol, tobacco, and clothing) than nonblacks. Similarly, older individuals, those who live in the South, and those who live in rural areas spend less on these items. None of these results is surprising nor of particular interest in itself. These three expenditure items are only of interest as an intermediate step. But, as will be seen, it is important to the strategy that it not be assumed that families of all socioeconomic conditions have the same ratio of expenditures on these three goods to total expenditure.

The equation estimated in table 5.2 provides us with a tool with which to estimate the expenditure on adults in households with children as well. Table 5.3 provides estimates of λ for several types of households. Column 1 uses the mean values for households without children; the estimated λ for such a household is 7.61. That is, about 13 percent of the household's adult expenditure goes for the three observed items (alcohol, tobacco, and clothing). Column 2 uses the mean values for households with children; the estimated λ for this type of household is 7.83. Columns 3–4 use other hypothetical household types and give the implied λ's for each. The household depicted in col. 3 (a single, black female with little education, low income, age 50, living in a nonrural, non-South location) spends about 18 percent (1/λ = 1/5.71) of the adult expenditure on alcohol, tobacco, and clothing, while the household depicted in col. 4 (a two-person, white household with one member employed, a well-educated, thirty-year-old head, relatively high income living in the rural South) spends only about 11 percent (1/9.22) of the adult expenditure on these items.

Estimation of $\phi(X)$

Given an estimate of λ for each household using equation (5.3), it is straightforward to estimate equation (5.5). Notice that the first term in the equation should have a coefficient of 1. Equation (5.5) has been estimated both with and without imposing that constraint. Table 5.4 reports both sets of coefficients. In column 1 the coefficient of $\lambda A \tilde{C}_A$ is constrained to be unity by an algorithm that minimizes the sum of squared errors. In column 2 the coefficient of $\lambda A \tilde{C}_A$ is unconstrainted; the equation is estimated by ordinary least-squares (OLS) regression without intercept.

In the unconstrained form, the coefficient on $\lambda A \tilde{C}_A$ is 1.007 with a stan-

Table 5.3   Estimated λ for Four Specific Household Types: An Illustration of the Use of Equation (5.3) As Estimated in Table 5.2

Variable	Value of the Household Variables			
	1	2	3	4
EDUC	12.11	12.40	8.	16.
AGE	43.87	33.91	50.	30.
INCOME (000)	11.36	13.23	8.	20.
SOUTH	0.31	0.30	0.	1.
RURAL	0.13	0.16	0.	1.
BLACK	0.09	0.11	1.	0.
ADULT EMP	0.78	0.71	0.	1.
FEMALE	0.24	0.11	1.	0.
A	1.64	1.93	1.	2.
Estimated λ:	7.61	7.83	5.71	9.22
1/λ	0.13	0.13	0.18	0.11

Note: Column 1: mean values for actual households without children.
Column 2: mean values for actual households with children.
Columns 3 and 4: hypothetical households defined by the values shown in each column.

Table 5.4   Estimation of φ (Eq. 5.5) from Families with Children

Variable	Constrained	Unconstrained	$\bar{\lambda}A\tilde{C}_A$ (Constrained)
$\lambda A\tilde{C}_A$	1.	1.00700 (0.0400)	1.
$\lambda A\tilde{C}_A(K/A)$	0.79994 (0.1708)	0.79305 (0.1753)	0.14803 (0.1843)
$\lambda A\tilde{C}_A(K/A)$ EDUC	0.01662 (0.0036)	0.01665 (0.0036)	0.01418 (0.0037)
$\lambda A\tilde{C}_A(K/A)$ AGE	0.00238 (0.0015)	0.00238 (0.0015)	0.00701 (0.0015)
$\lambda A\tilde{C}_A(K/A)$ INCOME	−0.00428 (0.0006)	−0.00427 (0.0006)	−0.00480 (0.0006)
$\lambda A\tilde{C}_A(K/A)$ SOUTH	−0.01443 (0.0211)	−0.01460 (0.0211)	0.02298 (0.0219)
$\lambda A\tilde{C}_A(K/A)$ RURAL	−0.06638 (0.0286)	−0.06607 (0.0286)	0.12155 (0.0337)
$\lambda A\tilde{C}_A(K/A)$ BLACK	−0.06948 (0.0346)	−0.06961 (0.0346)	−0.14312 (0.0320)
$\lambda A\tilde{C}_A(K/A)$ ADULT EMP	0.10870 (0.0350)	0.10874 (0.0350)	0.08521 (0.0345)
$\lambda A\tilde{C}_A(K/A)$ FEMALE	−0.00710 (0.0566)	−0.00775 (0.0567)	0.04716 (0.0548)
$\lambda A\tilde{C}_A(K/A)$ K	−0.01668 (0.0067)	−0.01506 (0.0114)	−0.02610 (0.0069)
$\lambda A\tilde{C}_A(K/A)$ A	−0.18396 (0.0353)	−0.18724 (0.0400)	0.09601 (0.0424)
$\lambda A\tilde{C}_A(K/A)$ OWNCHILD	−0.31281 (0.1204)	−0.31049 (0.1212)	−0.28194 (0.1289)

$N = 4,967$

dard error of 0.040, so the data do not reject the constraint. This is reassuring; the data are not inconsistent with the assumption that λ does not vary between households with children and those without. If λ differed systematically with characteristics across household types, then one would not expect the scaling of right-hand-side variables to remain constant, resulting in a coefficient other than unity on $\lambda A\tilde{C}_A$.

The estimates presented in table 5.4 contain essentially all of the relevant information pertaining to the allocation of expenditures within the family unit. The mean value of φ is 0.38, estimated from the means of all

variables for all 4,967 households with children.[5] That is, the average family is estimated to spend 38 percent as much on a child as on an adult, or
$38 per child for every $100 per adult. This yields one major conclusion
of the study: children are not treated as adults with respect to household
expenditures. Put differently, the size of a family in adult equivalents is
$(A + \phi K)$, so a four-person (two-adult, two-child) family is the equivalent of a 2.8 adult household, or a six-person (two-adult, four-child) family is the equivalent of a 3.5 adult household. The per capita expenditure
concept far understates the amount received by an adult. An adult commands about 2.5 times the resources enjoyed by a child in the typical
family. Children must be much easier to please than adults before one
could conclude that all family members have equal utility! Of course, if
the savings component of family income is spent more on children (e.g.,
on children's education), then this conclusion does not hold. These points
are explored further below. First, consider the separate coefficients of the
ϕ-function.

The coefficients have a direct interpretation as components of ϕ in equation (5.6). For example, using the estimates from the constrained version
(col. 1, table 5.4), the effect of an additional year of education is to raise
ϕ by 0.0166. This means that households with heads whose education
level is one year higher have a ratio of per-child expenditure to per-adult
expenditure that is higher by 0.0166. The one-year increase in education
is associated with a $1.66 increase in child expenditures per existing $100
of adult expenditure. Again, if the head's education were 12 years of
schooling and the spending per child was $38 for every $100 of adult
spending, the increase in the head's education to 17 years would be associated with $(5 \times 0.01662 = 0.0831)$ a spending of $46.31 per child for
every $100 of adult spending.

Using the estimates from column 1 of table 5.4 (which are almost identical to those from the unconstrained version in col. 2), a number of substantive conclusions follow: the ratio of per-child expenditure to per-adult
expenditure increases with head's education, head's age, and the proportion of household adults who are employed. We consider these three effects in turn.

That more educated parents spend a higher proportion of their income
on children is interesting and by no means obvious. It is not surprising that
more educated parents spend a larger absolute amount on their children.

5. The standard error of the estimate of ϕ is difficult to compute. The structures are
nonlinear, and the right-hand variables in the ϕ equation are estimated values rather than true
values.

But our result suggests that even holding work status and income constant, more educated parents devote a higher proportion of their income to their children. This may be interpreted in one of at least two ways: First, one can argue that more educated parents spend a smaller amount of their time with their children and substitute dollar expenditures for that time. Alternatively, more educated parents may spend as much or even more time with their children than do less educated parents and, since their time is presumably of higher "quality," their time and dollar expenditures may be highly complementary in raising children. The force of this effect can be seen easily in the following comparison.

One can calculate the expenditure on a child, C_K, from the budget constraint and the definition of $\phi = C_K/C_A$:

$$T = AC_A + KC_K = A(C_K/\phi) + KC_K,$$

so

$$C_K = \phi T/(A + \phi K). \tag{5.7}$$

Using the variable means for the subset of 2,762 nonblack, nonrural, non-South households with children (shown in col. 5 of table 5.1), ϕ is 0.40459, A is 1.94, K is 2.18, and T is \$9,699; so C_K is estimated to be \$1,391. That figure uses the mean EDUC (12.73 years) in the computation. If instead we set education equal to 17 years, ϕ is 0.47555 and C_K is estimated as \$1,550. So the increase in education by about four years raises by \$159 the average expenditure per child per year. This is the impact of the estimated EDUC coefficient of $+0.0166$. But this calculation does not take into account that income is generally higher in a household with more educated adults. We have selected out as two subsamples those households with EDUC equal to 12 and those with EDUC equal to 17 (recall that we only know if the household head has 16 or more years of schooling, so all such households were coded as 17 years of schooling). These subsets are drawn from the 2,762 nonblack, nonrural, non-South sample with children. The means for these small education-specific subsamples are shown in table 5.5. The more educated have substantially higher incomes—\$19,570 compared to \$13,070. Using these sets of means, we find that the increment in expenditure per child associated with the additional years of schooling (17 years compared to 12 years) is \$555. In percentage terms this is a 43 percent increase in the expenditure per child.

The fact that expenditures on children tend to increase with the proportion of adults in the household who are employed makes sense. To the extent that an additional employed parent creates a need for baby-sitting

Table 5.5

	(12.00)	(17.00)
(EDUC)		
AGE	32.95	35.40
INCOME (000)	13.07	19.57
ADULT EMP	0.73	0.71
FEMALE	0.11	0.04
A	1.92	2.00
K	2.19	2.11
OWNK	0.99	1.00
(N)	(1,093)	(579)
Estimated ϕ	0.3996	0.4455
T	$8,993	$12,126
C_K	$1,284	$1,839

and other types of direct child expenditures, families appear to substitute direct expenditures on children for parental time with the child. Regarding the magnitude of this effect, the coefficient in Table 5.4 is $+0.1087$. Consider a nonblack, non-South, nonrural household with the mean values as given in column 5 of table 5.1 of all characteristics except for proportion employed. Since that household has approximately two adults (1.94, to be exact), consider the experiment of changing the proportion employed from 0.5 to 1 (i.e., from one adult employed to two). If income were to remain the same (i.e., $14,160), the resulting ϕ and C_K are:

(ADULT EMP)	(0.5)	(1.0)
ϕ	0.3825	0.4369
C_K	$1,338	$1,465

The relative expenditure on a child—per $100 spent on an adult—rises with the employment of the second adult from $38.25 to $43.69, and the absolute expenditure per child rises from $1,338 to $1,465, an increase of $127.

Of course, the addition of another earner in a household is unlikely to leave the household income unchanged. Table 5.6 shows results for two selected subsamples (not stratified by race, urbanization, or region). Column 1 uses all two-adult, *one*-earner households with children and column 2 uses all two-adult, *two*-earner households with children. For these somewhat different subsets of households, the employment of the second adult is associated with a rise in the relative expenditure on a child (per $100 spent on an adult) from $35.24 to $39.83 and an absolute rise of $232, from $1,163 to $1,395. This 20 percent increase is a substantial increase

Table 5.6

(A)	(2.00)	(2.00)
(ADULT EMP)	(0.50)	(1.00)
EDUC	12.58	12.59
AGE	34.26	33.52
INCOME	13.83	14.78
SOUTH	0.28	0.32
RURAL	0.16	0.17
BLACK	0.06	0.11
K	2.33	2.06
(N)	(2,207)	(1,958)
ϕ	0.3524	0.3983
C_K	$1,163	$1,395

in expenditure on children. The sacrifice, of course, is the parental time which goes to the labor market instead of to the care of the child and other nonlabor market activities.

Three coefficients are noteworthy because they lack statistical significance:

1. Older parents appear to spend slightly more on their children than younger parents. The coefficient in column 1 of table 5.4 is $+0.0024$, implying an increase in the relative expenditure on a child (per $100 on an adult) of 24¢ per year of age of the adult. But the coefficient lacks statistical significance.

2. Female-headed households do not appear to behave differently than male-headed households, once the number of adults is held constant. If number of adults in the household is not held constant, the results are very different. Since female-headed households tend to be those with only one adult, and since the effect of number of adults on ϕ is negative, female-headed households spend more on their children, ignoring family-size differences. This may reflect the fact that female-headed households spend a larger proportion of the family income on items like day care.

3. Region of the country (South non-South in particular) has no direct influence on the child-adult expenditure ratio.

Consider next the two significant negative coefficients on RURAL (-0.0664) and BLACK (-0.0695). Rural families and, separately, families with a black head of household spend about 7 percentage points less per child than per adult. Holding all other economic and demographic characteristics constant at the whole sample mean level (col. 3, table 5.1), a *black,* nonrural, non-South family spends $1,158 per child while a corresponding nonblack, nonrural, non-South family spends $1,321 per child. The black family spends 88 percent as much as the equivalent non-black family per child. Similarly, the *rural,* nonblack, non-South family spends $1,166 per child while the nonrural, nonblack, non-South comparable family spends $1,321 per child.

But these numbers may be misleading because the typical black family (or the typical rural family) has a lower income than the typical nonblack (or nonrural) family, and the share of spending on the child, C_K/C_A, rises as income falls. Table 5.7 uses the group-specific means to look at the differences in C_K. The left-hand columns partition the 4,967 observations into blacks (541 observations) and nonblacks (4,426), while the right-hand columns partition the same sample of 4,967 into rural (775) and nonrural (4,192). Consider the black/nonblack columns first. Using race-specific means, the ϕ tells us that the black spends $36.49 per child per $100 per adult while the nonblack spends $38.69 per child per $100 per adult. So the 7 percent less per child than per adult that was noted in the preceding paragraph, holding income and all other variables constant, falls to only 2.2 percentage points less per child than per adult when income, education, etc., are free to vary by group.

But when expressed in absolute dollars (C_K), the typical black family spends $1024 per child while the typical nonblack family spends $1301. So instead of the black family spending 88 percent as much as the equivalent white family per child, when group-specific means for income and the other variables are used, the black family spends only 79 percent as much per child. In sum the child in the typical black family receives only 79 percent as much as the child in the typical white family, while the degree

Table 5.7

	Black/Nonblack Comparison		Rural/Nonrural Comparison	
(BLACK)	(1.00)	(0.00)	0.04	0.12
(RURAL)	0.06	0.17	(1.00)	(0.00)
EDUC	11.23	12.54	11.59	12.54
AGE	33.95	33.98	34.14	33.87
INCOME	9.22	13.72	11.42	13.57
SOUTH	0.48	0.28	0.44	0.27
ADULT EMP	0.71	0.71	0.72	0.71
FEMALE	0.32	0.08	0.04	0.12
A	1.74	1.96	1.99	1.92
K	2.40	2.17	2.31	2.18
(N)	(541)	(4,426)	(775)	(4,192)
ϕ	0.3649	0.3869	0.3171	0.3970
C_K	$1,024	$1,301	$914	$1,343

of inequality between the child and the adult is relatively similar for blacks and nonblacks (a difference of only 2.2 percentage points).

Since black families and white families have different numbers of children on average, per child expenditure is not the only measurement of interest. We can also look at the spending on children. Although black families spend less *per child,* since the number of children in the typical black family (2.40) exceeds that for the typical white family (2.17), total expenditure *on children* shows a smaller race-specific differential: for blacks the expenditure on children ($C_K \bar{K}$) is $1,024. × 2.40 = $2,458; for nonblacks the comparable number is $1,301. × 2.17 = $2,823. So in total expenditures on children, the black/nonblack differential is 87 percent. Moreover, since the total current consumption (*T*) by blacks is $7,349 and for nonblacks is $9,409., the percentage of total current consumption expended on children, $C_K K/T$, is actually higher for blacks (33.4 percent) than for nonblacks (30.0 percent). As this discussion has made several different comparisons, table 5.8 may help the reader synthesize our results on the black/nonblack comparisons. We calculate that blacks spend less per child absolutely (row 3), but only slightly less per child relative to an adult (row 4), and somewhat less absolutely on children in total (row 6), but more on children in total relative to their total consumption expenditure (row 7).

A similar exercise can be performed for rural versus nonrural families (the means for these two subgroups are shown in table 5.7). Table 5.9 shows the calculations. The rural family has substantially lower income and total expenditure and spends appreciably less per child than does the nonrural family. Relative to the adult expenditure as well, the rural family

Table 5.8

	Black	Nonblack	Ratio of Black to Nonblack
1. Income	$9,220.00	$13,720.00	67.20%
2. Total Current Consumption Expenditure (*T*)	$7,349.00	$9,409.00	78.11
3. Expenditure per Child (C_K)	$1,024.00	$1,301.00	78.71
4. Expend. per Child per $100 Expended per Adult ($\phi$ × 100)	$36.49	$38.69	94.31
5. Number of Children (*K*)	2.40	2.17	110.60
6. Expenditure on Children ($C_K K$)	$2,458.00	$2,823.00	87.07
7. Expenditure on Children as Percent of Total Current Consumption Exp. (100 × $C_K K/T$)	33.4%	30.0%	111.33

Table 5.9

	Rural	Nonrural	Ratio of Rural to Nonrural
Income	$11,420.00	$13,570.00	84.2%
T	$7,866.00	$9,428.00	83.4
Expenditure per Child (C_K)	$914.00	$1,343.00	68.1
Expenditure per Child per $100 Expended per Adult ($\phi \times 100$)	$31.71	$39.70	79.9
Number of Children (K)	2.31	2.18	106.0
Expenditure on Children $(C_K K)$	$2,111.00	$2,928.00	72.1
Expenditure on Children as Percentage of Total Current Consumption Expend. ($100 \times C_K K/T$)	26.84%	31.06%	86.4

spends less per child. Like the black/nonblack comparison, the differentials are smaller for the rural/nonrural groups when the number of children is introduced. But the differential remains 72.1 percent when we compare the absolute expenditures on all children and rises to only 86.4 percent when the comparison is made relative to total current consumption expenditure. The rural family spends less per child and a smaller percentage of its total expenditure on children than the nonrural family.

The coefficient on OWNCHILD is negative (table 5.4), implying that households where children are not the offspring of the head spend more on children, other things constant. This effect is quite large, although imprecisely estimated. One interpretation of the negative coefficient is that households that do not have their own children have, by their acquisition of others' children, sometimes at substantial cost, revealed a preference for children relative to other adults. As a result, they spend a greater proportion of their incomes on these children. Alternatively, if these are children from a prior marriage for one of the adults in the family and child support is obtained earmarked for the child, this could explain the negative coefficient on OWNCHILD. (It is interesting to look not only at expenditure per child, but at total expenditure on children. A regression of number of children on proportion of own children in the household, however, reveals the following:

$$K = \begin{array}{cc} 2.160 & + \quad 0.0368 \text{ OWNCHILD} \\ (0.141) & (0.143) \end{array}$$

$$R^2 = 0.000$$
$$\text{St. error of est.} = 0.7543$$
$$N = 4,967$$

This implies that no difference in family size by status of children is discernible.)

As this discussion has pointed out, the interpretation of the coefficients in table 5.4 can be less than straightforward. Sometimes the appropriate question is answered directly by examination of that table, but at other times, especially when analyzing the effect of dummy variables, some transformation of the coefficients is warranted. This becomes true with a vengeance when considering the effects of income, number of children, and number of adults on the allocation of expenditures within the household.

First, consider changes in family income. An increase in family income changes expenditures on children in two ways: First, ϕ itself is negatively related to income, as seen from table 5.4 where the coefficient is -0.00428. Higher-income families spend less per child relative to the expenditure per adult. Second, income affects total consumption expenditures, T, directly. Recall that ϕ is a function of a vector X and that equation (5.7) states:

$$C_K = \phi(x)T/(A + \phi(x)K).$$

So a change in income affects C_K through both ϕ and T. Likewise, a change in the number of adults or in the number of children affects C_K both through ϕ and A (or ϕ and K). It is instructive to look at the partial derivatives of C_K from equation (5.7) for a typical element in the vector X (other than INCOME, A, and K) and for these three variables:

$$\frac{\partial C_K}{\partial X} = \frac{TA}{(A + \phi K)^2} \frac{\partial \phi}{\partial X} \text{ for } x \neq \text{INCOME}, A, K,$$

$$\frac{\partial C_K}{\partial \text{INCOME}} = \frac{TA}{(A + \phi K)^2} \frac{\partial \phi}{\partial \text{INCOME}} + \frac{\phi}{A + \phi K} \frac{\partial T}{\partial \text{INCOME}}$$

$$\frac{\partial C_K}{\partial A} = \frac{TA}{(A + \phi K)^2} \frac{\partial \phi}{\partial A} - \frac{\phi T}{(A + \phi K)^2},$$

$$\frac{\partial C_K}{\partial K} = \frac{TA}{(A + \phi K)^2} \frac{\partial \phi}{\partial K} - \frac{\phi^2 T}{(A + \phi K)^2}.$$

Likewise, from the equation for C_A,

$$C_A = \frac{T}{(A + \phi K)}, \tag{5.8}$$

a comparable set of four partial derivatives of C_A with respect to X (other than INCOME, K, A), and INCOME, K, and A can be derived. These derivatives will be utilized in the discussion that follows. Table 5.10 shows

Table 5.10   Derivatives and Elasticities (means from col. 3, table 5.1)

Variable	dC_K/dX	Elasticity	dC_A/dX
EDUC	38.23	0.37	−43.44
AGE	5.47	0.15	−6.22
INCOME	86.29	0.90	260.96
SOUTH	−33.19	—	37.71
RURAL	−152.68	—	173.48
BLACK	−159.81	—	181.59
ADULT EMP	250.03	0.14	−284.09
FEMALE	−16.33	—	18.56
K	−214.60	−0.37	−413.87
A	−881.44	−1.34	−708.85
OWNCHILD	−719.48	−0.56	817.53

their values with respect to both C_K and C_A for all the covariates in table 5.4, using the constrained (col. 1) regression and the mean values for the sample of 4,967 families with children listed in table 5.1. The elasticities of C_K, defined as the derivative times the ratio of the mean of the exogenous variable to the mean value of C_K, is also shown for the nondichotomous variables.

Table 5.10 provides yet another way to think about the estimated effect of any covariate on the spending on children or adults. A unit increase in EDUC (1 additional year of schooling) increases expenditures by $38.23 per child or by $38.23 × 2.20 = $84.11 on the 2.2 children in the typical family. Similarly, that unit increase in EDUC reduced expenditures by $43.44 per adult or by $43.44 × 1.93 = $83.84 on the 1.93 adults in the typical family. Similar calculations can be made for the other variables listed in table 5.10. Recall that these effects each hold constant the other covariates at their mean value and are thus partial effects estimating the "direct" influence of the covariate.

Now we can consider the effects of income, number of children, and number of adults. The sign of the coefficient on INCOME, −0.00428, tells us that as income rises the amount spent on C_K falls relative to the amount spent on C_A. So with K and A held constant and putting aside savings and taxes, we know that a less than proportionate increase in C_K and a more than proportionate increase in C_A accompanies a rise in income—that is, the income elasticity of C_K is less than one and that of C_A is greater than one. In fact, the income elasticity of C_K is 0.90, as shown in table 5.10. Of course, this is a relatively simplistic income elasticity, holding K, A, T, and ϕ fixed at their sample means. On the other hand, it is an interesting number, for it says that children do not share equally in absolute or even in proportionate increases when the family income rises.

Poorer families expend more per child relative to an adult than do wealthier families, according to these calculations, for children up to age 16. So, for illustration, an additional $1,000 in family income raises total expenditure by $694.01; each child gets $86.29 (so the 2.2 children get $189.84), and each adult gets $260.96 (so the 1.93 adults get $503.65) according to table 5.10.[6] So put in round numbers, we calculate that, on average (or at the average levels of all the variables, including a before-tax 1972–73 family income of $13,200), an additional $1,000 in family income is divided: $500 to the adults, about $200 to the children, and $300 to taxes and savings.

The high proportion spent on the adults primarily reflects the ϕ of 0.38—families spend about 2.5 times as much per adult as per child. The savings and taxes pose a real problem. We have ignored them, implicitly treating them as apportioned among family members exactly like the total expenditure T, but that may not be correct or proper. To the extent that the savings benefit the children disproportionately, the unequal allocation of T may be offset by the savings. As we have not dealt here with families with children aged 16–24, when college costs are incurred, it does seem likely that one use of the savings would be to help the children with college expenses and with the lumpy durable goods expenses in setting up a household beyond the age of the child that we investigate. Likewise with taxes: while income taxes may provide public goods that may or may not be valued equally by all family members, a large share of property taxes are used to provide public schooling; maybe it is reasonable to consider that as disproportionately benefiting the children.

Consider how expenditures shift when K, the number of children, changes. Table 5.10 tells us that an additional child lowers expenditures per child by $214.60, so that is the direct impact in terms of annual expenditure on a child of having another sibling. But total expenditures on children rises—the reduction per child is less than the increase on the additional child. A typical family with 2.2 children spends $1,271.08 per child (that is our estimate of C_K using sample means), so a 2.2 child family spends $2.2 \times 1271.08 = \$2796.38$ and a 3.2 child family spends $3.2 \times (1271.08 - 214.60) = \$3380.74$. Expenditures on children rise by $585, though each child gets $215 less.

The effect of an additional child on the adult's expenditure is more dramatic. The additional child lowers C_A by $413.87, or lowers the expendi-

6. There is a tiny discrepancy between the value of $(dt/d\text{INCOME})$ estimated as the sample average $T/\text{INCOME} = \$694.01$ and the sum of $(dC_K K/d\text{INCOME}) + (dC_A A/d\text{INCOME}) = (\$189.84 + 503.65) = \$693.49$.

ture on adults by $413.87 × 1.93 = $798.77. Although the absolute amount of the effect on an adult is greater than on a child, this $413.87 is only a 12.5 percent ($= 413.87/3305.46$) reduction in the average expenditure per adult, C_A, while the $214.60 reduction per child is a 16.9 percent ($= 214.60/1271.08$) reduction in C_K. Thus, the introduction of another child into the household has a larger percentage reduction on consumption per child than on consumption per adult. But since the number of adults does not change, an increase in the number of children increases the ratio of expenditures on all children as compared with all adults. For example, a two-adult, two-child family spends 0.38 as much on its children as on its adults $[2(1271.08)/2(3305.46) = 0.38]$; the two-adult, three-child household spends 0.55 as much on its children as on its adults $[3(1056.48)/2(2891.59) = 0.55]$.

The general conclusion to be drawn from this discussion is that families with fewer children spend more per child than families with a larger number of children. But the increase in expenditures per child is not sufficient to offset the reduction in expenditures on all children that results from having fewer children. Further, the addition of another child in the family affects the per capita consumption of the other children by a smaller absolute amount but by a greater percentage amount than it affects the per capita expenditure on adults.

The same analysis can also be performed with respect to increases in the number of adults in the household. From table 5.10, it is clear that an increase in the number of adults has a very substantial effect on the consumption of the children. There are at least two interpretations of this finding that more adults reduce the per child expenditure and, since the number of children is being held fixed, reduce the expenditure on all children as well.

First, it might be argued that households that have a larger number of adults are those that have a preference for adults or are less inclined toward children. Thus, the observation reflects a kind of selectivity. Second, and more likely, is that the additional adult is a substitute for market-purchased child care. This interpretation seems appropriate in moving from a one-adult to a two-adult household, as well as from a two-adult to a three-adult household. In the one-adult household, much of the child care is expected to be done by baby-sitters or other professional child care providers. In the two-adult household, the second adult is likely to perform a significant fraction of the child care that might otherwise have been performed by hired persons. The same applies to the three-adult household. The three-adult household is one that may have an older relative living with the family. It is not unreasonable to expect that this person may take on many of the responsibilities for child care that were paid for more directly in the household with fewer adults.

The magnitude of the effect of a change in A shown in table 5.10 is interesting. The addition of another adult reduces expenditures on children dramatically. From a mean of $1,271 per child for the average family in our sample with 1.93 adults, one additional adult lowers that expenditure to $390 per child ($= 1271 - 881$). That estimate is, frankly, somewhat unbelievable. The reason that this effect is so large has two components. First, the coefficient on A in table 5.4 is very large and reduces the ratio of expenditures per child to expenditures per adult from 0.38 to 0.20. Second, a one-adult increase in the household, holding income constant, means that all household members suffer a large reduction in per capita income even if shares were affected equally. This is especially the case since the addition of an adult increases the size of the four-person household by more than 25 percent. Since all persons are not treated equally, a household with two adults and two children has 2.8 equivalent members $[=2 + 0.38(2)]$. A household with two children and three adults would, if shares had been adjusted proportionately, have 3.8 equivalent members $[= 3 + 0.38(2)]$. This is about a 36 percent increase in equivalent family size while leaving family income constant, assuming no economies of scale.

That this effect is large can be seen by looking at the reduction in expenditures on adults in the household. Even though the ratio of expenditures per adult to expenditures per child rises substantially (from $1/0.38$ to $1/0.20$), expenditures per adult fall since the number of equivalent family members rises so dramatically. What is interesting, however, is that in both absolute and relative terms, the additional adult's consumption is financed to a greater extent by the household's children than by the household's adults. This is illustrated by comparing the expenditures in a two-adult, two-child home to those in a three-adult, two-child home. In the former, the expenditure on all children is $2,542 and the expenditure on all adults is $6,610. In the latter, it is approximately $780 on children and $7,788 on adults $[= 3(3305 - 709)]$. Although the per adult expenditure falls, the total expenditure on adults rises. (These do not total to the same amount because taxes and savings are different in households of different sizes even at the same before-tax income level.) The conclusion here is that an additional adult in the family is associated with a sizeable reduction in the direct expenditure on children. We caution that there may well be large indirect benefits to children from an additional adult, but we have not investigated these effects. Our conclusion pertains only to our estimate of dollars spent.

Lifetime Expenditures

We wish to illustrate the total expenditure on children over some period of their lifetime. This we do using the function estimated and discussed in the previous section. We calculate the value of C_K for a family with a given set of characteristics for each year of the children's lives from 1 to 18. Notice that although the ϕ function only includes children up to age 16, for the reasons we have discussed, we have arbitrarily extended the period of calculation to age 18 for the illustrations in this section only.

Table 5.11 shows these calculations for several different types of families. Panel A reflects the values for a family with the mean values of all the continuous variables and is nonblack, nonrural, nonsouthern, and does not have a female head. (The values of the other variables are noted at the top of the panel.) The income level is set arbitrarily as indicated in the left-hand column. So, for example, the top row reflects the results assuming that the household's income is $5,000 per year, each year, thus conforming to the notion of permanent income. We further assume that savings and taxes are zero, so both INCOME and T, the total consumption, are set to the value indicated by the left-hand column. The second row shows the results when an income of $10,000 is instead assumed, and so on.

The aging of the child is handled in this calculation in a fairly simplistic manner. The child's age is not directly captured in the regression, so the assumption is made that the child is born into the family when the head is age 25. So a newborn child is viewed as receiving the expenditure C_K calculated for a household with a head aged 25; a one-year-old is viewed as receiving the expenditure C_K calculated for a household with a head aged 26; and so forth.

A discount rate of 10 percent is used throughout the calculations shown in table 5.11. Also, most of the calculations do not show the expenditure per child but for all children in the family, using the average number of children for the respective sample. So, for instance, panel A of table 5.11 uses $K = 2.19$ and acts as if all 2.19 of the children are born in the year in which the head is age 25.

Column 1 (FIRSTYEAR) shows the calculated expenditure on the zero-aged children. Column 2 (FIRSTYRADULT) shows the calculated expenditure on all the adults in the household during that same year, using the estimated C_A times A, the average number of adults. Column 3 (18 YEARS) shows the discounted value of the estimated expenditure on children over the first 18 years of the children's lives. (The calculation differs for each of the 18 years only by the fact that the household head ages each year, so the calculation uses head ages 25 through 42.) Column 4 (18 YRS

Table 5.11   Estimated Lifetime Expenditure on Children to Age 18 and on Adults, by Selected Household Characteristics
(discount rate is 10 percent throughout; SOUTH = RURAL = FEMALE = 0)

PANEL A

Mean Characteristics of Households with Children

(EDUC = 12.39; ADULT EMP = 0.71; K = 2.19; A = 1.93; OWNCHILD = 0.98)

INCOME and T	FIRST YEAR*	FIRSTYR ADULT	18 YEARS	18 YRS ADULT	18 YR CHILDADULT	φ
	(1)	(2)	(3)	(4)	(5)	(6)
			WHITES			
$ 5000	$ 1621	$ 3379	$ 16231	$ 28877	0.562	0.423
10000	3130	6870	31548	58668	0.538	0.401
15000	4520	10480	45904	89419	0.513	0.380
20000	5786	14214	59254	121177	0.489	0.359
30000	7917	22083	82728	187919	0.440	0.316
40000	9465	30535	101522	259340	0.391	0.273
50000	10362	39638	115124	335955	0.343	0.230
			BLACKS			
5000	1431	3569	14692	30416	0.483	0.353
10000	2737	7263	28367	61849	0.459	0.332
15000	3910	11090	40973	94351	0.434	0.311
20000	4943	15057	52455	127977	0.410	0.289
30000	6558	23442	71802	198845	0.361	0.247
40000	7512	32488	85878	274985	0.312	0.204
50000	7723	42277	94068	357011	0.263	0.161

PANEL B

ONE-ADULT HOUSEHOLDS (A = 1)

With Number of Children (K) as Indicated

INCOME and T	FIRST YEAR*	FIRSTYR ADULT	18 YEARS	18 YRS ADULT	18 YR CHILDADULT	φ
	(1)	(2)	(3)	(4)	(5)	(6)
K = 1 (with EDUC = 11.57; ADULT EMP = 0.75; OWNCHILD = 0.96)						
			WHITES			
$ 5000	$ 1896	$ 3104	$ 18324	$ 26784	0.684	0.611
10000	3708	6292	35958	54258	0.663	0.589
15000	5433	9567	52873	82451	0.641	0.568
20000	7068	12933	69042	111390	0.620	0.546
30000	10049	19951	99017	171631	0.577	0.504
40000	12620	27380	125621	235242	0.534	0.461
50000	14743	35257	148562	302517	0.491	0.418
			BLACKS			
5000	1756	3244	17170	27938	0.615	0.541
10000	3421	6580	33587	56629	0.593	0.520
15000	4990	10010	49221	86102	0.572	0.498

Table 5.11 (*Continued*)

INCOME and T	FIRST YEAR*	FIRSTYR ADULT	18 YEARS	18 YRS ADULT	18 YR CHILDADULT	φ
	(1)	(2)	(3)	(4)	(5)	(6)
$K = 1$ (with EDUC = 11.57; ADULT EMP = 0.75; OWNCHILD = 0.96)						
—————————————————————BLACKS—————————————————————						
20000	6460	13540	64040	116392	0.550	0.477
30000	9084	20916	91089	179559	0.507	0.434
40000	11255	28745	114434	246429	0.464	0.392
50000	12929	37071	133739	317340	0.421	0.349
$K = 2$ (with EDUC = 11.23; ADULT EMP = 0.62; OWNCHILD = 0.96)						
————————————————————WHITES————————————————————						
$ 5000	$ 2675	$ 2325	$ 25436	$ 19672	1.293	0.575
10000	5255	4745	50120	40096	1.250	0.554
15000	7735	7265	74007	61316	1.207	0.532
20000	10108	9892	97051	83381	1.164	0.511
30000	14507	15493	140393	130254	1.078	0.468
40000	18388	21612	179680	181183	0.992	0.425
50000	21675	28325	214356	236723	0.906	0.383
————————————————————BLACKS————————————————————						
5000	2514	2486	24161	20947	1.153	0.506
10000	4920	5080	47467	42749	1.110	0.484
15000	7211	7789	69864	65459	1.067	0.463
20000	9379	10621	91296	89136	1.024	0.442
30000	13311	16690	130999	139649	0.938	0.399
40000	16635	23365	165995	194868	0.852	0.356
50000	19258	30742	195590	255488	0.766	0.313
$K = 3$ (with EDUC = 11.50; ADULT EMP = 0.67; OWNCHILD = 0.99)						
————————————————————WHITES————————————————————						
$ 5000	$ 3130	$ 1870	$ 29469	$ 15639	1.884	0.558
10000	6168	3832	58220	31996	1.820	0.537
15000	9107	5893	86203	49121	1.755	0.515
20000	11939	8061	113362	67069	1.690	0.494
30000	17250	12750	164956	105691	1.561	0.451
40000	22019	17981	212430	148434	1.431	0.408
50000	26148	23853	255079	196000	1.301	0.365
————————————————————BLACKS————————————————————						
5000	2972	2028	28241	16867	1.674	0.488
10000	5836	4164	55646	34570	1.610	0.467
15000	8582	6418	82149	53175	1.545	0.446
20000	11201	8799	107679	72752	1.480	0.424
30000	16012	13988	155498	115149	1.350	0.382
40000	20162	19838	198357	162506	1.221	0.339
50000	23517	26483	235319	215760	1.091	0.296

Table 5.11 (*Continued*)

INCOME and T	FIRST YEAR*	FIRSTYR ADULT	18 YEARS	18 YRS ADULT	18 YR CHILDADULT	φ
	(1)	(2)	(3)	(4)	(5)	(6)

$K = 4$ (with EDUC = 10.80; ADULT EMP = 0.53; OWNCHILD = 1.00)

			WHITES			
$ 5000	$ 3358	$ 1642	$ 31525	$ 13583	2.321	0.511
10000	6621	3380	62324	27892	2.234	0.490
15000	9780	5220	92336	42987	2.148	0.468
20000	12826	7174	121496	58936	2.061	0.447
30000	18536	11464	176944	93704	1.888	0.404
40000	23645	16355	227946	132917	1.715	0.361
50000	28019	21981	273581	177498	1.541	0.319
			BLACKS			
5000	3193	1807	30271	14837	2.040	0.442
10000	6271	3729	59673	30543	1.954	0.420
15000	9222	5778	88125	47199	1.867	0.399
20000	12033	7967	115538	64893	1.780	0.378
30000	17175	12825	166828	103820	1.607	0.335
40000	21551	18449	212547	148316	1.433	0.292
50000	24963	25037	251389	199690	1.259	0.249

PANEL C
TWO-ADULT HOUSEHOLDS ($A = 2$)
With Number of Children as Indicated

INCOME and T	FIRST YEAR*	FIRSTYR ADULT	18 YEARS	18 YRS ADULT	18 YR CHILDADULT	φ
	(1)	(2)	(3)	(4)	(5)	(6)

$K = 1$ (with EDUC = 12.51; ADULT EMP = 0.75; OWNCHILD = 0.98)

			WHITES			
$ 5000	$ 897	$ 4103	$ 9200	$ 35908	0.256	0.437
10000	1722	8278	17783	72433	0.246	0.416
15000	2472	12528	25732	109592	0.235	0.395
20000	3145	16855	33031	147401	0.224	0.373
30000	4253	25747	45609	225038	0.203	0.330
40000	5029	34971	55372	305491	0.181	0.288
50000	5454	44546	62163	388916	0.160	0.245
			BLACKS			
5000	777	4223	8179	36929	0.221	0.368
10000	1477	8523	15704	74512	0.211	0.347
15000	2098	12902	22559	112765	0.200	0.325
20000	2637	17363	28724	151707	0.189	0.304
30000	3463	26537	38913	231734	0.168	0.261
40000	3935	36065	46112	314751	0.147	0.218
50000	4033	45967	50149	400930	0.125	0.175

Table 5.11 (*Continued*)

INCOME and T	FIRST YEAR*	FIRSTYR ADULT	18 YEARS	18 YRS ADULT	18 YR CHILDADULT	φ
	(1)	(2)	(3)	(4)	(5)	(6)
$K = 2$ (with EDUC = 12.87; ADULT EMP = 0.72; OWNCHILD = 0.99)						
—WHITES—						
$ 5000	$ 1476	$ 3524	$ 14870	$ 30238	0.492	0.419
10000	2844	7156	28858	61358	0.470	0.397
15000	4100	10901	41923	93401	0.449	0.376
20000	5237	14763	54025	126407	0.427	0.355
30000	7133	22867	75156	195491	0.384	0.312
40000	8483	31517	91863	269000	0.341	0.269
50000	9230	40771	103705	347374	0.299	0.226
—BLACKS—						
5000	1295	3705	13389	31719	0.422	0.349
10000	2470	7530	25806	64410	0.401	0.328
15000	3521	11479	37205	98118	0.379	0.307
20000	4439	15561	47538	132894	0.358	0.285
30000	5856	24144	64794	205853	0.315	0.243
40000	6660	33340	77119	283744	0.272	0.200
50000	6784	43216	83994	367085	0.229	0.157
$K = 3$ (with EDUC = 12.44; ADULT EMP = 0.70; OWNCHILD = 0.99)						
—WHITES—						
$ 5000	$ 1854	$ 3146	$ 18517	$ 26591	0.696	0.393
10000	3579	6421	36003	54213	0.664	0.372
15000	5166	9835	52396	82927	0.632	0.350
20000	6606	13394	67630	112801	0.600	0.329
30000	9006	20994	94326	176321	0.535	0.286
40000	10693	29308	115436	245427	0.470	0.243
50000	11559	38442	130185	320894	0.406	0.200
—BLACKS—						
5000	1634	3366	16768	28340	0.592	0.324
10000	3119	6881	32361	57855	0.559	0.302
15000	4445	10555	46706	88617	0.527	0.281
20000	5602	14398	59721	120710	0.495	0.259
30000	7357	22643	81398	189250	0.430	0.217
40000	8273	31728	96577	264286	0.365	0.174
50000	8214	41786	104282	346797	0.301	0.131
$K = 4$ (with EDUC = 12.23; ADULT EMP = 0.69; OWNCHILD = 0.99)						
—WHITES—						
$ 5000	$ 2131	$ 2869	$ 21148	$ 23960	0.883	0.371
10000	4117	5883	41172	49043	0.840	0.350
15000	5948	9053	59992	75332	0.796	0.328
20000	7610	12390	77517	102914	0.753	0.307
30000	10375	19625	108278	162369	0.667	0.264

Table 5.11 (*Continued*)

INCOME and T	FIRST YEAR*	FIRSTYR ADULT	18 YEARS	18 YRS ADULT	18 YR CHILDADULT	φ
(1)	(2)	(3)	(4)	(5)	(6)
$K = 4$ (with EDUC = 12.23; ADULT EMP = 0.69; OWNCHILD = 0.99)						
WHITES						
40000	12282	27718	132531	228332	0.580	0.222
50000	13170	36830	149134	301944	0.494	0.179
BLACKS						
5000	1882	3118	19223	25885	0.743	0.302
10000	3594	6406	37131	53085	0.699	0.280
15000	5120	9880	53621	81703	0.656	0.259
20000	6445	13556	68576	111856	0.613	0.238
30000	8415	21584	93358	177289	0.527	0.195
40000	9333	30667	110265	250598	0.440	0.152
50000	8975	41024	117764	333315	0.353	0.109

*Column 1 shows the calculated expenditure on the zero-aged children. Column 2 shows the calculated expenditure on all the adults in the household during that same year. Column 3 shows the discounted value of the estimated expenditure on children over the first 18 years of the children's lives. Column 4 shows the analogous calculation to column 3 for adults, the discounted value of the estimated expenditure on adults over the first 18 years of the children's lives. Column 5 is the ratio of column 3 to column 4, the ratio of total expenditures on children to those on adults during the first 18 years of the children's lives. Column 6 is the calculated ratio of the expenditure per child to the expenditure per adult during the children's first year of life.

ADULT) shows the analogous calculation to column 3 for adults, the discounted value of the estimated expenditure on adults over the first 18 years of the children's lives. Column 5 (18 YRCHILDADULT) is the ratio of column 3 to column 4, the ratio of total expenditures on children to those on adults during the first 18 years of the children's lives. Column 6 (φ) is the calculated ratio of the expenditure per child to the expenditure per adult during the children's first year of life.

Several points about table 5.11, panel A, might be noted. Column 1, the expenditure on the children in their first year, rises substantially with income but less than proportionately with the income. This is but one manifestation of the fact that the income elasticity is less than 1.0. The lowest income level household spends about 32 percent of its income on children (= $1,621/$5,000), while the household with $50,000 income spends only about 21 percent of its income on children (= $10,362/ $50,000). One sees the same phenomenon in column 5.

At a permanent income of $15,000 per year, the ratio of expenditures on all children to that on all adults during the years when the children are at home is just over one-half. So children account for about one-third of household expenditure and adults account for two-thirds of the expenditure during these years in which the child is growing up. The figure of 0.513 is larger than the φ of 0.380 because there are more children than adults in the average household in this sample and in part because φ rises as the children age.

Panels B and C of table 5.11 perform similar calculations for households with one and two adults, respectively, using in each case 1, 2, 3, or 4 children. The mean values of EDUC, ADULT EMP, and OWNCHILD for the actual samples with the specific number of children and adults are given in each instance. As there are many numbers in these panels, table 5.12 summarizes for whites a few of the more salient patterns that we have found in looking over table 5.11. In particular, we stress three features of table 5.12.

1. When income and number of adults are held constant, expenditures per child decline quite a lot as additional children enter the family (see col. 2, table 5.12). This might imply that in a family with two or three children each is much less well-off in terms of material goods and services, but it is also possible that the scale economies in the household help maintain the real level of income for the children in the larger families. All we are able

Table 5.12   Household Expenditures for Children (from table 5.11)
(household income = $15,000; whites)

K	Expenditures for 18 YEARS (1)	Expenditures per CHILD (col. 1/K) (2)	18 YR CHILDADULT (3)	φ (4)
		ONE ADULT		
One	$52,873	$52,873	0.641	0.568
Two	74,007	37,004	1.207	0.532
Three	86,203	28,734	1.755	0.515
Four	92,336	23,084	2.148	0.468
		TWO ADULTS		
One	25,732	25,732	0.235	0.395
Two	41,923	20,962	0.449	0.376
Three	52,396	17,465	0.632	0.350
Four	59,992	14,998	0.796	0.328
		THREE ADULTS		
One	11,664	11,664	0.094	0.207
Two	19,292	9,646	0.166	0.175
Three	25,892	8,631	0.237	0.165
Four	28,988	7,247	0.273	0.134

to report here is that our calculations of expenditures on children do not rise anywhere near in proportion to the increase in the number of children. The two-adult family spends about $26,000 on one child, only $42,000 on two children, and only $52,000 on three children, according to table 5.12.

2. In one-adult households with two or more children, more than half of the household's expenditures go to the children (see col. 3, table 5.12). Obviously, nothing in the logic or estimation scheme used here restricts this value to be less than unity. We might note that the calculations in table 5.11 assume that the head of household is male for computational purposes, but the variable FEMALE is in the regression equation. In fact, the mean value of that variable reflects the very high percentage of one-parent families who are female-headed. About 90 percent of our samples of one-adult households with one or two or three or four children have a female head. By contrast, only about 1 percent of the two-adult households have a female head, and less than 10 percent of the three-adult households do. Of course, this predominance of male-headed households in the two-adult case is just reflecting the traditional Census definitions of households and doesn't really tell us anything more than that there are both a male and a female in almost all the two-adult households and that nearly all the one-adult households with children have a female not a male adult.

3. As we discussed in an earlier part of the chapter, the addition of an adult, holding income fixed, dramatically reduces ϕ—the expenditure per child per dollar spent on an adult (see col. 4, table 5.12).

The calculations in table 5.12 hold income as well as other household characteristics constant. But, of course, income varies with family structure and size. The average INCOME for the households in the various structures in our data are shown in table 5.13. So although it is true, as reported in table 5.12, that a household that consists of one child and one adult spends more on that child at a given level of income than a household with two adults, it is by no means true that children in such households receive a larger amount of resources. The average one-adult, one-child household has an income of $5,170 and expends about $19,000 in present

Table 5.13   Average Family Income

	ADULTS		
Children	1	2	3
1	$5,170	$12,780	$14,980
2	5,520	14,740	16,130
3	6,060	15,350	15,300
4	5,280	14,800	16,960

value on the child over the first 18 years, while the average two-adult, one-child household has an income of $12,780 and expends about $22,000 in present value on the child. Apparently the income increase for a three-adult, one-child household is not sufficient to continue this increase—the average income of $14,980 yields an estimate of the expenditure of about $12,000 in present value on the child.

Similar experiments can be performed with respect to number of children. The two-adult, one-child household transfers an average of about $22,200 to its child. In the two-adult, two-child household, average income is $14,740, and that family spends $41,500 on its two children. The per child expenditure falls to $20,750, but the amount spent on children taken together rises by 87 percent in moving from one child to two children. Thus, at a given level of family income, say $10,000, it would appear that a sibling "costs" a child $3,354 [= $17,783 − ($28,858/2)]. In fact, the cost is only about $1,450, since income changes as the family moves from one child to two children. Some of this change is appropriately endogenous: the father and mother work more to support the additional child. But some of the change reflects cross-sectional differences that are not affected by the birth of another child. To the extent that differences across groups reflect factors that are not controllable by the parties in question, the true "cost" of a sibling is the larger figure rather than the smaller one. To the extent that all differences across groups reflect behavior rather than random exogenous events, the relevant number is the smaller one.

Sensitivity Checks

Before concluding this chapter, it is useful to discuss several checks performed to ascertain the sensitivity of our results. Several of these were undertaken by our colleague Reuben Gronau, who obtained our data for a study of his own and replicated many of our results in this chapter, comparing them to other functional forms and other selection criteria. We gratefully acknowledge his input in this section. Regarding the λ function in equation (5.3), as reported in table 5.2, that function is run with no constant term, since it is derived from a relationship with a ratio on the left-hand side and estimated by multiplying through by the denominator of that ratio. When the same regression is allowed to have an intercept, the estimated intercept has a high t-statistic and a substantial effect on the other estimated coefficients. Now, that implies that our equation (5.3) is not the correct functional form. It is not clear just how to correct it, however. The equation, as estimated, has the virtue of logically yielding a usable estimate of λ, hence of the adult expenditure in the second stage of our procedure. If an intercept is included in the equation, the result is uninterpretable and yields no useful way of estimating the adult expenditure.

One extreme way of handling the issue of λ is to use the same value of λ for all households—just ignoring the fact that consumption patterns vary by demographic characteristics. We have, for illustration, used that extreme alternative, employing the average value of λ from the households with no children for all households with children rather than estimating a household-specific value of λ using the equation in table 5.2. That result is shown in the last column of table 5.4. The most important difference between column 1 (with a separate λ for each household) and column 3 (with the same λ applied to all households) is in the interpretation of the spending behavior of blacks. Since blacks happen to spend a greater proportion of their income on the observable items of clothing, alcohol, and tobacco, column 3 implies that blacks spend more on adults, hence less on children, than is the case using the estimates from column 1 or column 2.

The explanation for this difference in interpretation is important, for it emphasizes the sensitivity of the results to the regression estimates, which are, unfortunately, not very stable. That interpretation is this: blacks spend relatively more on clothing, alcohol, and tobacco than on other adult goods, apparently. That is of no interest here in general, except that those three goods are the ones we use to estimate the total expenditure on adults as compared to expenditures on children. If we don't take account of the behavioral fact that blacks spend relatively more on these three items, we will be led to infer that because we observe a black household spending more on these three items, other things held constant, blacks spend more on adults and less on children. When we take account of the higher relative spending on these three items by blacks, we know to adjust downward the overall estimate of the adult expenditures by blacks, yielding, we think, a more accurate estimate of the relative expenditure by blacks on adults and on children. The same reasoning applies in reverse for southern and rural households, who spend less on the observable items. Ignoring this fact causes one mistakenly, we think, to conclude that those households spend more on their children.

There are other ways to estimate adult consumption in the spirit, but not the letter, of equation (5.3). One could estimate equation (5.4) directly, but as we commented above, the left-hand side of that equation is a ratio of two random variables, and that ratio has bad statistical properties. One might instead have begun with the more orthodox behavioral relationship, as suggested in note 1 and as pursued by Gronau (1986a, b). We have proceeded here with the estimate from table 5.2, but we alert the reader to its limitations and its apparent sensitivity to functional form about which neither we nor others yet have much insight.

The same issue arises with respect to the estimation of the ϕ function in table 5.4. Equation (5.5) too is estimated without an intercept, and when reestimated without this constraint, an intercept is statistically significant. In both the λ and ϕ equations, the data fit better with an intercept, but such an equation is neither as interpretable or as useful for our estimation procedure. We have proceeded having imposed our functional form on the data. That this practice is not unique to this study does not make it any more appealing, but we have no better strategy at this time and encourage others to improve upon our scheme.

Pertaining to other sensitivity checks, many of which we performed, table 5.14 reports the results of including in the ϕ function the age, gender, and the work status of the children, along with a nonlinear term for income. Here, most of the previous results remain intact. The age coefficient becomes somewhat larger, but the qualitative conclusions of the previous section remain. The additional variables do not tell any convincing story, but there appears to be some evidence of the following effects. First, more

Table 5.14   Additional Variables in the ϕ Function

Variable	Coefficient	Standard Error
EDUC	0.0170	0.0035
AGE	0.0061	0.0017
INCOME	−0.0033	0.0006
SOUTH	−0.0102	0.0211
RURAL	−0.0691	0.0285
BLACK	−0.0808	0.0346
ADULT EMP	0.1221	0.0355
FEMALE	−0.0035	0.0574
K	−0.0147	0.0068
A	−0.1958	0.0357
OWNCHILD	−0.3106	0.1200
CHILD YOUNG	0.0818	0.0345
CHILD OLD	−0.0614	0.0458
CHILD MALE	−0.0772	0.0304
CHILD EMP	0.0958	0.1074
INCOME-Squared	−0.00003	0.000006
Constant	0.6861	0.1776

$N = 4{,}967$.

appears to be spent on young children than on older ones, holding constant the age of the head.[7] Second, more is spent on female children than on male children. Third, children who work receive a larger proportion of the household's expenditure than those who do not. Although this effect is substantial, it is estimated with very little precision, so we hesitate to make much out of it.

In another regression, not shown here because of its similarity to column 1 of table 5.4, we estimated the φ function without the OWNCHILD variable. As one might expect, its deletion had no real effect on any of the other coefficients or on their standard errors.

Summary

The 1972–73 CES is used to estimate the relationship between spending patterns in the household and demographic and other economic characteristics of the household. What is novel about this work is that estimates are obtained, even though most expenditures cannot be apportioned directly.

The intuition behind the approach is this: certain goods are consumed exclusively by some members of the household. In particular, alcohol, tobacco, and adult clothing are not typically consumed by children. By

---

7. This regression has three age variables: AGE, the age of the head in years; CHILD YOUNG, the proportion of the children who are less than or equal to age 6; CHILD OLD, the proportion of the children who are age 12–15. So the omitted child-age category is age 7–11. The positive coefficient on CHILD YOUNG and the negative coefficient on CHILD OLD both indicate that in the age range 0–15, the 0–6 child receives the most and the 12–15-year-old receives the least. Of course, as the children age so does the head of household, and it appears that the aging of the head raises the relative expenditure on the children. The regressions in table 5.4 do not explicitly include the ages of the children, so that positive effect of the head's age is dampened by the fact that the children are aging too. In table 5.14, by contrast, the children's ages are explicitly included so the positive effect of the head's age is not dampened and is therefore larger than in table 5.4.

Other studies of expenditures on children find that expenditures rise with the age of the child (e.g., see Espenshade 1984, Turchi 1983), while in our results age plays a minor role. We think the explanation is that we are looking not at the absolute level of expenditures on children in the equations in table 5.4 or table 5.14 but rather the relative expenditures on children compared to those on adults. We find in table 5.4 that the expenditures on children *up to age 16* rise very slightly (statistically insignificantly) relative to expenditures on adults. That does not imply that they are not rising absolutely. In table 5.14 we have a piece-wise linear relationship with age that rises within each piece (child aged 0–6, aged 7–11, aged 12–15), but each piece is lower for the older age group. Given the typical pattern of income growth with the age of the head, it is not unlikely that as the child and the parent age, the absolute expenditures on both rise; we see rather small changes in the relative expenditure for children to age 16.

assuming that there is some stable relationship between consumption of these observable items and consumption of nonobservable items by adults, one can estimate the total amount consumed by adults in the household. With this estimate and information about the total expenditure by the household, subtraction of one from the other yields as a residual an estimate of the expenditure on children. In our work we do not attempt to estimate the allocation of the adult expenditure among the adults or the allocation of the child expenditure among the children. Only the apportionment between the adults and the children is investigated here. Somewhat indirectly we do consider the within-group apportionment by noting the influence of the age or gender or employment status of the adults or of the children on the portion of the household's expenditure that goes to that group.

The stable relationship between the observable and unobservable adult expenditures is estimated by confining attention to households without children. There the total expenditure is exclusively expended on adults, so the required relationship is identified easily. Furthermore, the way in which that relationship varies with household characteristics can also be identified. This prevents mistaking differences in the relationship between observable adult expenditures and unobservable adult expenditures for differences in expenditures on adults versus children.

The most important empirical finding is that the average household allocates about 2.5 times the amount of income to an adult as it does to a typical child. Thus, the evidence strongly suggests that the per capita concept is inappropriate in the average household. Children may have fewer needs than adults, but it is certain in our evidence that they command fewer resources.

Put differently, the size of the household, in adult equivalent units, is $A + [\phi]K$, where A and K are the number of adults and children and ϕ is 0.38 for the average family in our sample of households with children. So a two-adult, two-child family is equivalent to about a 2.8 adult-sized household; a one-adult, three-child family is equivalent to about a 2.1 adult-sized household. The reader is reminded that we do not investigate differences among adults or children, so we take adults as one homogeneous group and children as another distinct homogeneous group when we calculate that in household spending an average child is the equivalent to about 0.38 of an adult.

Perhaps equally important is that the allocation pattern varies significantly with the characteristics of the household. For a given level of family income, size, and other characteristics, households with a more highly educated head allocate a greater proportion of income to their children.

In a two-adult household, an increase in the number of adults employed raises by perhaps 20 percent the expenditure on children. Older adults appear to spend somewhat larger portions of their expenditures on their children up to age 16, holding constant the number of these children (recall that as the adult ages so does the child).

We find no evidence that the gender of the household head affects the apportioning of expenditures between the adults and children, when the number of adults in the household is held constant. Likewise, region of residence appears to have no influence on the apportionment.

Blacks at the same income level as whites spend more on their children than do whites, but because they have larger families, blacks spend less per child. Thus, a given child in a black family is likely to enjoy fewer resources than a given child in a white family with the same income because the black is likely to have more brothers and sisters. Moreover, the average income level of the black family is lower. This results in less spent per black child than per white child, even though black families actually spend a larger proportion of their total expenditure on children.

When a household has an additional child, the expenditure that goes to the previous children declines; so does the income that was previously claimed by the adults, but children bear a greater proportion of the cost of the additional child than do the adults. What may be more surprising is that the addition of an adult to the household lowers expenditure on the children by a greater proportion than it does expenditure on the adults in that household. This might reflect the substitution of the additional family member for previously market-oriented child care. Stated alternatively, the cost of a sibling is estimated for some typical households to range anywhere between $1,451 to $3,353 per year to the previously only child, depending upon assumptions. These conclusions hold as long as income is held constant. However, when it is recognized that family income goes up when the number of adults in the household rises, the pattern reverses, at least in some ranges. For example, the average child in the one-child, one-adult household consumes fewer resources than he does in the one child, two-adult household because the second adult adds more in income than he consumes.

Children represent a substantial commitment of resources. A family that has a permanent income of $15,000 per year with two adults and two children spends a present value of almost $23,000 per child on its children. A household with a permanent income of $50,000 per year spends a present value of $57,600 per child, thus more than tripling the permanent income increases child expenditures by less than a factor of 2.5. Expenditures on children do not quite have unitary elasticity with respect to income.

There is some evidence that young children receive more than older children relative to adults, that female children receive more than male children, and that children who work command a larger proportion of the family's material resources.

Finally, we want to remind the reader again that we are discussing here only the allocation of the household's money income. In several studies in recent years, estimates of the "cost of a child" have been made that include the opportunity cost of the parents' time. Our figures are not comparable to those as we are reporting only the apportionment of the household's income between the adults and the children. We make comparisons of our results with these others in chapter 9. We also want to remind the reader that both behavioral assumptions and functional form assumptions have been made in the process of our empirical work; these are arbitrary but essential to our estimation scheme.

Appendix: Definitions of Variables Used in Chapter 5

Variable	Definition and Values
EDUC	Education level of head of household = 7 if some grade school completed = 10 if some high school completed = 12 if high school graduate = 14 if some college completed = 17 if college graduate or graduate work. [General Purpose Tape (GPT) variable loc 46]
AGE	Age in years of head of household. [GPT variable loc 71]
INCOME	Household annual income before personal taxes. [GPT variable loc 775]
ADULT EMP	Proportion of adults in the household that are employed either full-time or part-time. Range is 0 to 1. [derived from GPT variables loc 74 and 75 for head and respective variables for other adult household members]
FEMALE	Female head of household. Dummy is 1.0 if head is female; 0 otherwise. [GPT variable loc 73]
SOUTH	Household lives in the South. Dummy is 1.0 if household is located in the South; 0 otherwise. (South includes Del., D.C., Md., W.Va., Va., N.C., S.C., Ga., Fla., Ky., Tenn., Ala., Miss., Ark., La., Okla., and Texas) [GPT variable loc 39]
RURAL	Household lives in rural area. Dummy is 1.0 if in rural area; 0 otherwise. [GPT variable loc 40]

BLACK   Household head's race is black.
                 Dummy is 1.0 if head is black; 0 otherwise.
                 [GPT variable loc 45]

A   Number of adults in the household.
                 All household members over age 18 are adults. The spouse of
                 head of household is always counted as an adult.

K   Number of children in the household.
                 All household members under the age of 16 were counted as
                 children. (Note: households with own children over 15 or with
                 any members aged 16 or 17 were eliminated from the sample
                 because of the impossibility of distinguishing expenditures.)

CHILD YOUNG   Proportion of children in the household who are age 6 or younger.
                 Range is 0 to 1.

CHILD OLD   Proportion of children in the household who are age 12–15.
                 Range is 0 to 1.

CHILD MALE   Proportion of children in the household who are males.
                 Range is 0 to 1.

OWNCHILD   Proportion of children in the household who are classified as
                 "children" in terms of their relationship to the household head
                 [e.g., GPT variable loc 88]. (Note: other young family member
                 might be classified as "other relative" or as "unrelated.")
                 Range is 0 to 1.

CHILD EMP   Proportion of children in the household who are employed part-
                 time or full-time.
                 Range is 0 to 1.

T   Total current annual consumption expenditure.
                 [GPT variable loc 124]

CA   Adult observed expenditure.
                 Household expenditure on alcohol, tobacco, and adult clothing.
                 [GPT variable locs 174, 184, and var loc 424 minus var locs
                 434, 444, and 454.

Six

The Division of Income between Adults and Children: Evidence from the 1960–61 Consumer Expenditure Survey

In this chapter we use the 1960–61 Consumer Expenditure Survey (CES) described in chapter 3. This completely separate data set has a very similar structure to the 1972–73 survey used in chapter 5. Two purposes are served by replication of the analysis of the 1972–73 data with these earlier data.

First, with the 1960 data we can estimate the system of equations again and get a sense of the robustness or fragility of the findings discussed in chapter 5. As our scheme involves using a relatively little piece of information on the spending pattern of households—the spending on only about 10 percent of the total consumption bundle—to infer quite a lot about the household's allocation behavior, it behooves us to use as much information as we can get to see if our results hold up under scrutiny. So at times in the discussion that follows we will act as if we think the 1960 data and the 1972 data are two independent samples drawn from the same population and consider how similar the findings or the conclusions are.

We stressed above that the methodology employed requires the assumption of a stable relationship between observable adult expenditures and unobservable ones. This requirement of stability is across households with and without children (this is the separability assumption). The obviously counterfactual assumption that the 1960 and 1972 data are samples from the same population represents a different kind of stability. Stability of the second type is not necessary, and if it is rejected by the data, that itself is of interest.

Indeed, the second purpose of replication with the earlier 1960–61 data set is to investigate the changes that have taken place over the twelve years between the two surveys. We know from a glance at the demographic structure of the U.S. population in 1960–61 and 1972–73 that substantial change has taken place in the educational attainment of the population, in the number of families with only one adult and of those the sizeable proportion with a female head. One would expect the higher divorce rate, the lower fertility rate, the higher rate of labor force participation by married women, et cetera, to have an impact on the expenditure pattern of households and on the allocation of spending between the adults and the children.

There are two reasons to examine these changing spending patterns. First, it is important to establish the nature of the changing allocation pattern between children and adults. Second, those changes are attributable to changes in the demographic and economic structure of households or to changes in behavioral responses. Decomposition of the change into these two parts should be informative. If we think of spending in year 1 (e.g., 1960), $S(1)$, as determined in part by the level of a characteristic X in year 1, we would write $S(1) = b(1)X(1)$, where the coefficient b is the measure of the behavioral response. Then we would have in year 2 (e.g., 1972) a comparable relationship, $S(2) = b(2)X(2)$, and the change from year 1 to year 2 can be expressed as the sum of three terms:

$$\Delta S = S(2) - S(1) = (\Delta b)X(1) + b(1)(\Delta X) + (\Delta S)(\Delta X), \quad (6.1)$$

where Δ represents "change," meaning year 2 minus year 1. The first term on the right-hand side of equation (6.1) shows the change attributable to the change in behavior, the change in the coefficient b. The second term shows the change attributable to the change in the value of the variable X, for example, the change due to higher education or to smaller family size. The third term is the interaction between the two and is not properly attributed to either one but rather to both forces taken together. A positive value for Δ's implies that the magnitude rose from year 1 (1960) to year 2 (1972).

To begin, table 6.1 shows the mean values of the subsamples of households without and with children from the 1960–61 data set.[1]

A comparison of tables 5.1 and 6.1 reveals several important demographic and economic changes, although there are also several substantial differences in the definitions of the variables, as detailed in the appendix

1. The samples were drawn from the entire sample of 13,728 households, with the following selection criteria:

Sample with no Children
Retain those with:
no children	5534	
age of head under 65	3479	
positive total consumption	3469	
education of head reported	3405	sample

Table 6.1   Characteristics of Households with and without Children
(1960–61 CES Data)

Variable	Households without Children		Households with Children	
	Mean	St. Dev.	Mean	St. Dev.
EDUC	10.38	(3.5)	11.38	(3.1)
AGE	48.40	(12.6)	35.75	(8.4)
INCOME (000)	$5.88	(4.6)	$6.88	(4.0)
SOUTH	0.30		0.28	
RURAL	0.25		0.30	
BLACK	0.12		0.08	
ADULT EMP	0.78		0.72	
FEMALE HEAD	0.22		0.05	
A	1.71	(0.6)	1.83	(0.5)
K	—		2.42	(1.3)
CHILD YOUNG	—		0.48	
CHILD OLD	—		0.20	
CHILD MALE	—		0.48	
T	$4,259.62	(2,525.4)	$5,770.97	(2,600.8)
AC_A	$511.68	(462.92)	$496.77	(370.90)
(N)	(3,405)		(4,901)	

of this chapter as compared to chapter 5's appendix. The 1972 sample has about two years more education, mirroring the fact that the U.S. adult population had about two more years of educational attainment by 1972. There is also some difference in the coding of the education of the head in the two samples. In 1972 there were fewer coded values; in particular, the lowest level reported was 8 years, whereas there was a code of zero in 1960; the highest code was "16 or more years" in 1972, whereas the actual years of schooling up to 21 were recorded in the 1960 data tape.

The more recent sample is also younger—about five years younger for those without children and about two years younger for those with children. The proportion living in rural areas is dramatically lower in the more recent data, but this reflects a difference in definition, not behavior. Some-

Sample with Children
Retain those with:

children	7135	
age of head under 65	6999	
family size reported	6918	
positive total consumption	6909	
education of head reported	6816	
number of adults positive	6759	
children under 18	4901	sample

what fewer blacks are in the recent sample among those without children, but slightly higher proportions are black among those with children, reflecting the racial differences in fertility rates in the intervening years. Likewise, among those with children there was a noticeable increase over time in the proportion of households headed by a female. Regarding the household size, there were fewer adults in the households without children in 1972 than in 1960, partly reflecting the rise in single-person households and in divorce. There were, however, slightly more adults in the households with children. There were also fewer children in the households with children in the 1972 data, consistent with the pattern of fertility over this period.

The income level is substantially higher in the later survey. Of course, much of that increase reflects the 45 percent inflation that occurred over the period. Expressed in 1972–73 dollars, the average income of the households without children is $8,520 instead of the $5,880 reported in the table. So the real income differential is 33 percent ($= 11.36/ 8.52 - 1.0$). For the households with children, the 1972–73 income figure for 1960–61 is $9,965, so it too rose by about one-third in inflation-adjusted dollars from 1960 to 1972. That is a substantial change in real income. If the results from chapter 5 are of any relevance over time, a higher proportion of the family's expenditure should go to the children in 1960, since the 1972–73 data revealed that the proportion falls as income rises.

Also note that the total expenditure in the earlier survey is lower, adjusted for inflation: the figure (expressed in 1972–73 dollars) for those without children is $6,170 (instead of the reported $4,260); for those with children, $8,359 (instead of $5,771). The fraction of before-tax income spent on current consumption, the ratio T/INCOME, was appreciably higher in 1960 than in 1972: for those without children, the ratio was 0.72 in 1960 and 0.62 in 1972; for those with children the ratios were 0.84 and 0.69, respectively. So savings and taxes were a larger portion of the total allocation of a household in the later period.

A final point of comparison: the ratio of observed-to-total adult expenditures among those without children is higher in the 1960 data—it is 12.0 percent of the total expenditure in that year and only 9.3 percent in the later year. The direction of this difference is somewhat surprising. The coefficient on income in the previous chapter indicated that the proportion of total expenditure on the three observed adult expenditure items rose with income. So if income were the dominant change in the period, a smaller proportion would have been spent on these three items in the earlier (lower-income) data set.

The λ Estimation

Consider the two questions that motivate this chapter: First, are the general, qualitative findings of chapter 5 replicated from this independent (1960–61) data set? Second, what changes occurred in the allocation of expenditures to children over the twelve years between the two surveys and are these changes accounted for primarily by changes in the household characteristics or by changes in the structural relationships?

We first estimate the λ equation (eq. 5.3) using the households without children. Table 6.2 shows that complete equation based on 3,405 households. For convenience of comparison, the approximate values of the coefficients (and their standard errors) are shown in table 6.3. While only one of the significant coefficients changed signs, there is substantial difference in the two regressions. We calculated an F-test on the difference between the two years, and, as one would expect from looking at the values, the F-test implies that these are two statistically distinct relationships. The F-statistic with a year dummy variable was $F(9, 8417) = 9.14$, and calculated without a year or intercept difference, the $F(10, 8417)$ value was 29.16.

The differences are noteworthy. Income appears to have a much larger effect on the proportion of adult spending on the three observed items in the 1960 data; likewise region and race have larger effects in the earlier year. By contrast, rural residence and the number of adults have smaller effects, in terms of their coefficients, in 1960. The literal interpretation of

Table 6.2   Estimation of the λ Function (Eq. 5.3) Using Households without Children

(1960–61 CES Data)

Variable	Coefficient	Standard Error
Constant*	4.843	0.525**
EDUC	0.009	0.019
AGE	0.018	0.005**
INCOME	−0.039	0.008**
SOUTH	1.145	0.149**
RURAL	0.547	0.183**
BLACK	−1.108	0.211**
ADULT EMP	−0.220	0.215
FEMALE HEAD	0.510	0.202**
A	0.498	0.118**
(N = 3,405)		

*Note that the constant term is the coefficient on $A\bar{C}_A$; the regression is run without a true constant.
**$t \geq 2.0$.

Table 6.3   λ Coefficients (and standard errors) for 1960 and 1972 Data Sets
                            (from tables 5.2 and 6.2)

Variable	1960	1972
EDUC	0.01 (0.02)	−0.02 (0.02)
AGE	0.02 (0.01)	0.03 (0.01)
INCOME	−0.04 (0.01)	−0.005 (0.003)
SOUTH	1.14 (0.15)	0.32 (0.15)
RURAL	0.55 (0.18)	1.38 (0.26)
BLACK	−1.11 (0.21)	−0.71 (0.26)
ADULT EMP	−0.22 (0.22)	0.04 (0.27)
FEMALE	0.51 (0.20)	−0.39 (0.21)
A	0.50 (0.12)	1.47 (0.15)

the FEMALE coefficient is that in 1960 a household headed by a female spent a smaller fraction of the total expenditure on alcohol, tobacco, and clothing, whereas, in the later survey that qualitative relationship has reversed. (Recall that the adult employment is held constant in this regression, as is the educational attainment of the household head.)

While the differences in the λ equation across years are substantial and imply a change in the structure of the relationship, note that any differences in the definitions of the variables or in the sampling procedure, intentional or unintentional, might be captured in the behavioral coefficients. We merely note the differences and the instability over the twelve years. We are not confident that we know why that is the case.

The φ Estimation

The next step is to reestimate the φ function, using the estimate of λ for each household with children, based on the equation reported in table 6.2. Table 6.4 reports the φ function estimated again both in a constrained form, as implied by our theory, and in the unconstrained form. Before examining the coefficients one by one, let us go immediately to the bottom line—the evidence on the allocation of expenditures between children and adults. Table 6.5 shows these allocations for the 1960–61 data and, for comparison, for the 1972–73 data as well. The calculations for 1960 use the means of the household characteristics shown in table 6.1 and the φ coefficients from table 6.4; the calculations for 1972 use the 1972 data means and φ coefficients.

The overall impression from table 6.5 is one of *similarity* between the figures for the two years. The 1960 data estimate of φ itself—the ratio of the estimated expenditure per child relative to the expenditure per adult—is quite similar to the estimate from the 1972 data (0.406 compared to

Table 6.4   Estimation of the φ Function (Eq. 5.5) for Households with
                   Children
                          (1960–61 CES Data)

Variable	Constrained	Unconstrained	Constrained and $\lambda A \tilde{C}_A$
Constant*	1.000	1.110 (0.031)**	1.000
K/A	0.666 (0.066)**	0.607 (0.068)**	0.379 (0.061)**
EDUC	0.010 (0.002)**	0.010 (0.002)**	0.011 (0.002)**
AGE	−0.002 (0.001)**	−0.003 (0.001)**	0.000 (0.001)
INCOME	−0.006 (0.001)**	−0.005 (0.001)**	−0.011 (0.001)**
SOUTH	−0.105 (0.015)**	−0.105 (0.015)**	0.049 (0.015)**
RURAL	−0.021 (0.015)	−0.019 (0.015)	0.056 (0.015)**
BLACK	−0.059 (0.025)**	−0.064 (0.025)**	−0.180 (0.020)**
ADULT EMP	−0.200 (0.032)**	−0.206 (0.032)**	−0.201 (0.030)**
FEMALE HEAD	0.050 (0.044)	0.057 (0.044)	0.106 (0.041)**
K	−0.048 (0.004)**	−0.031 (0.007)**	−0.031 (0.004)**
A	0.023 (0.016)	−0.009 (0.019)	0.060 (0.015)**
(N = 4,901)			

*The constant is the coefficient on $\lambda A \tilde{C}_A$; the regression is run with no intercept.
**$t \geq 2.0$.

0.381). Although nothing constrains this to be so, we would have doubted
a result that suggested a dramatically different φ in the two years. They
are, however, clearly in the same ballpark as estimates of an interesting
behavioral parameter. Because the φ's are so similar, so too are the estimates of the equivalent family sizes in the two years. Actually the number
of adults rose slightly between the two surveys, but that was offset by a
decline in the number of children from 2.42 to 2.20. Also, the percent of

Table 6.5   Comparison of Allocation of Expenditures in 1960 and 1972 Using
                Average Characteristics of Households with Children from Each
                Survey

Item	1960	1972
Average φ	0.406	0.381
Family size in equivalent units		
(A + φ × K)	2.81	2.77
Consumption per adult (C$_A$)	$2051.	$3320.
[in 1972–73 $]	$2971.	$3320.
Consumption per child (C$_K$)	$832.	$1262.
[in 1972–73 $]	$1205.	$1262.
C$_K$/T	0.14	0.14
C$_A$/T	0.36	0.36
K × C$_K$/T	0.35	0.30
A × C$_A$/T	0.65	0.70

Based on the following values: 1960: $A = 1.83$; $K = 2.42$; $T = 5,771$. 1972: $A = 1.93$; $K = 2.20$; $T = 9,184$. Inflation rate $= 0.4484$.

total expenditure allocated to a child and to an adult remained constant over the period studied. So one of the most important findings in this chapter is that the relationship between spending on children and spending on adults was quite stable over the twelve years for which we have data.

The similarity seen in table 6.5 is not quite a constancy however. The estimates of the average φ imply that φ declined about 6 percent between 1960 and 1972. While expenditures per adult rose by about 12 percent over the period, expenditures per child rose by only about 5 percent. Coupled with the slight increase in the number of adults and the slight decline in the number of children, the fraction of the total expenditure going to children *fell* from about 35 percent to 30 percent. So we find evidence here of a nontrivial tendency for the dollars allocated to children to decline, relatively, over the 1960s. Children as a whole are doing less well relative to adults in terms of dollars expended in 1972 than in 1960. The typical 1972 household devoted a smaller proportion of its expenditure to its children than did the typical 1960 household. But since the number of children declined a little too, *each child* is getting just a very little less of the total expenditure relative to each adult in 1972.

Despite the small change in φ over the period from 1960 to 1972, it is of some interest to perform the decomposition described near the beginning of this chapter, because the stability of the average φ might mask substantial offsetting pressures. Table 6.6 reports the results of that decomposition. Column 1 simply shows the change in the regression coefficients estimated for the 1960–61 data and the 1972–73 data; column 2 shows the change in the sample mean values of the regressors; column 3 shows the effect on ϕ of the change in each coefficient, so the bottom number of column 3 indicates the total impact of the changes in those coefficients.

The intercept term (the coefficient on the K/A) and the coefficient on number of children, K, tended to lower ϕ substantially. That is, the estimated changes in behavior with respect to these two characteristics tended to lower the allocation of money income to children. What that implies is that the effect of having more children in the household had a bigger downward impact on the allocation to children in 1972 than in 1960. However, the effects in column 3 of two other variables offset this change. In particular, AGE and ADULT EMP had rather large positive effects. The interpretations are not transparent. In the case of AGE, the coefficient was negative in 1960 and positive in 1972. An increase in the age of the parent lowered the child's allocation in the earlier year but raised it in the latter year, so the estimated effect of an increase in the age of the parent changed dramatically over the period. The same is true of the ADULT EMP variable. In 1960 a higher proportion of adults employed in the household meant a smaller allocation to the children relative to the adults, but in the 1972 data the relationship was a positive one rather than a negative one. While the separate magnitudes of these several effects are large, the overall impact of the changes in these coefficients is essentially nil.

Looking at column 4, the effects of the changes in the household characteristics over the twelve years, only one of the variables had an appreciable effect by itself. The big increase in income lowered the relative allocation to children, as expected, but this negative effect was almost completely offset by small positive effects through several other variables. The net effect of the mean changes on ϕ is also tiny (-0.004).

Table 6.6   Decomposition of Changes in ϕ from 1960 to 1972

Characteristic	Change in Coef.	Change in Means	$\Delta b(X_{60})$	$b_{60}(\Delta X)$	$-(\Delta b \Delta X)$	Sum
Intercept	-0.208	-0.00	-0.208	—	—	-0.208
EDUC	0.006	1.01	0.068	0.010	0.006	0.084
AGE	0.005	-1.84	0.175	0.004	-0.009	0.170
INCOME	0.001	6.35	0.008	-0.035	0.007	-0.020
SOUTH	0.095	0.02	0.027	-0.002	0.002	0.027
RURAL	-0.047	-0.14	-0.014	0.003	0.007	-0.004
BLACK	-0.005	0.03	-0.000	-0.002	-0.000	-0.002
ADULT EMP	0.308	-0.01	0.222	0.002	-0.003	0.221
FEMALE	-0.046	0.06	-0.002	0.003	-0.003	-0.002
K	-0.195	0.10	-0.357	0.002	-0.019	-0.374
A	0.033	-0.22	0.081	0.011	-0.007	0.085
Total			-0.001	-0.004	-0.019	-0.023

The fifth column of table 6.6 is the interaction between the two types of changes. Here there is a small net effect that yields the two percentage point decrease in ϕ from 1960 to 1972, from 0.406 to 0.381. The final column shows the net effect for each variable separately, combining the changes in both the coefficients and the means and their interactions.

There is another way to investigate the point of the previous few paragraphs. Since the average ϕ for the 1960 sample is 0.406, we can estimate what ϕ would be in the typical household in 1972—meaning the household with the 1972 sample means for all of the characteristics—if the behavioral responses were those estimated for 1960. That calculation yields 0.402 as the ϕ. So the changes in the mean characteristics had almost no influence on ϕ when measured using the 1960 coefficients. Additionally, we can calculate what the typical 1960 ϕ would have been had the 1972 behavioral responses held. That calculation yields 0.405 as the ϕ. Neither the changes in coefficients nor the changes in means alone would have caused the ϕ to decline as it did. Only the interaction of the two, the product of the changes in coefficients and means, yields the ϕ of 0.381. So like the previous paragraph's conclusion, it is the interaction that seems to deserve the credit for the change that we observe.

One further point on the issue of changes in the coefficients: What we have been looking at is the impact of the changes on the ϕ, and that is not the same issue as whether the coefficients did or did not change in a statistically significant manner over this period. To determine the facts about the latter issue, the two samples from the 1960 and 1972 data sets were pooled and the F-test calculated. The F-statistic is $F(11, 9846) = 12.55$ with no intercept or level difference allowed, or $F(10, 9846) = 13.00$ with an intercept difference, implying that the coefficients for 1960 and for 1972 are indeed statistically different. That these differences do not result in a major difference in the average ϕ does not imply that there was no behavioral change.

Turning to the coefficients on the household characteristics, notice that when the constraint on the intercept is tested, the difference from 1.0 is statistically significant in these 1960 data. The t-test is 3.55 ($= 0.110/0.031$). The magnitude of the difference is only 0.110, however, and with the large number of degrees of freedom, almost any difference is statistically significant.

Household Characteristics

Perhaps the best way to summarize the magnitude of the several coefficients from table 6.4 is to report the derivatives of C_K and C_A with respect to each regressor. Using the formulas following equation (5.7) in the previous chapter, table 6.7 shows these derivatives and the C_K elasticities, all corresponding to the values from the 1972 data shown in table 5.10. We discuss each of the derivatives in turn. Probably the most important result in table 6.7 is the income elasticity of C_K. Its value is 0.94. As income rises, the expenditure on children rises less than proportionately. The estimate from the 1972 data was a remarkably similar value of 0.90. In both these calculations, expenditures per child are a "necessity" by the conventional economic definition.

It is instructive to look at what the derivative with respect to income implies about how an increment in income is spent. Of an additional $100 in before tax income, the coefficient on C_K tells us that $11.36 additional is spent per child and that $29.99 additional is spent per adult. The 2.42 children get $27.49 and the 1.83 adults get $54.88 for a total increment in expenditure of $82.37. This implies that each child gets 0.38 (= 11.36/ 29.99) as much as each adult of the increment, or that children get 0.50 (= 27.49/54.88) as much as the adults of the increment.

Recall that these numbers are at best averages across all income levels and pertain essentially to small changes at the average. But to the extent that they are accurate reflections of this average behavior, they suggest that a $100 addition to the family income results in the average child receiving only about one-tenth of that increase. When social legislation dictates a social transfer to a family on behalf of the children in that family, it may be useful to have our number in mind: in general only about one-tenth of an income increase is received by the average child, and only about one-quarter of the increase is received by all the children. That proportion might be a useful benchmark or expectation for social transfers.

Along similar lines, the payments made by a noncustodial parent on

Table 6.7   Derivatives and Elasticities, Based on Table 6.4, Column 1

Variable	dC_K/dX	Elasticity of C_K	dC_A/dX
EDUC	13.17	0.18	−2.92
AGE	−2.95	−0.13	0.65
INCOME	113.61	0.94	299.90
SOUTH	−140.19	—	31.07
RURAL	−27.51	—	6.10
BLACK	−78.39	—	17.38
ADULT EMP	−267.75	−0.23	59.35
FEMALE	67.25	—	14.91
K	−184.18	−0.54	−281.91
A	−265.28	−0.58	−736.86

behalf of his or her children are often given to the custodial parent for expenditure on the children. But if the calculation in the previous paragraphs is indicative of the extent to which a transfer is diverted from the children, that could help explain why noncustodial parents are so notoriously unreliable in providing support for their children. It can also help explain why the noncustodial parent often prefers to make in-kind transfers (like paying for medical expenses or schooling expenses directly), for the slippage between a dollar given and a dollar received by the child is presumably far less with in-kind transfers. (We discuss this issue at some length in chapter 8.)

Regarding other coefficients, three are small or statistically insignificant. The EDUC, AGE, and FEMALE variables are not particularly important quantitatively here. The educational level of the household head has a small positive effect on ϕ, smaller in fact than in the 1972 data. The small elasticity of 0.18 for 1960 compared to 0.37 for 1972 reflects this difference. The age of head had an insignificant positive coefficient in 1972 and a small negative but significant effect in the 1960 data. The effect of a female head of household, as that structural dimension is defined, is statistically unimportant in both years. We view these three sets of coefficients, as well as the income coefficient, as basically similar in the two surveys.

The three coefficients on the dummy variables SOUTH, RURAL, and BLACK have some changes between the two surveys, but basically they tell a similar story. In both cases they are all three negative. SOUTH is large and significant in 1960 but insignificant in the 1972 data. By contrast, RURAL is insignificant in the 1960 data and large and significant in 1972. BLACK is marginally significant in both years and substantially larger in magnitude in the 1972 data. The effect of the BLACK variable is estimated rather imprecisely, but we cannot rule out its having a statistically discernible influence on ϕ.

One aspect of the samples deserves comment at this point. The proportion rural is 0.30 in our 1960 sample and 0.16 in our 1972 sample. The proportion of the U.S. population living in rural areas in 1960 was in fact 0.30, but by 1970 that proportion had only declined to 0.265. So the shift from rural to nonrural implied in our CES samples of households with children is far greater than for the United States as a whole and reflects a difference in the definition used. A more restrictive definition of rural was used in the 1972–73 data.

Turning to the ADULT EMP coefficient, an interesting difference emerges between the 1960 and 1972 estimates. In the earlier year the effect on C_K is large and negative ($-\$267.75$), while it was large and positive ($\$250.03$) in 1972. Just the opposite signs exist for the effect on C_A.

But when we compute the effect on total expenditures of a unit change in ADULT EMP ($=$ derivative of C_K times K, plus the derivative of C_A times A) for 1960 that value is $-\$541$, and for 1972 it is $+\$2$. That is, in 1960 a household with more adults employed spent $541 less in total, holding the before-tax income fixed, but in 1972 the effect on total expenditure was essentially nil. Perhaps in the earlier year more of the additional earner's income was saved for expenses, such as schooling for the children, but that is only a conjecture at this point.

The estimated effects of K and A are also of interest. While both are large in magnitude, note that the coefficient on A is not statistically significant. The effect of K was the only effect that changed materially when the intercept was allowed to be free in our estimation scheme. So caution is warranted regarding both of these coefficients. Nonetheless, if we take the point estimates of the coefficients and calculate the implied effects on C_K and C_A, table 6.8 illustrates the impact of an additional child (K) or an additional adult (A), calculated at the point of means. An additional child has a smaller percentage effect on C_K in 1972, so the total expenditure on children rises by a much larger proportion in 1972 than in 1960. The effect on C_A is the same in the two years, expressed in proportions. The effect of an additional adult on C_K is much larger in 1972, and note that the effect in 1960 is not even statistically significant. Also, the effect of an additional A is to reduce the expenditure per adult by a much smaller percentage so the effect on total adult expenditure is to increase it by almost one-fifth.

Overall the coefficients on the household characteristics in the φ equations estimated with the 1960 data and with the 1972 data have similarities, yet they are undeniably different. The very large effect of A in 1972 is not found in the 1960 data; the negative effects of SOUTH, RURAL,

Table 6.8

	Effect of One Additional K		Effect of One Additional A	
	1960	1972	1960	1972
Change in C_K	$ $-184.$	$ $-215.$	$ $-265.$	$ $-881.$
New level of C_K	$ 648.	$ 1056.	$ 567.	$ 390.
% change in C_K	-22%	-17%	-32%	-69%
% change in $K \times C_K$	$+10\%$	$+21\%$	-32%	-69%
Change in C_A	$ $-282.$	$ $-414.$	$ $-737.$	$ $-709.$
New level of C_A	$ 1769.	$ 2891.	$ 1314.	$ 2596.
% change in C_A	-14%	-13%	-36%	-21%
% change in $A \times C_A$	-14%	-13%	-1%	$+19\%$

and BLACK seem volatile; the effects of ADULT EMP, FEMALE, and AGE change signs; only the effects of INCOME and K are relatively similar. Greater similarity in these coefficients would have been reassuring, for the estimation scheme employed here relies heavily on the ϕ equation for the results described in this chapter. While the internal structure of the estimated relationship, coefficient by coefficient, is not very similar, the implied average ϕ from the two relationships is quite similar, providing evidence about the robustness of this result.

Next we turn to the question of how large the effect is of different household characteristics on absolute and relative expenditures on children. Let us begin with the education of the head of household. We use the sample of 2,443 households which are non-South, nonrural, and nonblack (with an average EDUC of 12.04) and compare this group's average ϕ and C_K to a hypothetical group with the same means for every variable except education, and we use for EDUC the mean for those with at least a college education (a mean of 16.40). The effect of the change in education level is:

(EDUC)	(12.04)	(16.40)
ϕ	0.452	0.495
C_K	$1,018.	$1,077.

The increase in education raises ϕ by $4.30 per $100 spent on an adult and raises absolute expenditures by $59. But this experiment holds all other variables at the sample mean. If instead we use all the characteristics of households with EDUC = 12 and separate them from those with EDUC $\geq$ 16, then the results are stronger:

(EDUC)	(12.00)	(16.40)
ϕ	0.457	0.483
C_K	$989.	$1,316.
(N)	(845)	(435)

The major difference is that income is higher in the second group—a mean of $10,270 compared to $7,280 in the group with EDUC = 12. While the increase in relative expenditure on the child rose by only $2.60 here, the absolute expenditure rose by $327, a much larger increase than the $59 implied by the experiment described above. In fact, the $327 increase is a 33 percent increase in the absolute expenditure per child. So the higher educational level of the head, accompanied by higher income and other changes that covary with education, involves a substantially higher absolute expenditure on the child, albeit a very small increase in the expenditure on the child compared to the expenditure on the adult.

Look next at the impact of having one or two employed adults in the household. Again using the sample of all 2,443 non-South, nonrural, non-black households and changing ADULT EMP from 0.5 (meaning 50 percent of the adults are employed) to 1.0 (meaning 100 percent of the adults are employed), the differences in ϕ and C_K are:

(ADULT EMP)	(0.5)	(1.0)
ϕ	0.495	0.395
C_K	$1,077.	$932.

Here the direction of effect is negative, suggesting that the employment of more of the household's adults is associated with a lower relative and lower *absolute* expenditure per child. The same qualitative results emerge when instead we select two subsamples of two-adult households (not controlled for region, location, or race) that have one or both adults employed:

(ADULT EMP)	(0.5)	(1.0)
ϕ	0.452	0.348
C_K	$848.	$781.
(N)	(2,429)	(1,266)

One interesting additional fact is noteworthy here. The mean income in the sample of 2,429 households with one employed adult is $6,970; in the other sample with two employed adults, the income is $7,470. The categorization by number of adults employed does *not* imply much difference in household income. The group with two earners have essentially the same money income, so they are not more wealthy. Indeed, since it takes more workers (and presumably more hours of employment) to produce about the same money income, their *real* income is probably lower. (The education level of the head is in fact slightly lower—11.16 in the sample of 1,266 two-employed adults compared to 11.50 in the sample of 2,429 with one-employed adult.)

Next, in table 6.9 we look at the effects of SOUTH, RURAL, and BLACK. Since RURAL is not a significant variable in these data, we ignore its separate effect here. If we take the sample of all 4,901 households with the actual mean values of SOUTH ($=0.28$), RURAL ($=0.30$),

Table 6.9

SOUTH	0.28	(0.0)	(1.0)	(0.0)
RURAL	0.30	(0.0)	(0.0)	(0.0)
BLACK	0.08	(1.0)	(0.0)	(0.0)
ϕ	0.406	0.387	0.341	0.446
C_K	$832.	$807.	$741.	$884.

and BLACK (= 0.08), ϕ is 0.406 (see col. 1). If we replace these means with various other values for SOUTH, RURAL, and BLACK, we can see what the effect is on ϕ and C_K. Column 2 of table 6.9 shows the results for a black, non-South, and nonrural household; the ϕ and C_K are lower here. If instead we look at a southern, nonrural, nonblack household, the ϕ and C_K are lower still (see col. 3). The non-South, nonrural, nonblack household (col. 4) has a much higher ϕ and a higher absolute expenditure on the child as well.

A more all-encompassing comparison is shown in table 6.10 in which all 4,901 households are divided into two groups: black and nonblack households in the left-hand columns, and South and non-South households in the right-hand columns. The means for the household characteristics are shown for these subsets of households. Notice the difference between blacks and nonblacks in education, income, and number of children, and the difference between the South and non-South samples in the percentage black. The bottom two rows show the difference in relative and absolute expenditures on a child. The black spends $11.10 less per child per $100 than the nonblack and spends absolutely $358 less per child. So if we hold all else constant, we find that the black spends $77 less (= $884 − $807) by comparing columns 2 and 4 in table 6.9, but if we let income and other characteristics vary too, then the difference is the much bigger $358. That is, the lower education, lower income, and higher number of children take their toll. (The − $358 black/nonblack differential is similar to the $277 black/nonblack differential calculated from the 1972–73 data in chapter 5.)

The differences in income and other characteristics also have an influ-

Table 6.10

Variable	Comparison		Comparison	
	Black	Nonblack	South	Non-South
SOUTH	0.50	0.26	(1.00)	(0.0)
BLACK	(1.0)	(0.0)	0.15	0.06
EDUC	9.57	11.55	10.56	11.71
AGE	34.77	35.83	39.92	35.68
INCOME (000)	$ 4.53	$ 7.09	$ 5.93	$ 7.26
RURAL	0.15	0.31	0.41	0.25
ADULT EMP	0.79	0.71	0.74	0.71
FEMALE	0.21	0.04	0.06	0.05
A	1.70	1.85	1.86	1.82
K	2.76	2.39	2.35	2.44
(N)	(402)	(4,499)	(1,383)	(3,518)
ϕ	0.304	0.415	0.322	0.438
C_K	$506	$864	$621	$918

ence, but to a smaller extent, in the comparison of the South and non-South households. The difference in absolute expenditure, when all else is held constant, is $143 (calculated by subtracting column 3 from column 4 in table 6.9), but is $297 when all characteristics are free to vary (calculated as the difference between columns 3 and 4 in table 6.10).

Summary

In this chapter we have used the 1960–61 CES data to replicate the analysis of chapter 5 where we used a more recent (1972–73) data set. We have also investigated the reasons for the differences found between the two surveys. Overall, the estimated value of the key parameter, ϕ—the ratio of expenditures per child to expenditures per adult in the household—is quite similar in the two years. Its value is about 0.4 for a typical household with children both in 1960 and in 1972. That is, households spend about two-and-a-half times as much on an adult as on a child under age 16.

While the estimate of ϕ is about the same in the two years, it did decline slightly, as we estimate it, from 0.406 in 1960 to 0.381 in 1972. Coupled with the small decline in the number of children in the average household over that period as well (from 2.42 children to 2.20 children), the percentage of the household's total expenditure spent on children fell from about 35 percent to about 30 percent, while the percent spent on each child remained steady at about 14 percent.

The introduction of an additional child or an additional adult into the household has a sizeable effect on both the absolute and relative expenditure on a child (and on an adult). An additional child lowers the expenditure on a child by about $184 or by about 20 percent, while an additional adult lowers the expenditure on a child by about $265. (The corresponding impact on the expenditure on an adult is a $282 decline associated with an additional child and a whopping $737 or 35 percent decline associated with an additional adult.) Of course, the effects on expenditures on all children together is quite different: the addition of a child raises the expenditure on all children in the household by about 10 percent, while the addition of an adult lowers that expenditure by at least 30 percent. All of these calculations rely on the regression coefficients for the variables K and A, so they are ceteris paribus statements, holding all the other household characteristics in the household, including income, constant.

Both living in the South and being black are associated with a lower expenditure on the child in these 1960 data. The point estimate of the effect of the head of household being black is a $-\$77$, if other characteristics are held constant, but a much bigger $-\$358$ if those characteristics vary as they do across average black and nonblack households. For South as well, the estimated effect is $-\$143$ holding other characteristics at their sample means, but is $-\$297$ if these characteristics vary.

Education of the head of household has a small but significant positive effect on the relative expenditure on children. Given the associated changes in income and other characteristics, the data suggest that a household with a college-educated head spends about one-third more on a child absolutely than one with a high-school-educated head ($1,316 compared to $989).

As income rises in the household, the expenditure on children does not keep pace; it rises less than proportionately with income. The income elasticity of the expenditure on a child, C_K, is 0.94 in these 1960 data. That important number is similar to the 0.90 estimated from the 1972 data.

Appendix: Definitions of Variables Used in Chapter 6

Variable	Definition and Values
EDUC	Education level of head of household, in actual years. [1960–61 General Purpose Tape (GPT) output word and position 0–7]
AGE	Age in years of head of household. [GPT 2–1]
INCOME(BT)	Household annual income before taxes. [adjusted by putting taxes back in, GPT 74–0, 86–0]
SOUTH	Household lives in the South. Dummy is 1.0 if household lives in the South; 0 otherwise. [GPT 1–0]
RURAL	Household lives in rural area. Dummy is 1.0 if household lives in rural area defined as non-SMSA or SMSA with less than 50,000 population; 0 otherwise. [GPT 0–0]
BLACK	Household head is black. Dummy is 1.0 if head is black; 0 otherwise. [GPT 1–5]
ADULT EMP	The computed* proportion of adults who are employed full-time or part-time. [*Computation explained at end of appendix; based on GPT 3–8]
FEMALE HEAD	Household head is a female. Dummy is 1.0 if head is female; 0 otherwise. [GPT 1–4]
A	Number of adults in the household. Constructed as family size minus number of children. There is a possible problem with this variable because the maximum number of children allowed in the coding (9) is greater than the

	maximum allowed in the coding (8) of the family size variable. Any cases in which the resulting number of adults was nonpositive were excluded in the sample selection. Part-year households were also excluded. [GPT 3–0, 2–9]
K	Number of children in the household. Only households with all children less than age 16 were included, for reasons explained in the text. The exclusion was achieved by excluding on the basis of "Age of children of head" variable [GPT 3–7] which identifies children over 17, and on the basis of clothing expenditures for children aged 16–17 [GPT 58–0 to 64–0 and 76–0 to 81–0]—if there were any expenditures in this category, the household was considered to have a child over age 15, and thus was excluded.
CHILD YOUNG	The computed** proportion of children who are aged 0–6. Range is 0 to 1. [**Computation explained at end of appendix; GPT 3–7]
CHILD OLD	The computed** proportion of children who are aged 12–15. Range is 0 to 1. [**Computation explained at end of appendix; GPT 3–7]
CHILD MALE	The computed*** proportion of children who are male. Range is 0 to 1. [***Computation explained at end of appendix; GPT 64–0]
T	Total expenditure on current consumption. [GPT 8–0]
AC_A	Observed adult expenditure. Expenditures on alcohol, tobacco, and adult clothing [GPT 12–0, 13–0, 52–0, and 70–0].

*Computation of ADULT EMP

The 1960–61 CES tape only gives the number of total earners, not the number of adult earners. It also gives the "earner composition":

0 = head only employed
1 = head and wife only employed
2 = head and person > 18, not wife, employed
3 = head and person < 18, not wife, employed
4 = head and other persons of any age, not wife, employed
5 = head and any combination of others, including wife, employed
6 = no one employed
7 = head not employed, wife only employed
8 = head not employed, any other person, not wife, employed
9 = head not employed, any combination of others, including wife, employed.

For values 1, 2, 3, 6, and 7 the value of ADULT EMP is clear.
For values 4, 5, 8, and 9, AEL, KEL, and PROB are computed.
AEL (eligible adults) is the number of adults who could be working and whose employment status is unclear; KEL (eligible children) is the number of children over age 12; PROB is the

probability that each eligible person is employed—total earners minus number of known earners (husband and wife are known), divided by number of eligible adults and children. Then

ADULT EMP = number of adults employed for certain (husband or wife) plus AEL × PROB/A.

**Computation of CHILD YOUNG and CHILD OLD:

The available information was of the following, challenging kind:

code	meaning
0	no children;
1	oldest child < 6;
2	oldest child 6–11, youngest child < 6;
3	all children 6–11;
4	all children 12–17;
5	oldest child 12–17, youngest child < 6;
6	oldest child 12–17, youngest child 6–11;
7	oldest child > 18, youngest < 6;
8	oldest child > 18, youngest 6–11;
9	all children > 18.

Codes 0, 7, 8, and 9 were eliminated as discussed.

Code	CHILD YOUNG value	Implied child 6–11 value	CHILD OLD value
1	1.0	0.0	0.0
2	0.5	0.5	0.0
3	0.0	1.0	0.0
4	0.0	0.0	1.0
5	*	*	*
6	0.0	0.5	0.5

*if $K = 2$ then values respectively are 0.5, 0.0, 0.5;
if $K = 3$ then values respectively are $\frac{4}{9}$, $\frac{1}{9}$, $\frac{4}{9}$;
if $K = 4$ then values respectively are $\frac{5}{12}$, $\frac{2}{12}$, $\frac{5}{12}$;
etc., for the general formulas $(K + 1)/(K \times 3)$; $(K - 2)/(K \times 3)$; $1.0 - [(K + 1) + (K - 2)]/(K \times 3)$. Our assistant, Elizabeth Peters, is responsible for this ingenuity.

***Computation of CHILD MALE

The sex of the children is not given, so we used information on whether there was expenditure on boy's clothing. If no expenditure on boy's clothing, then CHILD MALE is 0; if there was spending on boy's clothing, then at least one child was male, so:

K	Algorithm	CHILD MALE value
1	1	1.0
2	$(0.5)\frac{1}{2} + (0.5)\frac{1}{2}$	0.75
3	$(0.33)\frac{1}{3} + (0.33)\frac{2}{3} + (0.33)\frac{2}{3}$	0.67

Seven

Recalculating the Personal Distribution of Income

One question that this book set out to answer is: How is the distribution of income affected by the recognition that all individuals are not treated identically within a household? The inquiry began by noting that using the household as the basic unit of analysis masks the effect of family size on income distribution. Replacing family income by per capita income corrects this problem. But if all individuals in the household are not treated the same, it is possible that per capita income is also a poor measure on which to base the distribution of utility within an economy.

This chapter attempts to address that question. By using the method developed in the preceding chapters, income distributions are computed from the Current Population Surveys (CPS) for 1970 and 1979. Cross-year comparisons are made and differences, implied by the various definitions of income, are examined. The theory from chapter 4 along with the coefficients obtained in chapter 5 are used to derive the actual income that each member of the household receives. This is compared with per capita income for both years. Income per individual, as we have derived it, is dubbed "LMINC"; per capita income, "CAPINC."

The major finding of this chapter is that although there is some overlap between per capita income and LMINC, there are important differences as well. The distribution of LMINC is more diffuse than that of per capita income. Children are more likely to be found in the lower tail and less likely to be found in the upper tail of the LMINC distribution.

The comparison across years reveals remarkable stability in the results. There are a few small differences, however. For example, in both 1970 and 1979, male-headed households were richer, if measured by family income (FAMINC), than female-headed households. That is true when LMINC is used as well. Family income makes it appear that the differences have increased over time; LMINC reveals a narrowing of the gap in expenditures across these two kinds of households. Additionally, there appears to be slightly better correlation between LMINC and CAPINC in 1979 than there was in 1970. Still, differences may be pronounced. Of those who were found to be in the lowest 10 percent of income on a per capita basis, only 68 percent would have been in that low tail had LMINC been used. The converse is also true: Of those who were found to be in the lowest 10 percent of income based on LMINC, only 68 percent would have been in that tail had per capita income been used. The same is true, but to a somewhat lesser extent, of the upper tail of the distribution. Thus, if LMINC is a better measure of true income, the use of per capita income or family income can lead to significant misclassification. This should be of concern to policymakers who target individuals in poverty based on some measure of their income. If our definition is closer to the correct one, many who are being labeled poor are not, and many of the truly poor are being missed.

The Estimating Equation

To apportion the family's income into the amount received on average by an adult, C_A, and by a child, C_K, we must estimate the family's ϕ as well as observe its total income, Y, and its number of adults, A, and children, K.[1] The estimation of ϕ used here is based on our analyses with the 1972–73 CES data used to construct the tables in chapter 5. Estimates of ϕ are obtained directly from applying column 1 of table 5.4 to the CPS data. This function is used in the following section, applied to households in the CPS, to apportion the household income between the adults and the children.

The 1970 and 1979 Distributions of Income

Using the 1970 and 1979 CPS, we selected subsamples of 134,031 and 89,438 observations, respectively. The sample from the 1970 CPS was selected as follows: The person file was merged with the family file and the head-of-household person file, yielding approximately 145,000 observations. A few were deleted because of missing ID codes. Information on all household characteristics was not available for primary and secondary

---

1. Notice that we rather blithely shift from the allocation of total consumption, T, to the allocation of total income, Y. Implicitly, we assume that savings is allocated in the same proportions as expenditures between adults and children.

individuals (living alone or as a single, unrelated to the head), so these categories of individuals and their incomes were deleted. Since negative values of ɸ are non-sensical, observations were deleted if the estimated ɸ was less than 0.05 *and* the household had children. Although this leads to some bias, those thrown out by this criterion were a trivial fraction of the total.

The 1979 CPS sample was selected as follows: The person file was matched with the family file, yielding about 110,000 observations. In this file full information is available on primary and secondary individuals, so these were retained in the 1979 data file. Observations were deleted for missing data on any of the variables and again if ɸ < 0.05 *and* the household had children. In both samples, individuals in subfamilies were merged with the family record of the primary family since the primary family's income includes the income of subfamilies.

For each individual we used household characteristics to construct the variables required to estimate ɸ. Table 7.1 reports the means of these variables, which were used with the ɸ equation from table 5.4 to estimate a ɸ for each individual.[2] Since ɸ is the estimate of the average income per child relative to the average income per adult, its magnitude and dispersion among households is of some interest in its own right.

Table 7.2 shows selected values of ɸ estimated from the 1970 and 1979 samples. It is noteworthy that the mean (and median) of the distribution for both years is 0.38. That is, a child on average receives about $38 for

Table 7.1   Means (and standard deviations) of Characteristics of Households; 1970 and 1979 CPS Samples of Individuals

	1970		1979	
EDUCATION	12.4	(3.5)	13.1	(3.4)
AGE	44.6	(14.8)	44.5	(15.9)
INCOME (000)	10.5	(8.0)	18.7	(13.0)
SOUTH	0.30	—	0.33	—
RURAL	0.34	—	0.34	—
BLACK	0.10	—	0.11	—
ADULT EMP	0.67	—	0.69	—
FEMALE	0.08	—	0.19	—
K	1.87	(1.9)	1.32	(1.5)
A	2.13	(0.7)	2.05	(0.7)
N	(134,061)		(89,438)	

2. One variable in the ɸ equation was not measurable with the CPS data: OWNCHILD, the percent of children in the households with children who were the natural offspring of the household head. We simply assigned all individuals a proportion 0.98, the mean for the sample from the 1972–73 CES data.

Table 7.2   The Estimated Distribution of φ, the Ratio of Income per Child to
                 Income per Adult, for 1970 and 1979 CPS

	1970 CPS	1979 CPS
Mean	0.375	0.375
Standard Deviation	0.150	0.171
Skewness	−0.270	−0.415
Quartiles:		
95%	0.639	0.668
90%	0.547	0.610
75%	0.458	0.465
50%	0.384	0.379
25%	0.290	0.283
10%	0.185	0.166
5%	0.121	0.094

every $100 received by an adult. Recall that the average value of φ in the 1972–73 CES data used to estimate φ was 0.38 and, using a completely independent estimate of the λ and φ functions, the average φ in the 1960–61 CES data set was 0.406. This robustness is reassuring. As table 7.2 indicates, however, there is considerable variation in φ among households: the standard deviation is 0.15 in 1970 and 0.17 in 1979. While over a quarter of the individuals reside in households with a φ below 0.30 (i.e., in households that are estimated to allocate less than $30 per child for every $100 per adult), another quarter resides in households with a φ in excess of 0.45. This is true for both 1970 and 1979.

Consider the distribution of income among individuals when an individual's income is estimated by taking account of φ. From chapter 5, equation (5.8), the income received by an adult (an individual age 18 or older) is $FAMINC/(A + \phi K)$. This should be thought of as a per capita income measure, where adults have weight = 1 and children have weight = φ. Likewise, for individuals under age 18, the income received is defined to be $(\phi)(FAMINC)/A + \phi K)$. We call this measure of the individual's income LMINC.

For comparison, we also calculate CAPINC, the standard unweighted measure of per capita income defined as $FAMINC/(A + K)$, for all individuals. CAPINC assumes all household members have the same level of income, although neither CAPINC nor LMINC makes any adjustment for scale economies. The estimates of LMINC and CAPINC are summarized in table 7.3. For each year the mean of the two measures is the same. This is necessarily the case, for the average LMINC in a household is simply a weighted average of the adult and child income for the household weighted by the proportions of adults and children. For a given household:

$$LMINC = \frac{FAMINC}{A + \phi K} \frac{A}{A + K} + \frac{FAMINC}{A + \phi K} \phi \frac{K}{A + K}$$

$$= \frac{FAMINC}{A + K} = CAPINC.$$

The dispersion, however, is not the same. The standard deviation of LMINC is $114 higher than that of CAPINC in 1970, adding about 4 percent to the coefficient of variation. By 1979 the standard deviation of LMINC is $400 higher than the standard deviation of CAPINC, adding about 6 percent to the smaller coefficient of variation in 1979. Both distributions have substantial positive skew in both 1970 and 1979.

The magnitudes in table 7.3 do not indicate the extent of difference between LMINC and CAPINC in the tails of the distribution, where so much policy interest lies. Figure 7.1 plots the cumulative distributions of LMINC and CAPINC. The greater dispersion of LMINC is seen in the flatter shape of the cumulative distribution.

Suppose we ask what percentage of the population is below some specific per capita income level. For the lower tail of the distribution, that will be a bigger percentage if we use the measure LMINC rather than CAPINC. For example, in 1970 the official poverty level set by the government was $3,968 for a family of four with certain characteristics. This is $992 on a per capita basis. If the distribution of per capita income is used, then 7.4 percent of the relevant population would have been below the poverty line. If LMINC is used instead, a much larger figure of 15 percent fall below the poverty line. Most of these individuals are children, and more will be said about that below.

The same is true of the 1979 distribution. Poverty was defined as income below $7,412 for a family of four. This is equivalent to per capita income of $1,853. If the per capita distribution is used, then 9.2 percent

Table 7.3   Estimated LMINC and CAPINC 1970 and 1979 CPS

	1970 CPS		1979 CPS	
	LMINC	CAPINC	LMINC	CAPINC
Mean	$3,237	$3,237	$6,418	$6,417
Median	2,371	2,433	5,002	5,133
Standard Deviation	5,077	4,963	5,649	5,249
Skewness	+ 13.93	+ 14.88	+ 2.79	+ 3.25

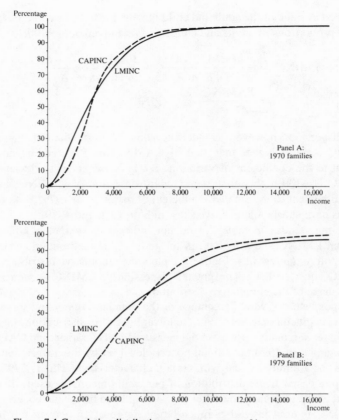

Figure 7.1 Cumulative distributions of two measures of income

fall below the poverty line. If LMINC is used instead, the larger fraction of 16.9 percent is defined to be in poverty.

A study in the United Kingdom (Fiegehen and Lansley 1976), using the 1971 Family Expenditure Survey, reached conclusions that mirror the paragraph above. In that study the income could be measured either at the household level (defined as all persons living at the same address having meals prepared together and with common housekeeping) or the tax unit level (defined as nonmarried adults and married couples each linked to their dependent children). The household can comprise more than one tax unit, but not vice versa (1976, 509). Defining the poverty income level as "the official view of a minimum tolerable level of living" used to administer the government's Supplementary Benefit scheme, the study estimates the proportion of persons below that poverty level of income. When the tax unit is used as the basis, 13.1 percent are below the poverty level. When the household unit is used, however, only 7.3 percent are below the poverty level (1976, 515). The study concludes, "The choice of income receiving unit is crucial in estimating the numbers of people in poverty. If tax-unit incomes are used we find a figure that is 80 percent higher than when household incomes are considered" (1976, 517).

The poverty cutoff level is surely arbitrary, but the point made by our results and by Fiegehen and Lansley (1976) is clear. While the apportionment of household income is at the heart of all measures of well-being, conclusions about its distribution among individuals differ significantly with the allocation method.

The same point can be made by examining the other tail of the distribution. Suppose "very rich" is defined as per capita income above \$6,000 in 1970. If per capita income is used as the criterion, then 5 percent of the population is very rich. If LMINC is used instead, then about 12 percent of the population is among the very rich, most of them being adults.

To investigate the relationship between LMINC and the household characteristics, a reduced-form regression was run which has as its dependent variable LMINC and as independent variables age, education, South, rural, black, proportion of adults who work, whether the household was headed by a female, the number of children in the household, and the number of adults in the household. Since the definition of LMINC varies with the age of the individual in question, the sample was split into adults and children. Thus, the dependent variable in the child sample is really C_K, whereas in the adult sample it is C_A. Those results are reported in tables 7.4, panels A and B.

The regressions combine two effects. Coefficients include not only the effect of the right-hand variable on ϕ (the apportionment within a household), but also the effect on total household income. For example, education contributes both to the consumption of the child and to the consumption of adults. That is because education tends to raise family income, which is not held constant in these regressions. Similarly, living in a household with a female head tends to reduce the income of all members, because these households have lower average family income, irrespective of its apportionment.

The addition of another child to the household reduces a child's consumption by more in 1970 than it does in 1979 (both in absolute and percentage terms). The same is true of the effect of an additional adult on child consumption. One of the more surprising results is that increased household labor force participation decreases income of the children in

Table 7.4   Reduced Form Regression of LMINC on Household Characteristics, for Children (Panel A) and Adults (Panel B) Separately, for 1970 and 1979 CPS

Panel A: Children: C_K as Dependent Variable		
Variable	1970	1979
Constant	12423	1209
	(238)	(48)
EDUCATION	99.4	208
	(9.8)	(2.18)
AGE	142	33
	(3.47)	(0.7)
SOUTH (Dummy)	−119	−113.5
	(69)	(14.81)
RURAL (Dummy)	−434	−529
	(65)	(14.5)
BLACK (Dummy)	482	−477
	(101)	(21)
ADULT EMP	−2340	936
	(83)	(16)
FEMALE (Dummy)	−6292	−1168
	(116)	(22)
K	−521	−299
	(17)	(5)
A	−6437	−1299
	(67)	(16)
N	47629	26211
R^2	0.19	0.52
Mean of Dep. Variable	1751	2274

Panel B: Adults: C_A as Dependent Variable		
Variable	1970	1979
Constant	−172	−1135
	(64)	(148)
EDUCATION	256	563
	(2.6)	(6.3)
AGE	15	51
	(0.67)	(1.5)
SOUTH (Dummy)	−243	−212
	(19)	(43)
RURAL (Dummy)	−645	−937
	(18)	(43)
BLACK (Dummy)	−668	−935
	(32)	(69)
ADULT EMP	2032	4075
	(25)	(57)
FEMALE (Dummy)	−1028	−2492
	(33)	(56)

TABLE 7.4 (*Continued*)

Panel B: Adults: C_A as Dependent Variable

Variable	1970	1979
K	− 364	− 916
	(6.2)	(18)
A	− 57	− 711
	(11)	(27)
N	86432	63225
R^2	0.24	0.26
Mean of Dep. Variable	4055	8135

1970, but increases it in 1979. Note that in 1970 the effect of labor force participation on adult income was positive. This suggests that the substitution of expenditures toward adults in working households swamped the effect of additional income in 1970. The same was not true in 1979. Part of this may be a reflection of the improvement in jobs being held by secondary family members over time (see Smith and Ward 1985).

The results in panel B of table 7.4 show more stability between the two years. Education and age of head raise the consumption of both the adult and the child in each year, while the location and race dummy variables decrease the consumption of both (except for the estimate for C_K in 1970). The consumption of adults rises with an increase in the proportion employed, while households headed by a female exhibit lower consumption by both adults and children.

Table 7.5 goes into more detail and makes some additional comparisons. The CPS samples are partitioned by gender of head, and separately by number of children and by race of head. Reported are the means and standard deviations of two income measures: FAMINC and our estimate of the person's income, LMINC. The three panels of table 7.5 are independent of each other; appendix tables 7.A, 7.B, and 7.C provide details on the characteristics of these various subsamples.

Consider panel A in table 7.5. In 1970, the household income of male-headed households was almost twice that of female-headed households, and the gap actually widened by 1979. While the LMINC (and therefore per capita income) differential was about the same in 1970—an 80 percent differential favorable to male-headed households—it was only a 40 percent differential by 1979. The reason seems to be that the number of children in the female-headed household is much smaller in 1979: Instead of 12 percent more children than the male-headed households, as in 1970, by 1979 the female-headed households had 18 percent fewer children. Notice as well that a much larger percentage of the households have female heads

Table 7.5   Mean (standard deviation) of Family Income and LMINC for
                 Selected Subgroups from 1970 and 1979 CPS in $1,000s

Year	Type	(% of Households)	FAMINC		LMINC	
Panel A: Male/Female Head of Household						
1970	Male	(91.5)	10.9	(8.1)	3.4	(5.3)
1970	Female	(8.5)	5.9	(4.6)	1.9	(1.8)
1979	Male	(81.2)	20.9	(13.0)	6.8	(5.7)
1979	Female	(18.8)	9.3	(8.0)	4.9	(5.1)
Panel B: Few/Many Children in Household						
1970	Few	(95.3)	10.6	(8.0)	3.3	(5.2)
1970	Many	(4.7)	9.8	(6.8)	1.1	(1.2)
1979	Few	(98.8)	18.8	(13.0)	6.5	(5.6)
1979	Many	(1.1)	13.9	(9.8)	1.6	(1.9)
Panel C: Black/White Head of Household						
1970	Black	(9.8)	6.9	(7.6)	2.3	(6.5)
1970	White	(90.2)	10.9	(7.9)	3.3	(4.9)
1979	Black	(11.3)	12.5	(10.4)	4.1	(4.2)
1979	White	(88.7)	19.5	(13.1)	6.7	(5.7)

by 1979. This is partly reflective of changes in living arrangements, but it is also partly a result of including single-person households and primary and secondary persons in households in the 1979 sample.

Table 7.5, panel B, compares households with few (0–5) or many (6 +) children. This partitioning separates the small portion of families with very many children and indicates, especially in 1979, how low the per capita income is in these very large families. Families with six or more children are disproportionately black, and they have especially low estimated ϕ values (e.g., in 1979 those with many children had $\phi = 0.28$ whereas the complement group had $\phi = 0.38$. See appendix table 7.B). Notice as well that the dispersion in per capita income measured by LMINC is substantial.

Table 7.5, panel C, compares black and white families. Those with a black head have only about two-thirds as much family income and roughly the same fraction on a per capita income basis. These families have somewhat younger heads who are also less well-educated and are much more likely to be female. They have more children, slightly fewer adults, and roughly the same adult-equivalent family size as the family with a white head.

Consider the characteristics of individuals in the tails of the distributions of LMINC. Table 7.6 reports the mean characteristics of the lowest 10 percent of each distribution and the highest 10 percent of each distribution for 1970 (panel A) and for 1979 (panel B). The individuals in the lower tail of the distributions live in households with heads who are, as one would expect, less educated, younger, and more likely to be female, black, and rural. They are less likely to live in households with a high proportion of adults employed; they are more likely to be located in the South, and to

Table 7.6 — Characteristics of Households in the Lowest and Highest Deciles of the Distribution of LMINC for 1970 and 1979 CPS

Variable	Lowest 10%		Highest 10%	
Panel A: 1970 CPS				
FAMINC	4.80	(4.2)	21.64	(14.4)
CAPINC	0.80	(0.7)	10.13	(13.2)
LMINC	0.33	(0.3)	10.79	(13.1)
EDUCATION	10.31	(3.4)	14.27	(3.2)
AGE	41.86	(13.1)	48.23	(13.3)
SOUTH	0.43	—	0.24	—
RURAL	0.49	—	0.22	—
BLACK	0.29	—	0.04	—
ADULT EMP	0.57	—	0.76	—
FEMALE	0.23	—	0.03	—
K	3.60	(2.3)	0.56	(1.0)
A	2.10	(0.8)	2.04	(0.8)
ϕ	0.30	(0.2)	0.43	(0.2)
$(A + \phi K)$	3.06	(0.8)	2.24	(0.8)
CHILD	0.85	—	0.02	—
N	13,357		13,410	
Panel B: 1979 CPS				
FAMINC	7.49	(7.7)	37.62	(16.5)
CAPINC	1.48	(1.5)	17.46	(7.4)
LMINC	0.64	(0.6)	18.74	(7.0)
EDUCATION	11.17	(3.5)	15.29	(2.8)
AGE	38.97	(13.5)	46.37	(14.3)
SOUTH	0.43	—	0.28	—
RURAL	0.43	—	0.23	—
BLACK	0.30	—	0.05	—
ADULT EMP	0.55	—	0.81	—
FEMALE	0.37	—	0.11	—
K	2.67	(1.7)	0.42	(0.8)
A	1.93	(0.8)	1.95	(0.7)
ϕ	0.34	(0.2)	0.40	(0.2)
$(A + \phi K)$	2.77	(0.8)	2.07	(0.8)
CHILD	0.82	—	0.00	—
N	8,938		8,946	

have several more children. Additionally, they tend to be low φ households. In comparing the lowest 10 percent in 1970 with the same segment of the comparable 1979 distribution, the major difference is the dramatic increase in the proportion living with female heads of household. That difference might reflect only that single-person households and secondary individuals are included in the 1979 file but not in the 1970 data file for reasons described above. We note that the proportion with female heads of household in the upper tail also rose dramatically between 1970 and 1979, surely reflecting both the rise in female headship rates and the difference in sample definition.

While table 7.6 shows characteristics of the tails of the distributions of LMINC, we might also look at the tails of the distributions using CAPINC as the income measure. There is far from perfect rank correlation of individuals in these two distributions. Table 7.7 shows that about two-thirds of those in the lower tail of one distribution (LMINC or CAPINC) are in the lower tail of the other. That means, of course, that a sizeable number who are in the lowest 10 percent of the one distribution are not comparably located in the other. The most noticeable difference is the number of children in these tails. The variable CHILD in table 7.6 indicates the proportion of those in each subsample who are under age 18. While 85 percent of those in the lower tail of the 1970 LMINC distribution are children, only 53 percent of those in the lower tail of the 1970 CAPINC distribution are children (not shown in the table). (For comparison, overall 36 percent of the 1970 distribution were children.) So by the measurement of LMINC, more of the "poorest" in our population are children. Likewise, at the other end of the distribution, while 2 percent of the top decile are children when we use LMINC as our measure, 10 percent of that top decile are children by the CAPINC measure. The same qualitative results apply to 1979, where overall 29 percent are children: in the lowest decile of CAPINC, 52 percent are children, while of the LMINC, 82 percent are children; at the highest decile, 6 percent of CAPINC and less than 0.5

Table 7.7

	1970	1979
Probability of being in lowest 10% of:		
LMINC distribution, given in lowest 10% of CAPINC:	0.66	0.68
CAPINC distribution, given in lowest 10% of LMINC:	0.66	0.68
Probability of being in highest 10% of:		
LMINC distribution, given in highest 10% of CAPINC:	0.83	0.85
CAPINC distribution, given in highest 10% of LMINC:	0.83	0.84

percent of LMINC are children. The contrast is striking. In 1970, there was a 0.85 probability that an individual in the lowest 10th percentile of LMINC was a child, but only a 0.02 probability that an individual in the highest 10th percentile of LMINC was a child.

One important qualification must be stressed here. Our measure of income is dollars of income expended on the individual, and this measure does not necessarily reflect welfare: children may well need fewer dollars to be equally well fed, clothed, or entertained. We attempt to allocate the family income and to measure the dispersion in income among individuals including children; we do not claim that these distributions reflect well-being.

The effect of the individual's age on the transformation of income into utility cuts two ways: If we believe that $1 of income produces the same amount of utility for an adult as it does for a child, then the distributions of LMINC in this chapter are important because they imply that it is children who are relatively deprived. If instead one thinks that an average ϕ of 0.38 reflects the average expenditure necessary to provide a child with the same utility as an adult, then the relevant income distribution would be one that adjusted the child's income upward by a factor of 2.6 ($= 1/0.38$) to make it comparable to an adult's income. Since there is considerable variation in ϕ across households, children might have low incomes because their family income is low, or because their household size is large, or because their household's ϕ is low.

Summary

The common practice of treating all family members as if they are in the same financial boat is surely a gross oversimplification. By our estimates, in almost 25 percent of families a child receives only about 25 percent as much of the family's income for consumption purposes as an adult. On average, a child receives about 40 percent as much as an adult in the same household. Taking these rough estimates into account, the distribution of consumption income among a population tends to locate children much further down the scale than is the case when income is assumed to be apportioned equally on a per capita basis.

Children probably require less income than adults for their well-being. They are, after all, smaller, so they need less food, smaller clothes, less living space, and so forth. Thus, our conclusion that children receive on average only about 40 percent as much as adults does not necessarily indicate that they are deprived or that their utility is dramatically less than that of an adult. But since adults tend to determine the allocation of resources within the family, there is no certainty that the utility of the children and the adults are equalized.

Our procedure attempts to do for the child-adult consumption within the family what has been done for years across earners or across families: To estimate the dollar worth of consumption of different individuals. Perhaps comparison between a child and an adult is less legitimate than between one adult and another. But some way of measuring the child-adult differential is needed. Our message is that income is not distributed evenly within the family. Theoretical models and policy decisions should not continue to be based on the assumption that it is.

Appendix Table 7.A   Means of Characteristics of Subsamples of Households Summarized in Table 7.5: Male-Headed and Female-Headed Households

Variable	1970				1979			
	Male Head		Female Head		Male Head		Female Head	
FAMINC	10.9	(0.02)	5.9	(0.04)	20.9	(0.05)	9.3	(0.06)
CAPINC	3.4	(0.01)	1.9	(0.02)	6.8	(0.02)	4.9	(0.04)
LMINC	3.4	(0.01)	1.9	(0.02)	6.8	(0.02)	4.9	(0.04)
EDUCATION	12.5	(0.01)	11.1	(0.03)	13.3	(0.01)	12.2	(0.03)
AGE	44.4	(0.04)	46.7	(0.15)	43.8	(0.06)	47.3	(0.15)
SOUTH	0.29	—	0.35	—	0.33	—	0.34	—
RURAL	0.35	—	0.31	—	0.35	—	0.28	—
BLACK	0.08	—	0.30	—	0.08	—	0.25	—
ADULT EMP	0.68	—	0.63	—	0.71	—	0.60	—
FEMALE	0.00	—	1.00	—	0.00	—	1.00	—
K	1.85	(0.01)	2.09	(0.02)	1.37	(1.4)	1.12	(0.01)
A	2.17	(0.00)	1.74	(0.01)	2.20	(0.00)	1.43	(0.01)
ϕ	0.37	(0.00)	0.42	(0.00)	0.34	(0.00)	0.51	(0.00)
$(A + \phi K)$	2.78	(0.00)	2.63	(0.01)	2.64	(0.00)	1.93	(0.01)
N	122,650		11,411		72,598		16,840	

(Standard errors of estimate are in parentheses.)

Appendix Table 7.B   Means of Characteristics of Subsamples of Households Summarized in Table 7.5: Households with Many and Few Children

Variable	1970				1979			
	Many Children		Few Children		Many Children		Few Children	
FAMINC	9.8	(0.09)	10.6	(0.02)	13.9	(0.31)	18.8	(0.04)
CAPINC	1.1	(0.01)	3.3	(0.01)	1.6	(0.04)	6.5	(0.02)
LMINC	1.1	(0.02)	3.3	(0.01)	1.6	(0.06)	6.5	(0.02)

Appendix Table 7.B (*Continued*)

	1970				1979			
Variable	Many Children		Few Children		Many Children		Few Children	
EDUCATION	11.7	(0.05)	12.4	(0.01)	11.5	(0.10)	13.1	(0.01)
AGE	39.5	(0.08)	44.9	(0.04)	40.4	(0.25)	44.5	(0.05)
SOUTH	0.29	—	0.30	—	0.34	—	0.33	—
RURAL	0.39	—	0.34	—	0.33	—	0.34	—
BLACK	0.25	—	0.09	—	0.37	—	0.11	—
ADULT EMP	0.79	—	0.67	—	0.81	—	0.69	—
FEMALE	0.14	—	0.08	—	0.25	—	0.19	—
K	6.86	(0.01)	1.62	(0.00)	6.42	(0.02)	1.26	(0.00)
A	2.03	(0.01)	2.14	(0.00)	2.02	(0.02)	2.05	(0.00)
ϕ	0.29	(0.00)	0.38	(0.00)	0.28	(0.00)	0.38	(0.00)
$(A + \phi K)$	3.99	(0.01)	2.71	(0.00)	3.77	(0.02)	2.50	(0.00)
N	6,348		127,713		1,000		88,438	

(Standard errors of estimate are in parentheses.)

Appendix Table 7.C	Means of Characteristics of Subsamples of Households Summarized in Table 7.5: Black-Headed and White-Headed Households

	1970				1979			
Variable	Black		Nonblack		Black		Nonblack	
FAMINC	6.9	(0.07)	10.9	(0.02)	12.5	(0.10)	19.5	(0.05)
CAPINC	2.3	(0.06)	3.3	(0.01)	4.1	(0.04)	6.7	(0.02)
LMINC	2.3	(0.06)	3.3	(0.01)	4.1	(0.04)	6.7	(0.02)
EDUCATION	10.5	(0.03)	12.6	(0.01)	11.7	(0.03)	13.3	(0.01)
AGE	43.1	(0.13)	44.8	(0.04)	43.0	(0.16)	44.7	(0.06)
SOUTH	0.52	—	0.27	—	0.53	—	0.30	—
RURAL	0.26	—	0.35	—	0.24	—	0.35	—
BLACK	1.00	—	0.00	—	1.00	—	0.00	—
ADULT EMP	0.69	—	0.67	—	0.65	—	0.69	—
FEMALE	0.26	—	0.07	—	0.41	—	0.16	—
K	2.52	(0.02)	1.80	(0.01)	1.76	(0.02)	1.26	(0.00)
A	1.94	(0.01)	2.15	(0.00)	1.89	(0.01)	2.07	(0.00)
ϕ	0.32	(0.00)	0.38	(0.00)	0.33	(0.00)	0.38	(0.00)
$(A + \phi K)$	2.66	(0.01)	2.78	(0.00)	2.45	(0.01)	2.51	(0.00)
N	13,155		120,906		10,082		79,356	

(Standard errors of estimate are in parentheses.)

Eight

Guidelines for Alimony and Child Support

This book has studied the allocation of income within a household. When a household dissolves, the court frequently must determine how to distribute the available income between two new households; this often involves child support and alimony. Many criteria are used. This chapter examines the implications of several criteria that are used to determine child support and alimony. Since child support and alimony are ways by which the original household's resources are allocated between the two new households, information about the initial allocation among the household members is germane to the decision.

Others have offered child support guidelines.[1] The guidelines contained in this chapter are unusual primarily because they are based on empirical information that reveals how households allocate their resources between adults and children. Additionally, the approach that we use is an economic one. This is appealing, we think, since the allocation of resources is an economic problem. This approach has the disadvantage, however, that many of the surrounding issues are noneconomic, but they must be dealt with explicitly. Most obvious among these are choices that society must make on how to treat the different members of the original household. We will attempt to distinguish clearly the economic issues from the others that require value judgments by society. We will also attempt to point out problems that arise when society attempts to achieve contradictory goals.

This chapter focuses primarily on child support, although it is impos-

1. See, for example, National Institute for Socioeconomic Research (1984a,b). The interested reader is referred to Cassetty (1983) for an excellent collection of essays on child support issues, covering the historical perspective, current normative standards, and psychological, social, and economic issues, among others.

sible to ignore alimony. As Chicago Judge Lassers points out, "Both mother and child live from the same sugar bowl" (pers. comm.). The standard of living of one is related to that of the other. The size of the bowl constrains the amount that any one member may consume. That constraint notwithstanding, the consumption of each member remains a matter of choice within those limitations. Our empirical investigation did not disaggregate the consumption among various adult members of the household; it only estimated a disaggregation between the adults and the children. As such, our results are most pertinent to child support. It is argued below that the household is the decision-making unit. The division between alimony and child support is implemented by the court, but not by the household. Since the court cannot gaze into the household and examine the way expenditures are made, the distinction between alimony and child support is artificial. The court can observe the size of the sugar bowl, but not the number of teaspoonfuls that go to each member. The court can influence the total resources that the household has available to it, but not very effectively the allocation of those resources within it.

Consider a court settlement that orders the noncustodial parent, say, the father, to pay $100 per month in alimony and $300 per month toward the support of the two children who reside with their mother. Suppose the mother has no other source of income. Obviously, this does not imply that the mother will allocate resources in the household so that the children receive $3 for every $1 that she receives. Money is fungible, and the adult typically has control, at least in part, over the way resources are used in the household. While the court may wish to consider alimony and child support separately in determining the amount of the payment, it does not make sense to treat them separately in determining the allocation within the household. The exception to this may be when resources that the child consumes can be observed easily or transferred in kind,[2] or perhaps when custody is joint, but these exceptions are not common.

---

2. For example, putting a child through college is an expenditure that is easily observed. It goes to the child and not to the custodial parent. Thus, if the court orders the father to pay tuition, the mother cannot usurp this payment for her own purposes. But even in this case, things are not so simple. If the mother would have spent resources to send the child to college anyway, then that custodial parent can transfer other resources away from the child. Suppose that of the $400 per month that the mother receives from the father, she would have allocated $100 to the children's education, $150 to other expenditures on children, and kept $150 for personal consumption. If the father is ordered to pay $100 directly to the school, and only $300 to the mother, nothing is changed. She allocates $150 of the $300 to the children and keeps the other $150. Thus, transfers in kind are not a general solution to the problem of fungibility. The exception is when the in-kind transfer exceeds the amount that

The format of this chapter deviates from earlier chapters. Since it is our hope that jurists and other practitioners will find the following discussion useful, we have separated the technical discussion by placing it within boxes. One can skip the technical material in this chapter and follow its argument from beginning to end without encountering any equations.

One detail about notation follows: Since "father" and "female" start with "f" and "mother" and "male" with an "m," we use the subscript "F" to refer to the noncustodial parent, and the subscript "M" to refer to the custodial parent, when that distinction is relevant. In what follows, therefore, we arbitrarily define the transfers as going from F to M. If a transfer should flow from M, the custodial parent, to F, we simply call that a negative transfer. Also we use the *female* pronoun any time we refer to the custodial adult and the *male* pronoun any time we refer to the noncustodial adult and to a child. The only exception is when we discuss earnings functions, which are gender specific.

Finally, the computations necessary to obtain a prescribed alimony or child support settlement are tedious and complex. A computer program is available from the authors to assist in making that calculation.

Selecting an Objective

It is necessary to select objectives before it is possible to determine appropriate transfers from one parent to the other. To begin, there exists the legal premise that parents must support their offspring. The level of support is what is in question, however. That level can be specified in absolute terms, for example, each child is entitled to $5,000 per year. It can also be specified in relative terms, for example, each child is entitled to 10 percent of the family income. An attempt to use a rigid absolute standard is doomed. Any standard that satisfies society for high-income families is likely to exceed available resources for low-income families. Additionally, the allocation that children receive in intact households is relative: it depends on total family income.

Thus, we adopt a standard that is relative to conditions in the same family prior to the divorce. We set out to achieve some level of resource allocation between the noncustodial parent, *F*, the custodial parent, *M*, and the children that relates to the allocation before the divorce. We recognize

---

the mother would have spent. For example, if the mother would have allocated only $75 of the $400 to the children (total), then the father's in-kind transfer of $100 for tuition implies that the children do receive more ($25 more) resources.

that the divorce alters some important factors. The level of income or earnings may be different than before the divorce. Other transfer payments, such as AFDC, may be different. The needs and outlays will differ because of economies of scale in household size among other things. These points are all dealt with in turn. First, we consider some possible criteria.

Criterion 1: Allocate the income between the two households so that each individual household member gets the same share as before the divorce.

One reasonable criterion is to allocate resources in the same relative way after the divorce as they were allocated before. For example, consider a two-child, two-adult household where each child receives 14 percent of the total resources, and each adult receives 36 percent [(14% × 2) + (36% × 2) = 100%]. This criterion would imply that transfers from F to M should be arranged so that each individual's share of the total income remains as it was before the divorce. In this case, transfers are arranged so that children still receive 14 percent and adults 36 percent of the total.

This criterion is unacceptable for a number of reasons. First, it allows for no flexibility in the household situation. What happens if new children or new spouses are introduced into the households? Second, as a general matter it is logically impossible. The reason is that the court can dictate how resources are allocated between the households, but not within. Any attempt to bring the children up to their original share will leave the share of the mother too low. This occurs because the single custodial parent tends to give the child more of the family's income than did the original household; that is a finding from the research in the previous chapters of this book. Thus, bringing the children back to 14 percent of the total is likely to leave the mother with perhaps only 30 percent (rather than 36 percent) of the two-household total income.

The logical impossibility is easily demonstrated. Before divorce,

$$C_K = \phi C_A$$

Define ϕ' as the proportion of income that the child receives after the divorce. Thus after the divorce,

$$C'_K = \phi' C'_A,$$

where C'_K denotes after-divorce consumption by the child and C'_A is postdivorce consumption by M. If both C'_K and C'_A are to bear the same relationship to the total as did C_K and C_A, then it must be true that

$$\frac{C'_K}{C'_A} = \frac{C_K}{C_A}. \tag{8.1}$$

But equation (8.1) implies that $\phi = \phi'$. This is not true in general. Chapter 5 has already revealed that ϕ changes with *household* income and family size, both of which are changed by the divorce.

Criterion 2: Allocate the income between the two households so that the children's share of income is unchanged.

Under this criterion, the custodial parent generally receives a smaller portion and the noncustodial parent a larger portion of the household's income than before the divorce.

Define

$$\theta \equiv \frac{\phi}{A + \phi K},$$

that is, the child's share of income before the divorce. Define Y_{F_0} as the noncustodial parent's income before the divorce, Y_{F_1} as the noncustodial parent's income after the divorce, and correspondingly Y_{M_1}, Y_{M_0} for the custodial parent. Let Z be the transfer from the noncustodial to the custodial parent.

The desire is to ensure that each child receives $\theta(Y_{F_1} + Y_{M_1})$ by transferring Z from F to M. M allocates $\theta' \equiv \left(\dfrac{\phi'}{1 + \phi'K}\right)$ of household income to each child and $\left(\dfrac{1}{1 + \phi'K}\right)$ to herself. Recall that $\phi' \neq \phi$ because there are fewer adults in her new household. The criterion requires that

$$\theta(Y_{F_1} + Y_{M_1}) = \theta'(Y_{M_1} + Z).$$

The left-hand side is the amount of resources that the court wants each child to receive. The right-hand side is the amount that the child will receive because M's resource pool consists of M's own income plus Z.

Rearranging terms yields

$$Z = \frac{\theta}{\theta'}(Y_{F_1} + Y_{M_1}) - Y_{M_1}. \qquad 8.2$$

Each child then receives

$$C_K = \theta(Y_{F_1} + Y_{M_1}).$$

The problem with this solution is that the two parents do not each receive what each would have received had the household remained intact. Instead, the custodial parent (M) receives less and the noncustodial parent (F) receives more. The proof follows.

Under this scheme, M consumes

$$C_M = \frac{\theta'}{\phi'}(Y_{M_1} + Z)$$

and substituting from equation (8.2):

$$C_M = \frac{\theta}{\phi'}(Y_{F_1} + Y_{M_1}).$$

Similarly, F consumes

$$C_F = Y_{F_1} - Z$$

$$= (Y_{F_1} + Y_{M_1})(1 - \frac{\theta}{\theta'})$$

Thus, the difference between these two is typically positive:

$$C_F - C_M = (Y_{F_1} + Y_{M_1})\left(1 - \frac{\theta}{\theta'} - \frac{\theta}{\phi'}\right) > 0.$$

This is positive if $1 - \frac{\theta}{\theta'} - \frac{\theta}{\phi'} > 0$. To see that it is, assume the opposite. Then

$$\frac{1}{\theta} < \frac{1}{\theta'} + \frac{1}{\phi'},$$

or, from the definition of θ,

$$\frac{2 + \phi K}{\phi} < \frac{1 + \phi' K}{\phi'} + \frac{1}{\phi'},$$

or,

$$\frac{2 + \phi K}{\phi} < \frac{2 + \phi' K}{\phi'}.$$

But this is a contradiction because $\phi' > \phi$ (empirically) and

$$\frac{\partial\left(\dfrac{2 + \phi K}{\phi}\right)}{\partial\phi} < 0.$$

One can compute a transfer between noncustodial parent F and custodial parent M that will result in the children getting the same share of total income as they got before the divorce. The problem is that in order to achieve that objective, M ends up receiving less than before the divorce and noncustodial F ends up receiving more. If some amount were added to the transfer, it would in part be allocated by M to the children, violating our objective, so we are left with an unappealing side effect of criterion 2: M suffers and F benefits. There seems to be nothing to be done about this outcome if this criterion is adopted.

Note that this predicament, with the custodial parent personally losing financially and the noncustodial parent doing relatively well financially (relative to the other parent and even relative to before the divorce), has nothing to do with the gender of the respective parents and does not result from any shift in preference. It results because families with lower income or fewer adults allocate larger portions of the available income to their children. That pattern alone creates the discrepancy in resources allocated to M and F.

Criterion 3: Allocate the income between the two households so that the two adults have the same level of income.

This criterion is surely feasible. As the technical paragraphs that follow show, however, it generally results in each child receiving a larger portion of the total income than before the divorce. Correspondingly, each adult receives less than before.

Suppose that F pays the amount Z to M's household where Z is chosen so as to keep M's share equal to F's share of the family's consumption. According to this criterion:

$$C_F = C_M.$$

F's household income is

$$Y_F - Z = C_F,$$

and M's household income is $Y_M + Z_F$, which is allocated to M and the K children such that

$$C_M = \frac{Y_M + Z}{1 + \phi' K}.$$

In these three equations Y_F, Y_M, ϕ', and K are known, so solve for the transfer Z as:

$$Z = \frac{(Y_F - Y_M) + Y_F \phi' K}{2 + \phi' K}. \qquad (8.3)$$

It is now straightforward to show that C_F ($= C_M$) is lower than before the divorce:

$$\text{Before: } C_F = (Y_F + Y_M)\left(\frac{1}{2 + \phi K}\right).$$

$$\text{After: } C_F' = (Y_F + Y_M)\left(\frac{1}{2 + \phi' K}\right) \qquad \text{(from eq. 8.3)}$$

Since $\phi' > \phi$, $C_F' < C_F$. But since $C_M' = C_F$ and $C_M = C_F$, $C_M' < C_M$ also.

Criterion 3 is not unreasonable, but it is not an obvious choice either. Under this criterion, the share going to each parent falls and the share going to each child rises as compared with the intact family. This is troublesome, especially if there are economies of scale and F's household is smaller than M's. The noncustodial parent must run an entire household with fewer resources than would have been available to him alone had the household remained intact. F also no longer has whatever satisfaction the children once provided. This may well imply a significant reduction in F's standard of living relative to the children and to M, who enjoys the benefits of pooling resources in a household with more family members as well as enjoying the company of the children. (After all, M and F did previously choose to have children, so one would think there is satisfaction in living with them.) Criterion 3 has some appeal since it benefits the children relative to the parents, and the children are generally not a part of the decision to divorce. Moreover, we have ignored the psychological and social effects on the children, so it may be judged by many to be quite reasonable that the children gain relative to the parents in terms of income.

The difficulties with any of these three criteria multiply when one allows for joint custody or when additional members enter the new, splinter families. It is for these reasons that we turn to our final criterion.

Criterion 4: Allocate the income between the two households so that each of the households has income in proportion to its adjusted family size: the household as the unit of analysis.

The problem with all three of the criteria already discussed is that they select one member (or type of member) of a household as the target on which to base income transfers. The goal of criterion 1 was to keep all household members relatively unaffected, but that proved infeasible. The goal of criterion 2 was to keep the child's resource level constant, but that adversely affected the custodial parent. The goal of criterion 3 was to equalize resources (not utility) consumed by the father and mother, but that resulted in both parents suffering an income loss relative to their children. The problem is that meeting any criterion that focuses on one member of the household results in apparent inequity and in resource allocation among other family members.

This suggests that another approach might be used. Instead of attempting to maintain the income of a particular family member, criterion 4 seeks to balance the income between the two households, not focusing on specific household members. The adjustment for family size can take into account that children do not receive as much of the family's resources as adults, even if the family remains intact. The adjustment for family size is easily achieved by considering ϕ, the proportion of adult expenditure that a child receives, the indicator of the size of a child relative to an adult; that is, if ϕ is 0.44 after the divorce, then a child is 0.44 of an adult. If the noncustodial parent lives alone, that household size is 1.0; if the custodial parent has, say, two children, that household size is 1.88 ($= 1 + 2 \times 0.44$). Considering the sum of the income in both of these households, criterion 4 implies that the noncustodial household has about 35 percent of the adult-equivalent people ($= 1/2.88$) and the custodial household has about 65 percent of the adult-equivalent people ($= 1.88/2.88$). By this criterion, the noncustodial household should get 35 percent of the combined income, and M and the children should get 65 percent of it. Of course, the amount to be transferred from the noncustodial parent to the custodial parent and the children depends on how much of the whole F earns and how much of it M earns.

Let us continue to assume that custody resides entirely with M. Then M's household has $1 + \phi'K$ members and F's household has one member. Thus, criterion 4 allocates resources such that the ratio of resources in F's household to resources in M's household is

$$1/(1 + \phi'K).$$

Since F has available $Y_{F_1} - Z$ and M has available $Y_{M_1} + Z$, Z should be selected so that

$$\frac{Y_{F_1} - Z}{Y_{M_1} + Z} = \frac{1}{1 + \phi'K} \equiv R,$$

or,

$$Z = \frac{Y_{F_1} - Y_{M_1}R}{1 + R}. \tag{8.4}$$

It is straightforward to derive the amount of consumption that each individual receives under criterion 4.

The noncustodial parent, F, consumes $Y_{F_1} - Z$ or, using equation (8.4),

$$C_F = \frac{R(Y_{F_1} + Y_{M_1})}{(1 + R)}. \tag{8.5}$$

The custodial parent, M, consumes

$$\frac{Y_{M_1} + Z}{1 + \phi'K},$$

or,

$$C_M = \left(\frac{1}{1 + \phi'K}\right)\left(\frac{Y_{M_1} + Y_{F_1}}{1 + R}\right). \tag{8.6}$$

Since

$$R = \left(\frac{1}{1 + \phi'K}\right),$$

$$C_F = C_M.$$

Finally, the child's consumption, C_K, is

$$C_K = \phi'C_M = \left(\frac{\phi'}{1 + \phi'K}\right)\left(\frac{Y_{M_1} + Y_{F_1}}{1 + R}\right). \tag{8.7}$$

> Consider an example of the household with $Y_F = \$20,000$, $Y_M = \$15,000$, $\phi = 0.4$, $\phi' = 0.44$, and $K = 2$; criterion 4 implies (eq. 8.4) a transfer Z, of $\$7,847$.

If F earns $\$20,000$ and M earns $\$12,000$, then in order for M and the children to have 65.3 percent of the whole, F should transfer $\$8,889$ to M leaving $\$11,111$ for F's consumption. M will allocate that total ($\$12,000 + \$8,889$) so that each child gets 0.44 for every dollar M gets, which will result in M having $\$20,889/1.88 = \$11,111$ and each child having $(0.44) \times \$11,111 = \$4,889$.

It may be useful here to bring together, in a summary table, the outcomes of the various criteria. We have assumed that F earns $\$20,000$ while M earns $\$12,000$, both before and after the divorce, and that the family has two children. Table 8.1 summarizes who gets what before and after the divorce. In the intact family, each child gets $\$4,571$, assuming that ϕ is 0.40. In the divorced case, with M having full custody, ϕ rises to 0.44. One sees that criterion 2 does keep the children at the same level as before the divorce, with a transfer, Z, of $\$7,532$. M suffers a loss and F does relatively well. By criteria 3 and 4 the transfer is a little larger, the parents do identically well—both getting a little less than before the divorce, while the children each get a little more.

Under criterion 2, the child receives

$$C_{K_2} = (Y_{M_1} + Y_{F_1})\left(\frac{\phi}{2 + \phi K}\right).$$

Equation (8.7) shows that he receives

$$C_{K_4} = \left(\frac{\phi'}{1 + \phi'K}\right)\left(\frac{Y_{M_1} + Y_{F_1}}{1 + R}\right)$$

by criterion 4. To show that $C_{K_2} < C_{K_4}$, it is sufficient that

$$\frac{\phi}{2 + \phi K} < \left(\frac{\phi'}{1 + \phi'K}\right)\left(\frac{1}{1 + R}\right)$$

from the definitions of C_{K_2} and C_{K_4}. This reduces to

$$\frac{\phi}{2 + \phi K} < \frac{\phi'}{2 + \phi'K}.$$

Since $\phi < \phi'$, and since

$$\frac{\partial\left(\dfrac{\phi}{2 + \phi K}\right)}{\partial\phi} > 0,$$

the condition holds.

These mathematics indicate that the child receives more when household income is apportioned according to the ratio R in equation (8.4) than when transfers are chosen to hold child consumption constant. It is also true that M and F consume equal amounts by this criterion. Since child consumption has gone up relative to criterion 2 and to the intact family, it is necessarily the case that the parents' consumption has gone down relative to the intact family, and that F's consumption is smaller under criterion 4 than under criterion 2.

Criterion 4 ignores any scale economies, but it has the major advantage that it is easily implemented, is always feasible, and generalizes readily to cases of joint custody and to situations where either parent remarries. Most important, it allocates resources to the unit in which decisions are made, namely, the household. Criterion 2 gives no guidance, for example, about the appropriate transfer in the circumstance of a dissolution with no children, while criterion 3 does. One can find examples of courts that use guidelines that first dictate transfers from F to the children, then calculate the appropriate transfer from F to M, using in this latter calculation F's income *net* of the transfer to the children. Other jurisdictions first calculate F's obligation to M and then net of that transfer compute F's obligation to the children residing with M. In two contiguous counties in California, for example, one uses the first strategy (Santa Clara County 1984) and another uses the second (San Mateo County 1984).

Table 8.1   Who Gets What?

Family	Z	C_F	C_M	C_K	$Y_M + Y_F$
Intact:	—	$11,429	$11,429	$4,571	$32,000
Divorced:					
Using Criterion 1	INFEASIBLE				32,000
2	$7,532	12,468	10,390	4,571	32,000
3	8,889	11,111	11,111	4,889	32,000
4	8,889	11,111	11,111	4,889	32,000

The advantages of criterion 4 make it so attractive that we adopt it for the rest of this chapter. As will be seen, many of the problems that generally plague jurists can be dealt with using criterion 4 (as expressed in eq. 8.4) or some slight variation. Let us explore a few of its features.

In order to get a better understanding of criterion 4, let us consider what it implies about the appropriate magnitude of the transfer, Z, from noncustodial parent, F, to custodial parent, M, and the children when F and M have equal earnings. Notice that this is not the same circumstance we have dealt with in the previous examples. There, F earned \$20,000 and M earned \$12,000. Now, let us consider the case where both F and M earn the same amount. The technical section above yields a simple equation (eq. 8.4) that suggests we simply need to know the value of ϕ (the amount spent on a child relative to an adult) and the number of children in M's custody. Using equation (8.4) and a fixed value of ϕ of 0.40, we show in table 8.2 the amount of F's income that should be transferred to M, if M and F have the same level of income. That is, if both M and F earn \$20,000 and M has full custody of their two children, F should transfer 29 percent of the \$20,000, or \$5,714, to M and the children. That results in F's one-person household having 1/2.8 of the total \$40,000 (or \$14,286) and M's three-person (or 1.8 adult-sized) household having 1.8/2.8 of the total \$40,000 (\$25,714).

In the remaining sections we add several modifications to take account of joint custody, the ambiguity in measuring the relevant income of F and M, the changes in ϕ that occur with changes in the number of adults and children, taxes, and so forth.

The magnitudes in table 8.2 rely solely on our use of criterion 4 and on the estimated value of $\phi = 0.40$. As we discussed at some length in chapter 5 and confirmed in chapter 6, the value of $\phi = 0.40$ is one on which we are quite confident for the average family. In subsequent sections and in tables described below, we allow ϕ to vary with the number of adults or the number of children or, sometimes, with the level of income or other characteristics. We are less confident that these changes in ϕ are calculated

Table 8.2   Amount of Transfer

Z (as percentage of F's income)		Number of Children
0 percent	if	zero children
17 percent	if	one child
29 percent	if	two children
38 percent	if	three children
44 percent	if	four children
50 percent	if	five children

accurately, because our study indicates that our estimates of the effects of an additional child on allocations are not robust. But the instabilities in effects on φ from one factor (number of children) to another (number of adults) or another (age of the household head, for example), do not seem to have much influence on the average value of φ. It almost always ends up somewhere near 0.40. Thus, we have a great deal of confidence that a household with an adult and two children, for example, has a size that is roughly equivalent to 1.8 adults (= 1 adult and 2 children each of whom is about 0.40 adult in terms of expenditures).

The objective is to allocate the two households' total income in proportion to their adult-equivalent size. Now, let us turn to the details. How is income to be measured? What happens when a child grows up? What happens when one of the parents remarries? What happens in the case of a divorce with no children? How does one deal with joint custody?

Criterion 4 can be used to construct a table that suggests the appropriate amount of income for the noncustodial parent to transfer to (or receive from) the custodial parent. In table 8.3, panels A–D, we set φ equal to its average value of 0.38 from chapter 5 and allow φ to vary with the number of children and adults in the household according to the coefficients on K and A from table 5.4 (as the number of children varies from the mean level of 2.20 and as A varies from its mean of 1.93).

Consider, for example, table 8.3, panel C. It corresponds to a family with two children. If F (the noncustodial parent) had income of $15,000 and M had income of $10,000, then F would be required to transfer 46 percent of his income, or $6,900, to M who has full custody of the children. If, on the other hand, F earned $15,000 and M, who has custody of the children, earned $40,000, then M would be required to transfer to F 18 percent of F's income, or a transfer of $2,700 would go from M to F. This

Table 8.3 Transfer from Parent F to Parent M, Parent M Has Full Custody

Panel A: No Children							
Parent F's Income	Parent M's Income						
	0	5000	10000	20000	40000	80000	100000
5000	50%	0%	−50%	−150%	−350%	−750%	−950%
10000	50%	25%	0%	−50%	−150%	−350%	−450%
15000	50%	33%	17%	−17%	−83%	−217%	−283%
20000	50%	38%	25%	0%	−50%	−150%	−200%
30000	50%	42%	33%	17%	−17%	−83%	−117%
40000	50%	44%	38%	25%	0%	−50%	−75%
60000	50%	46%	42%	33%	17%	−17%	−33%

Table 8.3 (*Continued*)

Parent F's Income	Parent M's Income						
	0	5000	10000	20000	40000	80000	100000
80000	50%	47%	44%	38%	25%	0%	−13%
100000	50%	48%	45%	40%	30%	10%	0%

Panel B: One Child

Parent F's Income	Parent M's Income						
	0	5000	10000	20000	40000	80000	100000
5000	61%	22%	−17%	−94%	−250%	−561%	−717%
10000	61%	42%	22%	−17%	−94%	−250%	−328%
15000	61%	48%	35%	9%	−43%	−146%	−198%
20000	61%	51%	42%	22%	−17%	−94%	−133%
30000	61%	55%	48%	35%	9%	−43%	−69%
40000	61%	56%	51%	42%	22%	−17%	−36%
60000	61%	58%	55%	48%	35%	9%	−4%
80000	61%	59%	56%	51%	42%	22%	13%
100000	61%	59%	57%	53%	46%	30%	22%

Panel C: Two Children

Parent F's Income	Parent M's Income						
	0	5000	10000	20000	40000	80000	100000
5000	68%	36%	4%	−61%	−189%	−447%	−575%
10000	68%	52%	36%	4%	−61%	−189%	−254%
15000	68%	57%	46%	25%	−18%	−104%	−147%
20000	68%	60%	52%	36%	4%	−61%	−93%
30000	68%	62%	57%	46%	25%	−18%	−39%
40000	68%	64%	60%	52%	36%	4%	−13%
60000	68%	65%	62%	57%	46%	25%	14%
80000	68%	66%	64%	60%	52%	36%	28%
100000	68%	66%	65%	61%	55%	42%	36%

Panel D: Three Children

Parent F's Income	Parent M's Income						
	0	5000	10000	20000	40000	80000	100000
5000	72%	45%	17%	−38%	−149%	−371%	−481%
10000	72%	58%	45%	17%	−38%	−149%	−204%
15000	72%	63%	54%	35%	−1%	−75%	−112%
20000	72%	65%	58%	45%	17%	−38%	−66%
30000	72%	68%	63%	54%	35%	−1%	−20%
40000	72%	69%	65%	58%	45%	17%	3%
60000	72%	70%	68%	63%	54%	35%	26%
80000	72%	71%	69%	65%	58%	45%	38%
100000	72%	71%	70%	67%	61%	50%	45%

payment would look like alimony or spouse support because F has no children but does have a much lower income than M. (Note that a minus number in table 8.3 implies a transfer from M to F, expressed as a percentage of F's income.) Of course, there is nothing gender-specific about these tables. They relate only to income and to custody status. This implies that transfers could be made from father to mother or from mother to father.

Joint Custody

One of the most difficult problems to deal with in determining appropriate transfers between parents is that of joint custody. A number of questions immediately come to mind. Does joint custody imply that each parent has the children 50 percent of the time? If so, what does this imply about the level of support of the child in each household? How do "fixed costs" affect this support, since some duplication of facilities is likely to be required? Does visitation constitute custody, or is visitation a qualitatively different interaction from joint custody?

Let us begin by ignoring duplication of facilities and grapple first with the definition of joint custody. The most obvious point is that joint custody does not necessarily imply that each parent bears 50 percent of the burden of raising the children. For example, one arrangement might have the children reside with M on each weekday of the school year and with F on each weekend day of the school year. During the summer, that pattern may be reversed. In terms of overall time in this example, M has the children for 62 percent of the time whereas F has the children for 38 percent of the time.

One way to apportion resources would be to assume expenditures on children are proportional to the amount of time spent in the household. If M had the children 70 percent of the time and F had them 30 percent of the time, we could easily recalculate what transfer from F to M (or M to F) would achieve our objective. The following paragraph outlines that calculation. Not surprisingly, the general effect here would be to reduce the size of the transfer from F to M as F assumes more direct custody of the children.

Assume that the child spends γ of his time with M and $(1 - \gamma)$ of his time with F. Resources would be apportioned according to

$$\frac{Y_{F_1} - Z}{Y_{M_1} + Z} = \frac{[1 + (1 - \gamma)(\phi K)]}{(1 + \gamma \phi' K)} \equiv R, \qquad (8.8a)$$

> so
>
> $$Z = \frac{Y_{F_1} - Y_{M_1}R}{1 + R}, \qquad (8.8b)$$
>
> where $\bar{\phi}$ is relevant in F's household and ϕ' is relevant in M's household. Except for the slight change in the definition of R, equation (8.8) is identical to equation (8.4). In fact, equation (8.4) is a special case of equation (8.8) with $\gamma = 1$.

Joint custody raises the important issue of fixed costs. These are different from scale economies but produce some of the same effects. A scale economy implies that when an additional person is added to a household, the cost to that household does not rise in proportion to the number of its members. That is, a household with five members does not, typically, require 25 percent more expenditures than a household with four members. A fixed cost implies that having a child reside in a household for, say, 25 percent of the time requires more than 25 percent of the expenditures needed to support the child full-time at the same standard of living. For example, it might be necessary to provide the child with a bedroom that remains empty when he is with the other parent. This is an important modification, but easily handled in our formula by permitting the impact on expenditures to reflect the fixed-cost nature of this issue. While it is easy enough to handle in principle, the magnitude of these fixed costs has not been studied. We adopt the following rule, which seems reasonable to us, but we emphasize it is based on judgment and not on any particular empirical findings. We assume that a household with the children living there half the time will spend three-quarters as much as it would if the children lived there full-time. That captures the fixed costs or the economic inefficiencies in sharing the children between the two households. (The equations accompanying this discussion are general, and if one had a better sense of these fixed costs one could simply use a different value for the parameter h in these equations.)

> Accounting for fixed costs can be done by the following parameterization. If ϕ is the proportion of an adult's consumption that the child would have received had the household remained intact, then
>
> $$\gamma^h \phi$$

is the proportion that the child receives in the household in which he resides γ percent of the time. With this specification, if $h = 0$, then the parent is assumed to allocate as much to a child who resides with her part-time as to one who resides with her full-time (i.e., *all* costs are fixed costs). What value of h is appropriate? Unfortunately, our data give us no way to estimate this. When custody is shared equally, so that $\gamma = 0.5$, it does not matter: the allocation of resources and the size of the transfer are independent of h. To see this, suppose F's household allocates $(1 - \gamma)^h(\bar{\phi}C_F)$ to the child and M's household allocates $\gamma^h\phi'C_M$ to the child. Then the relevant R is

$$R \equiv \frac{[1 + (1 - \gamma)^h(\bar{\phi}K)]}{(1 + \gamma^h\phi'K)}, \qquad (8.9a)$$

and again,

$$Z = \frac{Y_{F_1} - Y_{M_1}R}{(1 + R)}. \qquad (8.9b)$$

Now, if $\gamma = 0.5$, then

$$R = \frac{1 + 0.5^h\bar{\phi}K}{1 + 0.5^h\phi'K}.$$

If $\bar{\phi} = \phi'$, as one might expect since both households are in identical circumstances with respect to number of family members and several other (but not all) characteristics, then $R = 1$ for all values of h.

The more general custody situations do not have perfectly joint custody, but instead have a value of γ that exceeds 0.5, but falls short of 1 (full custody). In this case the choice of h matters. For example, suppose that $\gamma = 0.75$ so that M has custody 75 percent of the time, and that F's income is \$30,000 while M's income is \$10,000. If $h = 0$, then F is required to transfer only 33 percent of his income to M. If $h = 1$, the transfer proportion rises to 45 percent of his income. The treatment of fixed costs as reflected in the value of h plays a significant role.

For lack of a better assumption, we assume that $h = 0.415$. That is the value of h that would make the following statement true: "A household that has its children residing in it only 50 percent of the time must allocate to the child 75 percent of what

> it would have allocated had the child resided there full-time." This
> compromise may not be far from the truth, but we have no empir-
> ical evidence to prove it.

Our suggestion is to acknowledge the joint custody in computing the
size of each of the households and then to allocate the two households'
income between the two in proportion to these sizes. The technical material above indicates that if the parents have *equal* custody, it does not matter what degree of fixed costs we assume, so let us briefly consider that
case first. If custody is equal, Z is selected so that post-transfer resources
are the same in both households, since both have one parent and the same
amount of children. For example, if the father earns $20,000 and the
mother earns $12,000, each household should end up with $32,000/2 or
$16,000. A transfer of $4,000 from father to mother does the job. In general, the parent with the higher income transfers half the difference in this
simple case.

The circumstance is more complicated when custody is not equal, for
then the fixed costs matter. For illustration, assume that M has custody 75
percent of the time. Consider, for example, a family with two children
where F's income is $20,000, M's income is $15,000, and ϕ is 0.4. If M
has full custody, then she is entitled to a transfer of 37.5 percent of F's
income, or $7,500. But if M has only 75 percent custody, then the transfer
is only 20 percent of F's income, or $3,940. When M has full custody, she
ends up with $22,500 (= $15,000 + $7,500) and F with $12,500
(= $20,000 − $7,500). When F has partial (25 percent) custody, M ends
up with $18,940 (= $15,000 + $3,940) and F with $16,060 (= $20,000
− $3,940). This example emphasizes that fixed costs play a big role here
because giving F a small proportion of custody entitles him to a much
larger share of total income.

A further issue which we will discuss briefly is visitation. Are visitation
days distinct from custody days? We see no reason and no convenient way
to distinguish the two. It is true that if the parent with custody is allotted
income to support the child, then the primary custodian sees greater visitation by the other parent as adversely affecting her income. But the second
parent has a correspondingly greater incentive to increase visitation time,
so there need not be any adverse effect. This may raise the stakes in dis-
putes over visitation. But if one were to exclude visitation from the calculation of partial custody, that would raise other problems that we see as
even more difficult. There would be the issue of distinguishing definitionally between the two. Also, if visitation did not count as custody, it would
be logical for the custodial parent to pay the child's expenses while visiting

the other parent. That would surely prove both disagreeable and difficult to enforce.

Second Families

One problem that often plagues the courts is how to take into account the needs of second families that are started by the divorced parents. The law generally provides that alimony, but not child support, ceases on remarriage of the recipient spouse. Is this the correct stand for the court to take?

A number of issues are important in this context. Many come under the rubric of the trade-off between equity and efficiency. A good example of this problem arises when the father, who is paying alimony and child support, remarries and has children with his new wife. If the court does not reduce the payment that is required of him, then his new family suffers. One might reasonably argue that, on equity grounds, there is no reason to favor the children of his first marriage over those of his second marriage. On the other hand, society might want to discourage the father, who already has a family to support, from taking on the burden of another household. If the court ruled that payments were to be independent of the number of members of his new family, then he would be less inclined to remarry. (He would also be a less attractive prospective husband.)

The incentive effects are not easily dealt with. First, even if the court does take into account his responsibilities to the new family, each person's consumption, including his own, still will be lower than it would have been had he not started the new family. Stated alternatively, since more individuals must share the same income, each person's standard of living falls. This acts as a deterrent to remarriage. Second, and related, it is not obvious that society wants to discourage his remarriage. There are reasons to believe that individuals who have families behave in ways that benefit society. Crime rates differ by marital status; individuals who are married tend to earn higher wages, which presumably reflects their increased productivity. It is difficult to establish causal links, but the point remains that there may be social benefits to seeing that the divorced individual remarries.

These questions are too deep to be answered here, primarily because they are decisions that society must make. None of the results presented in earlier chapters bears on these issues. The appropriate subsidization or taxation of remarriage cannot be determined without a better understanding of the effects of marriage on individual behavior.

We have chosen to treat all individuals in the family so that their claim to resources is independent of the primary or secondary family status.

Thus, a child living with the father from the second marriage has the same claim to the joint resources of the households as a child living with the mother from the first marriage. This carries with it some disincentives to remarry because his remarriage reduces, but does not eliminate, his responsibilities to his original family. At the same time, he takes on new burdens, which means that his own consumption level will fall.

With the creation of second families, income is brought into the families by individuals who were not party to the original marriage. For example, if a noncustodial father remarries a women who has a high income, one must decide whether her income should affect the transfer to the original household's members. One view is that the total income of the father's new household is the relevant pool available to the original household for consumption. There is no way to prevent some of the second wife's resources from going to support him, and so it should be considered in determining the size of any transfer to his first household's members. We have treated the household as the relevant unit in which expenditure and consumption decisions are made throughout this chapter. If the household is the appropriate unit of analysis, then to be consistent we should argue that the total income of the household, independent of its source, should be used to determine transfers from one parent's household to the other's. The second wife had the option of not marrying the father. This treatment of her income does make his remarriage less likely (since some of the new household's resources are transferred to the original household). Since we allow new members of the father's household full claim to his income, it is not unreasonable to take their full incomes into account as well.

This position is arbitrary and could be replaced by any of several others. One possibility is to count only some proportion of the second wife's income, say, half, for the determination of transfers to the other household. The drawback here is that it provides an incentive for the father's new household to choose formal employment for the new wife and domestic chores, or unpaid employment, for the father, even if such a choice is not efficient.

Under the logic of the last few paragraphs, it is inconsistent to continue child support but cease alimony payments when the custodial parent remarries. Again, since the household's money is fungible, elimination of spouse support affects the consumption of the children, whether it is labeled alimony or child support. At the same time, the new spouse's income also affects the consumption of the children of the first marriage, and there is no obvious reason to ignore that fact. To be sure, transfers must be adjusted, but setting the transfer to zero is as nonsensical as assuming that spouse support goes only to support the parent and that child support goes only to support the children.

A final problem relates to the definition of spouse. Does a live-in partner or only a formal marriage partner count? We have nothing in particular to contribute to the solution to this problem, so we assume away the ambiguity. In practice, however, this may be a difficult issue.

In the technical paragraph that follows, we derive the transfer from F to M when either M or F remarries and brings into the household other children or adults. The presumption lying behind these formulas is that the household is a self-contained unit.

The following formulas determine the transfer from F's new household to M's new household when there are new members in those households. Note that this formulation allows for joint custody as well, by setting γ less than 1.

$$R = \frac{N_2 + \hat{\phi}[\,(1 - \gamma)^h K_1 + \bar{\lambda}^h \bar{K}_2]}{N_1 + \phi'\,(\gamma^h K_1 + \lambda'^h K'_2)} , \qquad (8.10a)$$

so

$$Z = \frac{Y_{F_1} + \bar{Y}_F - R(Y_{M_1} + Y'_M)}{1 + R} , \qquad (8.10b)$$

where

$\bar{Y}_F$ is income earned by other members in F's household,

Y'_M is income earned by other members in M's household,

N_1 is the number of adults in the primary custodial parent's (M's) new household,

N_2 is the number of adults in the noncustodial parent's (F's) new household,

K_1 is the number of children by the first marriage,

$\bar{K}_2$ is the number of other children in F's household (either F's own new children or F's new partner's children),

$\bar{\lambda}$ is the proportion of custody on these ($\bar{K}_2$) children,

K'_2 is the number of other children in M's household (either M's or M's partner's children), and

λ' is the proportion of custody on these (K'_2) children.

Note that $\lambda' + \bar{\lambda}$ does not sum to 1 because the custody is shared with households outside this system. Note also that we have used a common value for h; that could be modified if we had a better way to estimate h.

The rule that we are using implies that the first father or mother may end up supporting, in part, the second father's or mother's children. Conversely, if the second father or mother is very wealthy relative to the first, he or she may end up giving resources toward the support of the first father's or mother's children. This is not a result of the criterion that we have chosen for transfer. It is a direct result of the fungibility of money. In most circumstances, there is no way that the noncustodial parent can ensure that money that is transferred will go solely for the support of his own children. Even direct expenditures on the children, such as college tuition payments, can be offset by reductions in what would have been provided by the income of the other parent's household, as we have discussed above. It is not sensible for the courts to pretend that they can earmark funds to support particular individuals in a household. Thus, transfer rules based on seemingly sensible premises (e.g., the first father should not pay for the support of the second father's children) are misguided. Except under unusual circumstances that have to do with the consumption pattern of the household, these allocations are unenforceable.

Income

In all that has gone before, we have spoken about income as if it were a simple, easily measured, unambiguous amount recorded for each parent. Unfortunately, income is not a straightforward concept. First, and most troubling, income is subject to short-run choice as well as to lifetime decisions and chance. Second, income varies systematically as well as randomly over an individual's lifetime. Third, assets as well as earnings affect an individual's income, and the treatment of assets is likely to have a substantial influence on monetary settlements at the time of a family dissolution. We discuss each of these issues in turn.

A settlement that makes the amount of transfer from F to M depend on the father's and mother's income using formulas like the ones we have suggested has the major drawback that it reduces the incentive to earn. For every dollar earned by the noncustodial parent, he retains only a fraction of that dollar because the transfer to the other household rises with earnings. The same is true for the custodial parent. Each dollar that she earns reduces the transfer to which she is entitled, so a dollar earned is not worth a dollar to her. The following technical paragraphs detail this point.

> The noncustodial parent's household income after transfer is
> $Y_{F_1} + \bar{Y}_F - Z$, where $\bar{Y}_F$ is the income earned by the other mem-

bers of F's household. Therefore, the change in this household's income associated with each dollar earned by the parent, F, is

$$1 - \frac{\partial Z}{\partial Y_{F_1}}.$$

From equation (8.10b),

$$\frac{\partial Z}{\partial Y_{F_1}} = \frac{1}{1 + R},$$

so for each dollar earned, the income rises by only $1 - 1/(1 + R)$ (e.g., if $\phi = 0.4$ and $K = 2$, then $R = 1/1.8 = 0.55$, so \$1 earned by parent F results in his keeping only $1 - 1/1.55 = \$0.35$). Now, it is true that of that $1/(1 + R)$ dollars transferred to the other parent's household, some will go toward support of F's children. However, it is impossible that all of the transfer will, since others in M's household (including M) consume out of the transfer. As R rises, $\frac{\partial Z}{\partial Y_{F_1}}$ falls, and the incentive problems become less pronounced.

Similarly, the custodial parent's household income after transfer is $Y_{M_1} + Y'_M + Z$. Thus, an increase in this household's income by \$1 yields an after-transfer increase of

$$1 + \frac{\partial Z}{\partial Y_{M_1}}.$$

From equation (8.10b),

$$\frac{\partial Z}{\partial Y_{M_1}} = \frac{-R}{1 + R},$$

so \$1 of increased earning in this household results in only $1 - R/(1 + R)$ of after-transfer income (e.g., using the same value, $R = 0.55$, \$1 earned yields an increase of only $1 - 0.55/1.55 = \$0.65$). If F has partial custody, then M's children will consume some but not all of that $R/(1 + R)$ reduction in transfer. M's incentive problem is reduced as R falls, the exact opposite of what happens in F's household. So long as there is a transfer (i.e., $R > 0$), there is a disincentive on both F and M to earn, since some of

> those earnings in both cases end up benefiting the other house-
> hold. The same point applies to the new spouses in each of the
> households.

Any particular transfer formula implies specific incentive effects, but
the fact that there are adverse incentive effects is not unique to our formulas or our criterion. In fact, virtually any reasonable criterion that bases
transfers partially on income will have some adverse incentive effects, although not the same effects in general.

Incentive problems are important when income is subject to choice. If
income were purely predetermined or subject only to random change, then
incentive effects could be ignored. This can be stated more concretely:

Suppose that an individual's income were totally independent of the
effort that he put into his job and of the training that he had acquired. That
is, suppose that all variations in income were due only to chance events
over which the individual had no control. If this were the case, then one
might expect all members of the individual's family to share all good luck
and misfortune proportionately. If the noncustodial parent experienced a
windfall gain of $10,000 per year, a proportional share would be passed
on to the former spouse and children. Conversely, any decline in income
would be shared by the former family through reduced income transfers.

At the other extreme, suppose that luck had nothing to do with income
determination and that, instead, income depended directly on the amount
of effort put into one's job. Under this circumstance, basing transfers on
income implies that each parent will work less hard than is socially optimal. Since each receives less than the full dollar earned (because the transfer changes as well), each parent will tend to exert less effort than would
be the case were there no transfer. Here, it does not seem equitable to force
the family to suffer simply because a noncustodial parent opts to reduce
effort on the job, or for the noncustodial to have to transfer more income
simply because the custodial parent opts to reduce effort on the job.

Notice the conclusion from the last two paragraphs: if the fluctuation in
income is attributable to luck, then all family members should share in that
change. If it is attributable to choice (e.g., to a decision to work less), then
other family members should not be affected. This conclusion motivates
the strategy we adopt in the next few pages.

Evidence suggests that earnings in the real world are affected by both
luck and choice. For example, it is well documented that additional
schooling is associated with higher income and that workers who work
longer hours take home larger paychecks. This attests to the importance of
choice in the determination of earnings. On the other hand, few attempts

to explain cross-sectional earnings differences are ever successful at accounting for more than 25 percent of the variation across individuals, no matter what is held constant. This suggests that there may be many factors that determine earnings over which the individual has little or no control.

We suggest dealing with this problem in a rather ad hoc way, allowing some transformation of observed current income into the income on which the transfer is based. Our formulation takes into account both choice and luck elements. The scheme is somewhat arbitrary, but we argue that there are good reasons for treating income in the way described in the next few paragraphs.

The basic notion is that each individual has some expected income, based on his characteristics, his history or earnings, marital status, and residence pattern. This means, for example, that a male who earned, say, $20,000 per year in each of the five years preceding the divorce might be expected to earn $18,000 after the divorce (because married men earn more than single ones). The impact of marital status as well as prior earnings history, skill level, age, and other observable characteristics should be taken into account in determining expected income for each parent. Actual income may deviate from expected income for a variety of reasons.

Expected income provides a guide to what an individual's income should be. If we believe that all income variation is a result of the individual's choice, then it would be proper to use the expected income figure for calculating transfer payments. For example, if the individual is expected to earn $18,000 but actually earns $20,000, he would be treated as if his income were $18,000. Since, by assumption, the additional $2,000 reflects added effort, and since we do not want to discourage effort, he is permitted to keep the entire difference. Conversely, if he is expected to earn $18,000 but actually earns $16,000, he is treated as if he earned $18,000 for the purpose of the transfer. Since, by assumption, the shortfall of $2,000 reflects decreased effort, and since we do not want to reward reduced effort, he is forced to cover the entire shortfall out of his own reduced consumption. This scheme neither rewards nor penalizes other family members for variations in the individual's effort.

That may seem somewhat unfair. Consider the other extreme. If all variations in income were due to luck, one would want to use the actually observed income as the income on which to base transfers. If his actual income is much higher than the expected amount of $18,000, he has experienced good luck and all his former family members should share in it. If his actual income is much lower than the $18,000 we expected, he has experienced bad luck and again all should share in it. This strategy does not affect effort because, by assumption, income variation is due entirely to luck. Thus, actual income is used for the purpose of the calculation.

Both of these positions are extreme and inappropriate, so we suggest as a compromise an intermediate position. It can be argued that large swings in income are dominated by luck rather than effort. An individual who was earning $25,000 per year for the past five years and suddenly experiences an income increase to, say, $150,000 is likely to have encountered good luck. (He won the state lottery or an unexpected business deal came through.) That six-fold increase is very unlikely to be due to increased effort. Similarly, if the same individual's income dips to $1,500 per year, he is likely to have experienced bad luck. (Perhaps he lost his job because of industry-wide layoffs.) The individual is unlikely to have chosen to live at such a low-income level.

Conversely, to the extent that effort affects income, it is likely to have its largest impact on income variations that are close to the expected level. Thus, small changes in income are treated as if they are in large part due to effort changes. The combination of the two yields a particular way to transform observed income into the income used for the purpose of transfer computation. The description of that method is technical and tedious and is relegated to the appendix to this chapter. The method takes into account changes in income earnings potential that are affected by the divorce itself as well as changes in the demand for the time of various family members. The thrust is this: Income is partially determined by choices the individual makes about hours of work and effort but also partially determined by luck. It is reasonable that all former family members share in the changes in income that reflect luck but not effort variation. Thus, large swings in income are shared with the former members, but small changes are not. (This is a simplification. Even small swings are borne in part by the former members.)

Table 8.4 illustrates the effect of this approach. The man's expected income of $21,800 is based on his previous earnings, education, experience, and other relevant characteristics. If the man's actual income were $35,000, the transfer would be calculated as if his income were $28,400.

Table 8.4   Male with Expected Income of $21,800

Actual Income	Income Used for Calculating the Transfer Z
$ 2,000	$ 6,800
10,000	15,900
21,800	21,800
35,000	28,400
100,000	60,900

Source: See appendix to this chapter.

If his actual income were $10,000, he would be treated as if it were $15,900 for the purposes of calculating the transfer. Since some of the difference between the expected $21,800 and $10,000 is likely to reflect reduced effort, he is penalized heavily for it. But if income were to fall by $8,000 more to $2,000, his income for the purpose of transfer would be $6,800. The actual drop of $8,000 is treated as if it were a drop of $9,100 (from $15,900 to $6,800) because this is likely to reflect bad luck, some of the burden of which is borne by the former family's members.

It should also be noted that the method used takes into account that earnings vary in a systematic way over the worker's life cycle. Since expected earnings are dependent on age and experience, the method appropriately accounts for such variation.

There remains the issue of how to treat nonemployed persons. First, there is the question of incentives. Society may wish to encourage or to discourage employment by a custodial parent. If the desire is to discourage employment by custodial parents, simply use the zero earnings observed for a nonemployed custodial parent as the relevant value of income on which to base transfers. On the other hand, society may wish to encourage employment by such persons. Using the person's characteristics (including marital status and work experience) to compute expected earnings accomplishes that. In that case, M would be treated as if she had some income, even if she earned nothing. This encourages her to work to make up the difference. Society has a powerful instrument to use in influencing divorced parents' incentives to be employed. If it adopts a procedure that counts income which could have been earned, it strongly encourages employment; if it uses a zero income for nonemployed parents when determining the transfer from one household to the other, it strongly discourages employment. Of course it would always be possible to adopt a middle ground.[3]

Assets

The treatment of assets is quite important. Suppose that, before divorce, the family owned, say, rental property that contributed to the household's income. Whether that property is sold, awarded to one of the parents, or owned jointly, its disposition affects the calculation of income that is relevant to the formulas determining the transfer. But this is straightforward and easily handled. Estimated income should be augmented by the value

3. Throughout this book we have focused on money income and money expenditures. The value of leisure foregone should be recognized as a loss to parents who are forced to take on new employment. However, we ignore that issue in these calculations.

of the income flow from the assets retained by each party. This includes equity in the family home and other significant assets. The point is that there is little reason to treat the flow of income from assets differently from other income.

Choice versus chance is an important consideration for assets as well as labor earnings. The value of an individual's assets may rise after the divorce either because he was lucky (his stocks went up) or because he saved at a high rate. Individuals who save instead of consuming their income will have higher assets in the future. If the transfer is based on this income, then the individual is penalized twice. The transfer is affected by income in the year it is earned but also by the interest on savings out of that income. This double taxation of income discourages savings in the same way that federal taxation of interest income does. Again, the compromise suggested above can be used. Savings that increase income near the expected level are not taxed as heavily.

To summarize, the approach we have suggested in this section on income and assets transforms observed income into another income measure. This is done for each earner in the household. Alternatives for adults who have no observed earnings have been discussed as well. Then, as a second step, those income figures can be used in conjunction with the formulas that calculate an appropriate transfer from one parent to the other. It is important to note, however, that there is no necessity that the two steps be linked. Any measure of income can be used in conjunction with the transfer formulas. Similarly, the transformed income figure can be used in conjunction with any other criterion. We have suggested one way to transfer observed income into some measure of criterion income. But we recognize that it is arbitrary and that one might choose to apply the formulas to observed income or to some other transformation of income. In our view, that is probably better than using observed income and some more arbitrary formula for the determination of transfers.

Taxes and Other Government Transfers

Some transfers from one household to another are tax-deductible to the donor and taxable income to the recipient. Since the two households may have different marginal tax rates, a restructuring of the transfer can reduce the overall burden of taxes paid by a household. Should individuals be encouraged to set up transfers to minimize these taxes?

If the tax law is written as society desires it, then there is no obvious reason why the courts should assist in reducing the tax burden below the "appropriate" amount. The "appropriate" burden is the amount that a household with a similar income and number of members would pay had that income come from the market rather than another parent. But this implies that all transfer income should be taxed as if it were earnings, and similarly, that all transfer payments should be deducted as if they were business expenses. It could be argued that since F receives utility on the transfers to his children, F should be taxed on it. This is what is currently done with child support transfers. If, instead, M should be taxed on the transfer received, then failing to allow the deduction by F would result in double taxation. This suggests that all payments should be taxed at the household with discretion over spending it; that is the current treatment of taxable alimony.

If t_F is the average tax rate that F pays (after transfer) and t_M is the average tax rate that M pays after transfer, then Z should be set so that

$$\frac{(Y_{F_1} + \bar{Y}_F - Z)(1 - t_F)}{(Y_{M_1} + Y'_M + Z)(1 - t_M)} = R ,$$

(8.11)

or

$$Z = \frac{Y_{F_1} + \bar{Y}'_F - R\left(\frac{1 - t_M}{1 - t_F}\right)(Y_{M_1} + Y'_M)}{1 + R\left(\frac{1 - t_M}{1 - t_F}\right)} .$$

(8.12)

If $t_F = t_M$, then the tax terms drop out. This is the implicit assumption made in tables 8.4 and 8.5. In most cases, it should not be far from the truth. Tax laws are set up to adjust for family size. This is close to our criterion as well. For example, the average tax rate for a parent with two children who has $15,000 in income including transfers may be similar to that for a single parent with $8,000 of after-transfer income. Our criterion is likely to divide income in a way resembling these figures.

Other transfers from government should also be treated as income to the recipient household. For example, AFDC contributes to the custodial parent's household and augments the standard of living of that household. If that AFDC income were not included in the measure of M's income, resources would no longer be distributed in the proportion R. AFDC or other transfers, like income on assets, should be included in the measure of the income of the parent who receives it.

If these arguments are accepted, then all income figures used in table 8.3 should be before-tax. Transfers are in before-tax dollars because they are deductible to the donor and taxable income to the recipient.

Other Issues

Time-Varying Payments

The courts sometimes build in explicit indexes on which to base changes in the required transfers. These often come under the headings of "standard-of-living" or "cost-of-living" adjustments. To make payments contingent on this kind of index circumvents the criterion used to set up table 8.3. In fact, there is an indexing method already incorporated in our approach. Since the predicted income depends on age and time, that predicted level will change each year. Given the level of predicted income, it is straightforward to go from observed income to transfer-based income. Thus, each year, a different level of transfer is determined. It is a trivial matter to update the transfer each year, but it should be done in the way prescribed by our method. No other index will maintain the criterion of distributing income in proportion to weighted household size.

Child's Age as a Criterion

It is conceivable that the ages of the children should affect the transfer. In our estimation, we were unable to find any significant effect of child's age up to age 16 on the proportion of household expenditure that went to children. Age of the adult mattered to some extent, but child's age did not. As such, child's age is not a variable that affects the dictated transfer. An issue of child's age that is relevant is the age up to which the child is considered the responsibility of his parents.

Conceptually, this is the same issue as the one that would have child's consumption vary by age. In theory, there exists some smooth function that relates child consumption to adult consumption. As the child reaches an age where more and more leave the parents' household, the average expenditure on the child falls. This occurs smoothly for two reasons: First, the probability of living at home declines smoothly or at least not abruptly with age. Second, conditional on no change in residence status, the net amount going from parent to child declines after a certain age. In fact, for many households, net transfers are negative; children contribute more to parents' support than the converse.

The fact that we are unable to find any significant effects of child's age on consumption independent of adult's age weakens our ability to say much about this question. This is particularly true because the effect of parents' age on child's consumption is positive, implying that at least up to age 16, no discernible decline is present.

Obvious ad hoc solutions are possible. One is to take the dictated amount of child support from table 8.3 and taper it off after some age.[4] The advantage of this approach is that it provides a way to recognize that some children are phasing out of the household, while others are not. Similarly, it recognizes fixed costs associated with supporting a child who has only a partial attachment to the household, say, because he is at school for a large part of the year.

Special Needs

All of the numbers that are presented in this chapter are based on some notion of the average individual. Obviously, all people are not alike. For example, some have handicaps that require special care. To the extent that these handicaps mean that a larger-than-predicted share of the household's expenditures went to a particular individual before the marriage breakup, those differences should be taken into account after the breakup as well. Since we have no data on these kinds of differences, we are unable to say much about them. However, they could be parameterized easily if the relevant facts were known.

For example, suppose that the mother has custody and one child has a handicap that requires expenditures that are double the amount normally spent on a child. If her household has two children, the other of which is "normal," then that household would be treated as if it had three children and transfers would be calculated accordingly. Thus, one approach is to scale the number of persons in the household to reflect some of these differences. Our data provide no guidance on the exact scaling.

4. Perhaps a reasonable rule would be to change the custody parameter, γ, in the following way: If $\gamma = \gamma^*$ throughout childhood, then let $\gamma = 0.75\gamma^*$ at age 19, $\gamma = 0.5\gamma^*$ at age 20, $\gamma = 0.25\gamma^*$ at age 21, and $\gamma = 0$ thereafter. The court could adjust these proportions to take into account school status, if desired. Then it is a simple matter to determine transfers from the tables.

Accelerated Payment

Throughout, it has been assumed that the transfer payment would be smooth over time. There are two reasons to deviate from smooth payments.

If individuals could borrow and lend freely, at the market rate of interest, then the timing of payment would not affect the value of the amount paid. A transfer of $1,000 on January 1 of two subsequent years could equivalently be replaced by a payment of $1,000 + $1,000/(1 + r)$, where r is the interest rate between the two dates. Both streams have the same present value, and both the payer and recipient would be indifferent to the two schemes.

There is a difference, however. First, if the payment is made at the outset, some enforcement difficulties may be avoided. It is well known that a large proportion of court-dictated child support and alimony payments go unpaid. As the time since the separation lengthens, the difficulty in tracing and securing payment from the noncustodial parent increases. One way to reduce nonpayment problems would be to order that the payment be made in a lump sum, or something closer to a lump sum, at the outset.

Offsetting this factor is that borrowing on promised future income is often difficult. Thus, an accelerated payment structure may place additional burden on the contributing parent. This must be weighed against the advantages in enforcement.

These considerations are different from the one that suggests that payments should taper off over time because the custodial parent can better support herself. In theory, that can be taken into account explicitly by entering not only marital status, but the time since divorce in the predicted earnings equations of appendix tables 8.A and 8.B. Since our data do not provide this information, it is impossible for us to take this into account explicitly. Thus, the coefficient on the divorce variables in the female income equation, for example, picks up the average income for divorced women over the entire period of divorce. This may overstate their income levels immediately following the divorce but understate it somewhat later. If there is strong evidence that this is the case in a particular instance, one could accelerate payment in a way that leaves the present value of earnings constant.[5]

5. This is more subtle than it seems. Since the average picked up by the divorce variable is always in current dollars, it tends to overstate the permanent income expected for the divorced individual. However, this is true on both sides of the equation; the figure overstates expected permanent income for both father and mother and it is not obvious that any bias exists on balance.

Alimony

The focus of this chapter is on child support. Still, table 8.3 presents entries for households with zero children, that is, they provide guidelines for alimony. How long and at what level should the alimony continue?

Most courts implicitly or explicitly adopt the principle that the longer the marriage, the more compelling is one spouse's claim to the income of the other. That judgment is based on two sound economic reasons. First, the longer the marriage, the older the parties and in general the more dif-difficult it is to establish a new market career. Second, the longer the marriage, the greater the likelihood that both partners assume that their well-being is directly tied to that of their spouse. Thus the length of the marriage proxies "investments" that each member has made in the other and in the marriage.

Conceptually, a correct way to deal with the issue would be to use the statistical likelihood that the marriage would have continued. The spouse

Table 8.5   Suggested Percentage Discounting of Alimony by Years since Divorce, and Age at Divorce, by Duration of Marriage Prior to Divorce

Age at Divorce	Years since Divorce											
	0	1	2	3	4	5	6	7	8	9–10	11–12	13–20
Married two years or less												
<30	0	0	0	0	0	0	0	0	0	0	0	0
30–35	80	60	33	0	0	0	0	0	0	0	0	0
36–45	100	80	60	40	20	0	0	0	0	0	0	0
>45	100	90	80	60	40	20	0	0	0	0	0	0
Married two to five years												
<30	80	60	40	20	0	0	0	0	0	0	0	0
30–35	100	80	70	60	50	40	20	0	0	0	0	0
36–45	100	90	80	60	40	20	20	20	0	0	0	0
>45	100	90	80	60	40	20	20	20	0	0	0	0
Married six to fifteen years												
<30	100	80	60	50	50	50	20	20	20	0	0	0
30–35	100	90	80	70	60	50	50	50	50	20	0	0
36–45	100	90	80	70	60	50	50	50	50	50	20	0
>45	100	90	80	70	60	50	50	50	50	50	20	0
Married more than fifteen years												
30–35	100	100	100	100	50	50	50	20	20	20	0	0
36–45	100	100	100	100	75	50	50	50	50	50	20	0
45–55	100	100	100	100	100	50	50	50	50	50	50	50
>55	100	100	100	100	100	100	100	100	100	100	100	100

who is a net recipient of transfers should have those transfers weighted by the average probability that the marriage would continue as well as by 1.0 minus the average probability of remarriage. Empirically, calculating those probabilities is impractical.

As a compromise, we suggest that the alimony payments prescribed by table 8.3 should be modified according to table 8.5, which provides percentages by which the prescribed amount should be multiplied. Those percentages rise with the duration of the marriage and with the age of the recipient spouse at divorce, but they fall with the number of years since divorce. For example, consider a couple that divorces after eight years of marriage. Suppose the husband has an income of $40,000 and the wife has no income. Suppose further that the wife is 32 years old at divorce. Panel A of table 8.3 suggests a transfer of 50 percent or $20,000. Table 8.5 suggests that in the year immediately following the divorce she receives $20,000. The next year that number falls to $18,000 (equal to 90 percent of $20,000). By the eleventh year following divorce, the amount of the transfer is down to zero. Of course, these tables are arbitrary, but we believe that they are not unreasonable values. Further, it is necessary to make assumptions along these lines to obtain final recommended transfers. These numbers are easily replaced with others, especially if better data become available. We include the tables in the interest of getting a final conclusion.

A Final Word on Fungibility

Throughout, the argument has been made that since payments are fungible, it is not sensible to split them into child support and spouse support. There is an exception when the parent with custody would provide less of a particular kind of support than the court or the noncustodial parent deems appropriate. If the noncustodial parent pays for that commodity directly, providing the commodity "in kind" rather than in dollars, the child's level of consumption is forced upward. The following example makes the point.

Suppose that M opts not to provide the child with piano lessons. If F were to pay for piano lessons directly in addition to providing the court-ordered transfer, the only way that M could secure some of that increment for M would be to cut back on other aspects of the child's consumption. But the amount that M reduces expenditures for the child on food, clothing, medical care, et cetera, may be trivial because of altruistic feelings toward the child. Under these circumstances, the child consumes more than he would have, had the additional transfer been made in the form of a cash payment to M.

This does not argue for in-kind transfers as a general matter. The criterion that distributes income according to the ratio of weighted family size already provides for the children in a socially desirable way. Awarding more income to the child does not improve society's welfare if that criterion is correct. In fact, the problem with the other criteria was that the custodial parent tended to give too much, not too little, to the child, reducing M's own consumption below that of the noncustodial parent. Again, we are led to the conclusion that neither in-kind transfers nor separation of child support from spouse support is warranted.

Actual Use of the Approach

To provide a brief example of the use of the formulas discussed in this chapter, suppose we consider a divorcing couple with two young children in which the before-tax income of the noncustodial parent is $21,500 while the custodial parent's income is $11,500. Suppose as well that the noncustodial parent in fact has custody on alternate weekends and for about six weeks in the summertime, amounting to about 25 percent of the total time. (That is, $\gamma = 0.75$, $K = 2$; and suppose $\bar{\phi} = \phi' = 0.4$ and $h = 0.415$.) The computation implies that the noncustodial parent should transfer *33 percent* of that income, or *$7,260,* to the custodial parent.

One might ask how that transfer of $7,260 compares to the transfer implied by some of the court guidelines currently in force. In Santa Clara County (1984), California, the guidelines suggest a payment of about $4,680 in child support plus alimony of $1,320, for a total annual payment of $6,000. That figure is $1,260 lower than the figure obtained from our formula ($7,260).

As if to emphasize the disparity in magnitudes of settlements from county to county, contiguous San Mateo County (1984), California, has as its guideline in this case an annual transfer of $8,600, taking into account the custodial spouse's earnings and child-care costs.

A good summary of the wide range of court guidelines and formulas is available from the National Institute for Socioeconomic Research (1984b). That summary indicates that of the 50 states plus the District of Columbia, 37 use "some type of quantifiable child support formula," and that, in general, "there are wide variations in the approach of state IV-D agencies to the development of child support formulas" (p. 3).

Conclusion

This chapter has used the results from chapter 5 to offer guidelines on the appropriate money transfer from a noncustodial parent to a custodial parent's household. The issues involved in determining proper child support payments are complex and frequently debated. We have discussed several possible criteria that might be used to guide the determination of the transfer. We have chosen as our criterion that the two households share income in proportion to their size in adult-equivalents. The main product of our work is information about how various households allocate income among their members. That information is of great significance in the appropriate determination of child support and alimony payments.

Appendix

Let W_F and W_M be the annual earnings of F and M. These are observed in most data sets and can be ascertained by the court. In this appendix we detail our suggestion for transforming earnings W_M or W_F into expected earnings $\hat{W}_M$ or $\hat{W}_F$. Further, using those expected earnings we calculate the curve CDE in figure 8.1 and show how that curve can yield an amount Y^*, the income to be used in the formulas computing the interhousehold transfer Z. We begin by discussing the estimation of $\hat{W}_M$ and $\hat{W}_F$.

Expected earnings are estimated by two separate, gender-specific earnings regressions. In our work they are estimated from a separate body of data, the Panel Study of Income Dynamics (PSID), which has good detail on earned income of each family member. The regression is of the following form:

$$\ell n\, W_{it} = X_{it}\beta + \varepsilon_{it} , \qquad (8A.1)$$

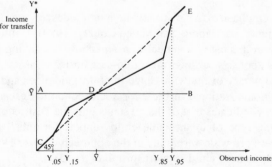

Figure 8.1 Transformation of observed income, Y, into income for transfer, Y^*.

where W_{it} is earnings of individual i in year t. Included in the X's are marital status and marital status changes after the divorce. Other variables include age, age squared, education, number of children, own children, and dummy variables for South, Urban, Currently Married, Never Married, and Black. Further,

$$\varepsilon_{it} = \delta_i + v_{it} .$$

(8A.2)

so that each individual is assumed to have an individual-specific constant term, δ_i. An estimate of δ_i can be gotten by looking at earnings in the five (or some other number of) years prior to the divorce. Let

$$\hat{\delta}_1 = \frac{1}{5} \sum_{t=1}^{5} (\ell n\ W_{it} - X_{it}\hat{\beta}) ,$$

or

$$\hat{\delta}_1 = \frac{1}{5} \sum_{t=1}^{5} \hat{\varepsilon}_{it} .$$

(8A.3)

Since $E(v_{it}) = 0$, the average ε_{it} over several years for individual i will be his δ_i. Given $\hat{\delta}_i$, we can estimate i's expected wage as

$$\hat{W}_{it} = \exp (X_{it}\hat{\beta} + \hat{\delta}_i).$$

(8A.4)

X takes the values measured after the divorce. These regressions were estimated separately by year and gender from 1976 through 1980. Table 8.A shows the 1980 regression for males and for females as well as a pooled 1976–80 regression for each gender. The regressions for 1976 through 1979 were quite similar and are not shown. With these regressions, we can use a person's characteristics (race, age, education, etc.) and get a predicted annual earnings from this set of regressions, $X_i\hat{\beta}$.

Given the results, $\hat{\varepsilon}_{it}$ can be obtained for each individual for each year. Using equation (8A.3), $\hat{\delta}_i$ can be obtained. Given $\hat{\beta}$ and $\hat{\delta}_i$, it is straightforward to obtain the predicted wage through equation (8A.4).

The only other issue is the transformation of actual incomes Y into income on which transfers are based, Y^*, that is, the exact function to be used as *CDE* in figure 8.1. The approach that we take is to make *CDE* a piecewise-linear function. The break points are selected on the basis of v_{it} in equation (8A.2). Luck is captured by v_{it}.[1] This implies that an estimate

1. It is also possible that luck can affect δ_i (e.g., the president of a big company is likely to remain in that job for a number of years, even if luck was in large part responsible for getting him there). But that part of luck already affected the children's standard of living before the breakup. As such, it is reasonable to treat that as income on which to base transfers.

Appendix
Table 8.A   Wage Regression from PSID, by Gender (run for each year separately 1976 through 1980, only 1980 shown), also Pooled 1976–80 [(ℓn earnings = $X\beta + \varepsilon$) weighted by expansion weight]

X	1980 Men		1980 Women		1976–80 Pooled Men		1976–80 Pooled Women	
Intercept	5.440	(28.74)	5.367	(20.55)	−157.53	(−14.88)	−154.08	(−9.72)
AGE	0.158	(18.84)	0.147	(11.92)	0.154	(44.90)	0.142	(26.97)
AGE^2	−0.0018	(−20.44)	−0.0018	(−13.01)	−0.0018	(−48.00)	−0.0017	(−28.61)
SOUTH	−0.103	(−2.45)	−0.0048	(−0.08)	−0.088	(−5.53)	0.0099	(0.40)
URBAN	0.229	(5.56)	0.146	(2.47)	0.078	(5.16)	0.066	(2.86)
EDUC	0.065	(10.52)	0.070	(6.74)	0.079	(33.50)	0.077	(17.17)
MARRIED	0.166	(2.52)	−0.261	(−4.14)	0.250	(9.18)	−0.249	(−9.07)
NEVER MAR	−0.195	(−2.37)	0.070	(0.76)	−0.161	(4.60)	−0.003	(−0.08)
CHILDREN	0.0016	(0.09)	−0.299	(−11.26)	−0.133	(−1.99)	−0.242	(−22.22)
OWN CHILD	0.0014	(0.14)	−0.0021	(−0.14)	0.0038	(0.88)	−0.007	(−1.08)
BLACK	−0.075	(−1.21)	−0.040	(−0.52)	−0.082	(−3.09)	0.043	(1.24)
YEAR	—		—		0.082	(15.38)	0.080	(10.04)
SEE	36926.1		69288.39		219459.8		400706.1	
df	1962		2029		11835		11046	
R^2	0.3281		0.1714		0.3319		0.1616	

of σ_v is needed. To obtain this, we estimate $\hat{\delta}_i$ by equation (8A.3), using the regressions from each of the individual years as reported partially in table 8.A. Now,

$$\hat{v}_{it} = \hat{\varepsilon}_{it} - \hat{\delta}_i ,$$

so σ_v can be estimated.[2] It is obtained as the standard error of the estimate of a regression of $\ell n\, W_{it}$ on $\ell n\, \hat{W}_{it}$ and trend. This is done in table 8.B.

If income is distributed log normally, it is not unreasonable to believe that v_{it} will be normally distributed. If so, it is a simple matter to compute the 15th and 85th (or any other) percentiles of the distribution. Using the estimate of $\hat{\sigma}_v$ from the last regression, we define

$$\hat{v}_{15} \equiv -1.04\, \hat{\sigma}_v ,$$

and

$$\hat{v}_{85} \equiv +1.04\, \hat{\sigma}_v .$$

Then, between

$$W_{15} = \exp\,(X\hat{\beta} + \hat{\delta} + \hat{v}_{15}) ,$$

and

$$W_{85} = \exp\,(X\hat{\beta} + \hat{\delta} + \hat{v}_{85}) ,$$

function *CDE* is linear with slope $= 0.5$ going through the point $(\hat{W}, \hat{W})$.

Similarly, define $\hat{v}_{05}$, $\hat{v}_{95}$ as the 5th and 95th percentiles of the distribu-

Appendix Table 8.B	Estimating the Variance of the Error Term v_i, by Gender $[\ell n\, W_{it} = a + b(\ell n\, \hat{W}_{it}) + C(\text{trend}) + v_{it}]$			
	Males		Females	
a	5.08	(0.87)	-51.44	(-5.50)
b	0.99	(172.74)	0.98	(114.21)
c	-0.0025	(-0.85)	0.026	(5.51)
SEE	23955.71		32664.59	
df	6657		5167	
R^2	0.83		0.73	
$\hat{\sigma}_v = \sqrt{\text{SEE} \div df}$	1.897		2.514	

2. There is a question of how year-effects should be treated. To the extent that trend is predictable, but business cycle behavior is just luck, it is appropriate to de-trend the series to obtain an estimate of v_{it}. (One would not want to attribute to luck increases in lnW that occur because of inflation.)

tion. We constrain the function to hit the 45° line at W_{05} and W_{95}, defined analogously. The function then sets W = observed earnings below W_{05} and above W_{95}.

To be concrete in our illustration, let us use the equation for men estimated in table 8.B and calculate the line segments of figure 8.1's line *CDE*. For men in the pooled data set 1976–80 from the PSID, the average of $\ell n\ W$ is 9.486 or \$13,174, and the square root of the mean squared error is 1.897. Thus, for a man with the average characteristics and average income of \$13,200, the line segment will go through the 45° ray at the income level \$13,200. To determine the 15 and 85 percentiles, we subtract and add (1.04)(1.897) yielding ℓn (wages) of 7.513 and 11.459, or \$1,800 and \$94,700. So our relatively flat (slope = 0.5) line segment spans a very large range from about \$2,000 to \$95,000. If we wish to return to the 45° ray at the 5th and 95th percentiles, the dollar levels would be \$600 and almost \$300,000.

Thus, the line segments for a man with $\hat{Y}$ = \$13,200 are:

if $Y \leq \$600$ then $Y^* = Y$;

if $\$600 \leq Y \leq \$1,800$ then $Y^* = 5.75\ Y - \$2850$
[derived from the relation
$(Y - 600)/(1800 - 600) = (Y^* - 600)/(7500 - 600)$];

if $\$1,800 \leq Y \leq \$13,200$ then $Y^* = \$13,200 - 0.5\ (\$13,200 - Y)$;

if $\$13,200 \leq Y \leq \$94,700$ then $Y^* = \$13,200 + 0.5(Y - \$13,200)$;

if $\$94,700 \leq Y \leq \$300,000$ then $Y^* = 1.20Y - \$59,690$
[derived from the relation
$(Y - 94,700)/(300,000 - 94,700) = (Y^* - 53,950)/(300,000 - 53,950)$];

if \$300,000 < Y then $Y^* = Y.$

Nine

Implications and Directions for Future Research

This book has examined the within-household income distribution from the abstract level to the most policy-oriented concerns. We have argued that, for most purposes, it is insufficient to consider merely the income of the household. Rather, when welfare comparisons are at stake some more refined index is needed. But there is lack of unanimity on the measure that best serves this purpose, even at the conceptual level. We have pointed out that it is necessary to consider the individual preferences involved in the interaction among household members to come to any unambiguous definition of individual welfare.

For most of the empirical analysis in this volume, we leave that issue aside. Our goal here is to obtain a measure of only the allocation of expenditures within the household; we decline to draw inferences on welfare. Still, it is impossible to be totally agnostic. To implement our empirical design, some assumptions about individual preferences must be made. We do not believe that the assumptions are unreasonable, but we concede that our estimates hinge crucially on them.

We are encouraged by this work. The analysis covers much ground, and most of it is new. We have been forced to consider many issues, and we hope that our treatment will strike the reader as thoughtful. We have labeled some calculations as illustrative when we have been less certain of their reliability. On the whole, we believe that this approach provides both theoretical and empirical insights.

Equivalence Scales

Probably the chief reason household income level is of considerable interest to social scientists is that income is considered an indicator of satisfaction or well-being. Of course "money doesn't buy happiness," but if two households are alike in several characteristics but one has a substantially higher level of income, it is generally thought to be better-off than the other. A problem arises, however, if the two households in question are not alike in terms of a characteristic such as household size (or structure). A one-person household with $10,000 is not necessarily less well-off than a two-person household with $15,000. But adjusting the income for the nature of the household in order to make comparisons across households is not at all straightforward.

A simple-minded adjustment might be to use income per capita as the relevant measure, but the strong consensus is that this results in an over-adjustment. How should one determine income equivalence for households of different sizes? The "truth" would seem to lie somewhere between no adjustment (i.e., income is income, period) and a full adjustment counting each person in the household as equivalent (i.e., per capita income). This issue has prompted a long and illustrious literature that dates at least from the work of Ernst Engel (1895) and V. Pareto (1896) and includes major contributions by Prais and Houthakker (1955) and Barten (1964), among others, which was recently summarized and explained in an excellent chapter of a text by Deaton and Muellbauer (1980, chap. 8).

In its most elementary form, the literature suggests a three-step procedure for adjusting household income for household size and structure: (1) select some criterion and define two households as equally well-off if they are identical by this criterion; (2) identify the level of money income in each household associated with this equality; and (3) define the ratio of income levels across households of different sizes as the equivalence scale.

For example, Engel (1895) pointed out that the proportion of income spent on food differed by income level and systematically declined as income rose. For example, 30 percent of income was spent on food at one income level, Y_1, and only 28 percent of income was spent on food at a little higher level of income, Y_2. Thus, one criterion that might be used is the share of income spent on food, since it seems to have a unique relationship to level of income. To illustrate, suppose one takes as a benchmark a two-adult household with no children and observed that 25 percent is spent on food at an income level of $8,000. In households of two adults and two children suppose one observed that the income level at which 25 percent is spent on food is $10,000. Thus, an income of $8,000 in the two-adult household is equivalent to an income of $10,000 in the two-adult, two-children household. The equivalence scale for this second household, with the two-adult household as the standard, would then be 1.25.

There are many other criterion suggested in the literature, some based on practical expenditure relations analogous to the one just described, and some based on explicit assumptions about the household's utility function and thereby purporting to hold the household's level of utility fixed. Some of these scales adjust for the relative nutritional needs of the household members (e.g., the Orshansky scales used by the U.S. Department of Health and Human Services in constructing the official poverty level for households of different sizes; see Mahoney 1976); some use expenditure data to infer the impact of an additional family member on demand functions or to infer the economies of scale or joint consumption within the household (e.g., Prais and Houthakker 1955; Barten 1964; Muellbauer 1974, 1977, 1980; Lazear and Michael 1980; Turchi 1983; among others).

Many of the equivalence scales estimated using an expenditure system approach try to measure what additional amount of money a household with children would need in order to make it possible for the adults to spend the same amount on themselves as in a household with no children. But if that level of income is considered an equivalent amount, and if it leaves the adults equally well-off in spending terms (and gives the children whatever children in households like those typically get), then the adults are actually better-off with the children and the "equivalent" income. After all, children are not distributed randomly but are found in households that like having children. The satisfaction of having the children per se should be considered in setting the equivalent income, as Deaton and Muellbauer (1980, 208–12) and Pollak and Wales (1979) argue, and as Gronau (1983, 5) emphasizes in his discussion of the "true equivalence scale."

Our chapter 4 explores some of the various assumptions about the household's utility function that can justify statements about the relation between spending patterns and welfare levels among household members. The allocation of the income (whatever its level) among the members of the household is not addressed by the scales, and that has been the subject of inquiry in this volume. The strategy adopted here to study the question asked avoids relying on any particular utility function (it does assume a particular form of separability). Consequently, our scheme does not conveniently yield a utility-based interpretation. However, we have estimated that a household with the sample mean level of characteristics spends about 0.40 as much on a child as it spends on an adult. That fact can provide a simple equivalence scale based on the estimate of the value of ϕ. The number of adult-equivalents in a household is simply $A + \phi K$, or, in this case, $A + (0.40)K$, where A and K are the number of adults and children in the household. Taking a two-adult household as the base or standard, the scale is:

Two-Adult Household:	1.00	
Two-Adult, One-Child Household:	1.20	(=2.4/2.0)
Two-Adult, Two-Child Household:	1.40	(=2.8/2.0)
Two-Adult, Three-Child Household:	1.60	(=3.2/2.0)

This scale is equivalent to using per capita income where all household members are adults. Consequently, this scale, like any other, continues the practice of thinking of the household as an homogeneous unit with one income and with the members of that household all somehow sharing the same general level of well-being. Our study surely suggests that all household members do not get the same amount of the household's income, so there is no reason to suppose that all household members get the same level of utility. We only see dollars spent and cannot say anything about welfare specifically, but the discrepancies we see in dollars spent do not imply equality across household members. Yet practicality dictates that for many purposes we simply want to get an average income per household member, and we contend that an equivalence scale of the form $A + (0.40)K$ is a useful one.

One fortuitous feature of the several strategies suggested in the literature for measuring equivalence scales is that many of the estimates do not differ by large amounts. For example, Deaton and Muellbauer (1980, 193) show the estimates of the equivalence of various family members used by Stone (1954) in his study of expenditures in England. The adult man was taken as the standard and a child under 14 was given the weight 0.52, which is not drastically different from the 0.40 that we have suggested here. Stone also distinguished people aged 14–17 and assigned them the weight 0.98 for males and 0.90 for females, and likewise distinguished adult females (over 17) and assigned them a weight of 0.90. We, of course, treat all adults as equivalent and so implicitly assign each adult a weight of 1.00.

Deaton and Muellbauer (1980) also show scales based on the Barten (1964) model. Using United Kingdom data, they define a two-adult household scale as 1.00. Then the scale for a household with two-adults and one-child scale (at median income levels) is 1.09 for a child under age 6 and 1.22 for a child 6–16. The latter scale is roughly similar to our implied scale of 1.20.

For the United States, Lazear and Michael (1980, 102) list several equivalence scales (Bureau of Labor Statistics, Orshansky, and their own—LM[1980]), using a two-adult two-child household as the standard. When we express the scale obtained here in comparable terms, the magnitudes are not dramatically different:

Household Size	BLS	Orshansky	LM(1980)	A + (0.40)K
two-adult	60	67	72	71
two-adult, one-child	82	80	88	86
two-adult, two-child	100	100	100	100
two-adult, three-child	116	118	115	114

Since we treat all adults as equivalent, the scale effects between households of one adult and two adults are not estimated by our scheme here. But for the sizes that are considered, the scales are similar.

There is a question in our minds about the wisdom of "fine tuning" these scales by age and gender; a simple scale like the one suggested here probably reflects the most important differences in household size. Practicality requires some scale for adjusting income across households of different sizes for all sorts of purposes, including social science research that often uses a family's "income" as an explanatory variable in studying all manner of behavior. However, one would not want to consider these scales as more than very rough approximations. That is why we think a simple scale like our suggestion, $A + (0.40)K$, is to be preferred: it is not likely to be mistaken for more than it is.

The Cost of a Child

What is the cost of a child? How does it vary by family income, by number of children? While these are not the questions which our research has addressed, it may be useful to consider how our work is related to these questions and to the literature that addresses them directly.

Three strands of economic literature can be distinguished and considered in terms of each of these questions:

1. Descriptive studies of spending patterns provide useful information about expenditures on a child. Relatively little is imposed on the data by assumptions in these studies, and relatively little can be concluded about the welfare of children.

2. Demand systems are sometimes estimated that impose a formal structure on the spending system, generally by assuming a priori that some functional form is appropriate for the spending system. Sometimes that spending system is consistent with a particular form of a household's utility function. It is sometimes possible to retrieve the parameters of the

assumed utility function as well as the parameters of the expenditure system. If one is willing to accept the underlying assumptions, then conclusions about welfare can be reached.

3. Analytic studies of fertility behavior often formulate the demand for children as a function of household income and the price of a child, among other things. These studies seek to explain differences in the number of children in households of different characteristics as responses to these different levels of income and price.

Economic literature distinguishes several concepts that often become confused in application to children: price, expenditure, cost, and welfare.

Price of an item reflects the value of the resources required to be traded or given up to acquire the item. It may be traded to the former owner, as when one purchases an automobile from a dealer, or it may be foregone by the purchaser but not received by the seller, as when one stands in a queue for half an hour in order to see a popular movie. The price—in dollars or time units or other resources—is an objective attribute of the item.

Expenditure on an item is the outlay of resources. The expenditure may differ from the price for two reasons: either more than one unit may be purchased (and the expenditure is $P \times q$, the product of the price times the quantity), or the item may be available in several qualities at different prices and the expenditure on the item may be high or low depending on which quality is selected, even though the set of prices is fixed. All consumers might face the same price structure—P_1, P_2, P_3—but they might select different qualities of the product because of differences in their incomes or in their preferences. The price does not vary in this example, but the expenditure does.

Cost measures the value of the resources used to produce the item as distinct from the value of the resources required to acquire the item. Under many conditions the cost and the price will be the same, but not always (as in the case of a monopolist who sells at a price greater than marginal cost). In the case of children, generally the parents are both the suppliers and the demanders, so that cost and price are the same. But the expenditure on the child is not necessarily equal to price or to cost, and if society subsidizes or taxes the child costs, the cost to the family may differ from the social cost.

Welfare refers to satisfaction or utility and involves preferences, tastes, or values. One often presumes that higher levels of resources, income, or expenditures are associated with higher levels of satisfaction or welfare. But the connection between expenditures and welfare is not straightforward unless the preferences are specified explicitly in terms of a utility function. As we discuss at length in chapter 4, without an explicit utility function one cannot make statements about welfare and how it might be affected by a change in expenditure. As the assumptions about utility functions are quite arbitrary, albeit commonly made in the economic literature, throughout this volume we avoid these assumptions so we have little to say about welfare except to emphasize that expenditures do not necessarily reflect welfare in any simple straightforward way.

There are several components to the price or cost of a child. First is the direct dollar outlay including, as we note in chapter 2, the more subtle, jointly consumed goods and services. Second, there is the indirect outlay in the form of parental (or someone's) time spent caring for the child. Third, and offsetting, are the direct dollar contributions the child makes to the household. Fourth, and offsetting, are the indirect (time) contributions the child makes in the form of work around the home. The sum of these four components is the price or cost or the expenditure on the child, depending on just what is measured. It is possible that the monetary and time contributions by the child exceed the outlays on the child, in which case the price of the child would be negative and the child would be considered, in economic parlance, an investment good for the household. In the contemporary United States, this is not likely to be the prevailing condition.

Our study, by focusing on who gets the dollar income of the household, is not really concerned with estimating the cost or even the total expenditure on the child, for we ignore the important *time* component of the expenditure. We look only at dollars and pay particular attention to the relative expenditure on the child as compared with the expenditure on the adult. Thus the figures we present in chapters 5 and 6 are not estimates of the full expenditure—including time expenditures—on the child.

What is the cost of a child? Several estimates have been made over the past two decades of the "cost of a child in the U.S." Cain (1971) offered one estimate of about $31,000. This estimate included the direct dollar outlays on a few specific items like food, housing, education, and medical costs up to age 18, totaling about $13,000, and an estimate of about $6,000 in housework that the child directly imposed on the family, and another $12,000 in time costs resulting from the necessity for a parent to take time out of the labor force to rear the child. Cain discounted his year-by-year estimates over the 18 years of the child's youth at a rate of 8 percent.

Others have updated and refined these estimates somewhat (see, e.g., Reed and McIntosh 1972). Espenshade (1977) summarizes these estimates and offers his own for the year 1977. Epenshade distinguishes a low-cost and a moderate-cost budget and measures the time costs for a parent (a mother) with lower and higher education levels. A low-cost, less-educated parent is estimated to spend about $1,500 in childbirth costs, $35,000 in direct expenses up to age 18, $7,500 in college costs, and about $27,000 in lost labor earnings over the child's lifetime, for a total cost of about $71,000. If the moderate budget and a college-educated person's time value is used, the respective figures are about $2,200 for childbirth costs, $53,000 for expenses to age 18, $8,400 for college, and $42,800 in lost earnings for a total of about $107,000. These Espenshade figures are not discounted, so they are higher than one would think appropriate, but they emphasize that the cost varies considerably with the time value and expenditure level of the household. They also emphasize that nearly half the cost is composed of the time foregone from other productive uses and spent instead in caring for the child.

Our estimates in chapter 5 ignore the important time costs entirely and estimate the dollar expenditure on the child more indirectly than by summing up the specific expenditures for children on a few items like food and clothing. Our estimate of the expenditure on a child (in a family with about two children) in 18 years (discounted at 10 percent) is about $30,000 for a family with $10,000 in annual income and as much as $115,000 for a much wealthier family with $50,000 annual income (see table 5.11A). (Recall once again that these figures are in 1970–71 dollars.)

Our study concentrates exclusively on dollar expenditures, while many other studies measure a narrower concept of money expenditures but include the time costs and call their resulting total outlay the "cost" of the child. But the cost is really an expenditure in terms of the definitions discussed above. The resources devoted to the child reflect the parents' decision about the level of "quality" they choose. Now the distinction may seem academic, but it is an important difference. Imagine that we ask, "What is the price of a car?" We know that the price of a new car can vary by a factor of, say, five, so the answer to the question is that the price of a car ranges from about $5,000 to maybe $25,000 today, depending on the quality of the car. For some purposes it is adequate to know that an average car purchased today costs maybe $10,000. That surely informs us about the expense of that item compared to other consumption items such as houses, or clothing, or a college education. But it does not tell us very precisely what a particular family is likely to spend on a new car. The same is true for children.

Espenshade's 1977 estimate of the "cost" of a child ranges from about $70,000 to about $107,000 (undiscounted in 1977 dollars), while another, more recent study by Espenshade (1984) estimates expenditures per child in a low and a high socioeconomic level family are $75,000 and $98,300, respectively (undiscounted in 1981 dollars). Our figures estimating the expenditure per child in a typical white household with 2.19 children range from $7,400 for a family with $5,000 annual income to $52,600 for a family with $50,000 annual income (discounted at 10 percent, in 1972 dollars). A part of the explanation for the span in the Espenshade (1977) estimates is the difference in the income level of two households, as is the case in the other two estimates. That difference is not a difference in price or cost, but a difference in the choice of the level of expenditures the parents select. Another part of the difference in the Espenshade (1977) estimates is the fact that they include time values which differ among parents. The less-educated parent's time is valued at $3.28 per hour, while the more-educated parent's time is valued at $5.29 per hour in Espenshade's calculation. That difference is not a matter of choice (at least not in the short run), so it does reflect a difference in cost or price. In general, "quality" of the child cannot be ascertained independently of these measured expenditures. That causes a confounding of differences in costs faced by the parents and of differences in the quality of the child. Of course, this problem is not restricted to the application to children but exists in any circumstance where the quality of the product produced cannot be easily ascertained independently of its costs of production.

The more recent study by Espenshade (1984) further updates his estimates of expenditures on children, and in several ways this new study is an important companion study to ours. Espenshade, like us, looks exclusively at expenditures on children rather than trying to get at the whole "cost" of a child by including the time costs as well. He also uses the 1972–73 CES data as we do. One rather superficial difference between the two studies is that he reports his figures as 1981 expenditures by multiplying the 1972–73 numbers by a Consumer Price Index that inflates them to 1981 prices. Of course, this procedure ignores the impact on behavior of changes in relative prices over that decade. A more important difference between Espenshade's work and ours is that he studies the pattern of expenditures only in families with both a husband and wife present and no other adults. Consequently he focuses on how the addition of another child affects expenditures, but he cannot tell us how the absence of a parent alters those expenditures.

Another important difference between our work and Espenshade's is in the research strategy used. We take the household's whole income and apportion it between adults and children by a multiple regression that takes account of differences in household size, location, structure, and income as well as of demographic characteristics of the household head. We focus on how these characteristics affect the proportion expended on each child relative to each adult in the household. Espenshade identifies several prototypical family types at the outset and uses a hierarchy of separate regressions based on the CES data to estimate synthetic patterns of expenditures. He estimates the wages of the husband and wife in each of his nine prototypic families, then estimates the total consumption in each family for each year of a child's youth in a synthetic cohort approach. Using the notion that two households that spend the same proportion of their total consumption on groceries have the same standard of living, he estimates—from families with no children, one child, two children, or three children—how much is spent in total on each child at specified levels of standard of living. Summing up those estimated synthetic expenditures over the first 18 years of life of each child, he has an estimate of the total outlay on the child. These outlays are not discounted in Espenshade's study. He augments this analysis by adding in extraneous information about the typical cost of college, employing figures from the College Entrance Examination Board.

Many of Espenshade's substantive conclusions mirror our own. Of course one might expect that, since we use the same data set. But our research strategies are dramatically different, so there is some reassurance when both projects find, for example, that: the expenditures on a second and on a third child are substantially lower than on a first child; that the average expenditure per child falls as the number of children rises; that blacks and southerners spend less per child; that expenditures rise, at least slightly, with the age of the child; and that the employment of both parents results in a higher expenditure on the child. While our results are expressed per child relative to each adult, Espenshade's are expressed as absolute amounts. Of course, each study can convert its answers into the other's metric. Our study further emphasizes the partial (holding income constant) and total effect of the household head's education, and gender and especially of the number of adults in the household, while Espenshade's further emphasizes the effect on expenditures of spacing and birth order of the children and the mother's age at the child's birth.

Another extensive recent study of note is Turchi's (1983) monograph *Estimating the Cost of Children in the United States.* He too uses the 1972–73 CES data, focusing on four household types: single persons, husband-wife with no children, one-parent households with children, and husband-wife households with children. The principal thrust of Turchi's work is the presentation of tables showing estimated expenditures on a child by year of age from 1 to 18 on each of six expenditure categories— food, transportation, clothing, etc.—by different household characteristics. In order to estimate these expenditures, he uses a specific income-expenditure equation that adjusts for family size and structure. As one step in his estimation procedure, Turchi must calculate a general scale by which he can equate the equivalence in terms of the consumption expenditure of a young child or any other family member as compared to an adult male. The strategy he selects, after considering many alternatives, is similar to our own in the data he chooses to use—information on adult consumption of clothing, tobacco, and alcohol—but rather dissimilar to our strategy in how that information is used.

Two conclusions Turchi reaches in this portion of his study are of considerable interest in our work. First, he experimented with using adult clothing without including the other adult consumption items, and he experimented with using only women's clothing or only men's clothing for the estimation of the general scales, but he concluded that the preferred commodity set for use is the total consumption on men's and women's clothing, alcohol, and tobacco. That is the same composite commodity we have independently selected.

The sensitivity checks that Turchi performed give us some additional confidence about our own choice of this composite good, especially in light of another of Turchi's conclusions. The general scale which he presents, based on the same data set we use but with very different statistical methods than we use, is quite similar to the scale we estimate. The Turchi scale is presented in far greater demographic detail than is our own. We stress the fact that the rough nature of the estimation makes us reluctant to go into fine detail and instead suggest that adopting the scale of 0.38 for a child compared to a scale of 1.0 for an adult is a sensible procedure. Turchi (1983, table 2, p. 40) presents scales for children by age and gender. His scales are:

Age 0–2	boy	0.281
	girl	0.295
Age 2–6	boy	0.195
	girl	0.207
Age 6–12	boy	0.355
	girl	0.352
Age 12–15	boy	0.497
	girl	0.472
Age 15–18	boy	0.797
	girl	0.774

What is of considerable interest is that if one asks what the average is of these weights, averaged over each of the 18 years, that average is 0.39 for both a boy and for a girl. That average is remarkably similar to our estimate of 0.38. Said differently, Turchi's subsample has an average family size of 3.36 persons comprised of 1.09 adult females, 1.07 adult males,

0.054 infant males, 0.242 females age 6–12, etc., and he computes the adult-equivalent size of this family, using his scales, to be 2.50. If we use our scale in which all children are 0.38, we compute the adult-equivalent size of that same family to be 2.62, a very similar value.

Studies that use a formal-demand system provide an interesting conceptual answer to the question of the cost of a child. One of the commonly used systems is the Stone-Geary system. In this scheme the utility function takes the form

$$U = \sum_{i=1}^{n} b_i \ln(C_i - C^*_i),$$

where b_i is the utility coefficient, and the key assumption is that one "needs" C^*_i amount of good i and getting that amount doesn't yield utility, it just satisfies the minimum need. Only quantities above C^*_i yield utility. If this type of function were estimated with adults and children treated separately, the set of "needs" for children, their C^*_1, C^*_2, et cetera, could be thought of as the goods required to sustain a child, albeit at a very low level of existence. But at least if one added up the price of these "needs" for children, one would have a "cost of a child" of a particular (low) quality. It would be the minimum outlay required to sustain a child at that low quality, so it would be an estimate of the cost of a child of that quality. Even here, however, notice that the social context in which the data are drawn will in part determine these base levels of the C^*_i's, so this cost is the cost of a low-quality child in that society, faced with those prices of the C^*_i's.

Time Use in the Household

While we have dealt with the allocation of money income among household members, time is another important resource whose allocation affects the level and distribution of well-being in the household. Several studies in recent years have investigated how time in the home is used and who performs various time-consuming household chores.

One of the key topics of inquiry is the use of time in child care, especially with young, preschool-aged children. The earlier studies, such as those by Hill and Stafford (1974) and Leibowitz (1974, 1975) found, for example, that more-educated women spent more time with children than did less-educated women. More recent studies like Hill and Stafford (1985) find in the detailed data what we see in aggregate statistics as well: The presence of a young child in the home has a smaller deterrent effect on the employment of women today than in years past. In fact, Hill and Stafford find in their 1975–76 data that "market hours are now reduced less per child by college-educated women than by high-school-educated women" (1985, 424).

While a systematic comparison of results on time use and on the allocation of money income is not feasible because of the limited nature of the data on both time and dollar expenditures, there are a few results from the time-use surveys that deserve mention here. As just indicated, these studies find that more-educated parents (mothers) spend more time per child in care and attention than do less-educated parents (mothers). If we think of child care as time allocated to the child and leisure time as the time allocated to the adult, this result parallels the findings in chapters 5 and 6. We find that the family consumption that is devoted to the child relative to the consumption that is devoted to the adult is higher, the higher the education level of the adult. Hill and Stafford report that the care of a child by both parents is allocated about 13.5 hours per week in a family with a college-educated mother, and only about half that much, about 6.5 hours per week, in a family with a grade-school-educated mother (1985, 436). So it appears that the additional money spent on the child is not offset by less time spent on the child; on the contrary, it is mirrored in relatively more time being spent on the child as well.

Hill and Stafford (1985, 417) report that the data even suggest that more-educated mothers spend more time with preschool daughters than with their sons. Our table 5.14 also found that the expenditure of dollars on male children was slightly, but statistically, less than on female children. Hill and Stafford (1985) also report that more-educated mothers provide a more varied time input with children than less-educated mothers, measured in the range of activities engaged in, including playing, reading, talking, and instructing the child.

An additional finding of real importance that parallels our own results is that time spent per child falls as the number of children in the household rises; we found that the per child expenditure of money falls as the number of children rises. In hours per week, Hill and Stafford find that college-educated mothers spend about 9.2 hours per child with one child and 7.3 hours per child with two children; high-school-educated mothers spend 7.8 and 6.1 hours per child, respectively, with one and two children; and grade-school-educated mothers spend 5.8 and 5.3 hours per child, respectively (1985, 431). Thus here is an additional indication of the quantity-quality trade-off: in both time and dollar expenditures, the resources devoted per child decline as the number of children increases.

Finally, even this brief discussion of time use within the household

serves to remind us again of an important limitation of our inquiry. We
have looked only at dollars and, as such, cannot speak to the allocation of
all household resources or to the distribution of well-being or of utility.
But again, money is a commonly used metric in the measurement of well-
being. Our point has consistently been that knowing about the allocation
of money across households is only a part of the story—the allocation
within the household should also be of concern. The limitation of looking
only at money and not at money-and-time resources is a severe limitation
in this and in many other studies. The "money illusion" involved should
never be ignored, but in this book it is not the direction in which we have
attempted to advance our understanding.

Future Research

It is often said that a research project raises more questions than it re-
solves. This book raises many questions; some are answered, others are
left unsolved. The allocation of expenditures within a household has been
estimated, and a number of conclusions have been drawn from the empirical analysis. Still, the analysis is both incomplete and imperfect. Assumptions have been made that are, at best, too specific and, at worst, untrue.
As a result, a number of areas are open to future investigation.

Important assumptions of our approach include:

1. Within a household, all adults receive the same amount of resources.

2. Similarly, within a household, all children receive the same amount
of resources.

3. The presence of children does not affect the ratio of expenditures on
observable adult goods (alcohol, tobacco, and adult clothing) to total adult
expenditures.

4. Public goods are consumed by family members in the same ratios as
private goods.

5. Many functional form assumptions must be made in order to obtain
estimates.

Some of these are violated in the data. These assumptions create some
difficulties and cause concern in a number of areas.

First, at the empirical level, it is somewhat disturbing that there is not a
better correspondence between the two samples' estimates of the effects of
demographic variables on household allocation. This may result from
functional form problems both in the ϕ equation and in the λ equation,
which estimates the ratio of observed adult to total adult goods. It is surely,
partially, a result of variations in definitions of variables.

Second, at the policy level, chapter 8 is packed with value judgments with which even the authors of this book are not fully comfortable. For completeness, it would be useful to replace our assumptions with others in order to determine the robustness of our transfer estimates.

Finally, new data are available from the 1981–82 CES. The entire analysis should be repeated using those data. Not only would this provide an additional check for consistency, but it would enable a better examination of time trends in household expenditure patterns. This would be especially interesting because household composition has undergone significant changes in recent years.

Beyond our focus, the importance of studying the allocation of nonmonetary resources should not be overlooked.

That much remains to be done does not reduce the value of our approach. We hope that some readers will be stimulated to modify and improve on our effort, and thereby to obtain more accurate answers to what we believe are very important questions.

References

Adelman, J., and C. R. Morris. 1973. *Economic growth and social equity in developing countries*. Stanford, Calif.: Stanford University Press.

Aitchison, J., and J. A. C. Brown. 1957. *The lognormal distribution with special reference to its uses in economics*. New York: Cambridge University Press.

Atkinson, A. B. 1975. *The economics of inequality*. Oxford: Clarendon Press.

Barten, A. P. 1964. Family composition, prices and expenditure patterns. In *Econometric analysis for national economic planning*, ed. P. E. Hart, G. Mills, and J. K. Whitaker, 277–92. London: Butterworth.

Beach, Charles M. 1976. Cyclical impacts on the personal distribution of income. *Annals of Economic and Social Measurement* 5(1):29–52.

Becker, Gary S. 1974. A theory of marriage. In *Economics of the family*, ed. T. W. Schultz, 299–314. Chicago: University of Chicago Press for NBER.

———. 1975. *Human capital*. 2d ed. Chicago: University of Chicago Press for NBER.

———. 1981a. *A treatise on the family*. Cambridge, Mass.: Harvard University Press.

———. 1981b. Altruism in the family and selfishness in the market place. *Economica* 48 (February):1–15.

Becker, Gary S., and H. Gregg Lewis. 1974. Interaction between quantity and quality of children. In *Economics of the family*, ed. T. W. Schultz, 81–90. Chicago: University of Chicago Press for NBER.

Becker, Gary S., and Nigel Tomes. 1976. Child endowments and the quantity and quality of children. *Journal of Political Economy* 84(4), part 2: S143–62.

———. 1979. An equilibrium theory of the distribution of income and intergenerational mobility. *Journal of Political Economy* 87(6):1153–89.

Behrman, Jere. 1985. Intrahousehold allocation of nutrients in rural India: Are boys favored? Do parents exhibit inequality aversion? University of Pennsylvania. Mimeo.

Behrman, Jere, Z. Hrubec, P. J. Taubman, and T. Wales. 1980. *Socioeconomic success: A study of the effects of genetic endowments, family environment and schooling.* Amsterdam: North-Holland.

Behrman, Jere, R. A. Pollak, and P. J. Taubman. 1982. Parental preferences and provisions for progeny. *Journal of Political Economy* 90(1):52–72.

———. 1986. Do parents favor boys? *International Economic Review* 27(1):33–54.

Benus, Jere, and J. N. Morgan. 1975. Time periods, unit of analysis, and income concept in the analysis of income distribution. In *The personal distribution of income and wealth,* ed. J. D. Smith, National Bureau of Economic Research Studies in Income and Wealth, vol. 39, 209–24. New York: Columbia University Press for NBER.

Bound, John, Z. Griliches, and B. H. Hall. 1984. Brothers and sisters in the family and the labor market. Harvard University/NBER. Mimeo.

Budd, Edward. 1970. Postwar changes in the size distribution of income in the U.S. *American Economic Review* 60(2):247–60.

Budd, Edward C., and T. C. Whiteman. 1978. Macroeconomic fluctuations and the size distribution of income and earnings in the U.S. In *Income distribution and economic inequality,* ed. Zvi Griliches et al. 11–27. New York: Halsted Press.

Cain, G. C. 1971. Issues in the economics of a population policy for the United States. *American Economic Review* 61(2):408–17.

Carlton, Dennis W., and Robert E. Hall. 1978. The distribution of permanent income. In *Income distribution and economic inequality,* ed. Zvi Griliches et al., 103–12. New York: Halsted Press.

Cassetty, Judith, ed. 1983. *The parental child-support obligation.* Lexington, Mass.: Lexington Books.

Champernowne, D. G. 1973. *The distribution of income.* London: Cambridge University Press.

Chenery, H., M. S. Ahluwalia, C. L. G. Bell, J. H. Duloy, and R. Jolly. 1974. *Redistribution and growth.* Oxford: Oxford University Press.

Chiswick, Barry, and J. Mincer. 1972. Time-series changes in personal income inequality in the United States from 1939, with projections to 1985. *Journal of Political Economy* 80, supplement (May/June): S34–66.

Davis, H. L. 1976. Decision making within the household. *Journal of Consumer Research* 2(March): 241–60.

Deaton, Angus, and J. Muellbauer. 1980. *Economics and consumer behavior.* New York: Cambridge University Press.

———. 1986. On measuring child costs: With application to poor counties. *Journal of Political Economy* 94(4):720–44.

Engel, Ernst. 1895. Die Lebenskosten belgischer Arbeiter—Familien früher und jetzt. *International Statistical Institute Bulletin,* no.9: 1–74.

Espenshade, Thomas J. 1972. The price of children and socio-economic theories of fertility. *Population Studies* 26(2):207–21.

———. 1977. The value and cost of children. *Population Bulletin* 32(1). Washington, D.C.: Population Reference Bureau Inc.

———. 1984. *Investing in children*. Washington, D.C.: Urban Institute.

Fiegehen G. C., and P. S. Lansley. 1976. The measurement of poverty: A note on household size and income units. *Journal of the Royal Statistical Society* A, 139, part 4:508–18.

Gillespie, W. Irwin. 1965. Effect of public expenditures on the distribution of income. In *Essays in fiscal federalism,* ed. Richard A. Musgrave, 122–86. Washington, D.C.: The Brookings Institute.

Goldsmith, Selma. 1958. The relation of census income distribution to other income data. In *An appraisal of the 1950 Census Income Data,* National Bureau of Economic Research Studies in Income and Wealth, vol. 23, 65–107. Princeton, N.J.: Princeton University Press for NBER.

Griliches, Zvi. 1979. Sibling models and data in economics: Beginnings of a survey. *Journal of Political Economy* 87(5), part 2:S37–S64.

Gronau, Reuben. 1982. Inequality of family income: Do wives' earnings matter? *Population and Development Review* 8, supplement (*Income distribution and the family,* ed. Yoram Ben Porath):119–36.

———. 1983. Some disorganized thoughts concerning the measurement and welfare implications of adult equivalence scales. Mimeo.

———. 1986a. Consumption technology and the intrafamily distribution of resources—Adult equivalence scales reexamined. Discussion Paper no. 85.11. Maurice Falk Institute for Economic Research in Israel, Jerusalem.

———. 1986b. The intrafamily allocation of goods—How to separate the men from the boys? Discussion Paper no. 87.3 Hebrew University of Jerusalem and Economics Research Center/NORC, Chicago.

Hall, Robert E., and Mishkin, Frederic. 1982. The sensitivity of consumption to transitory income: Evidence from a panel study of households. *Econometrica* 50 (March):461–81.

Harvard Education Review. 1974. *The rights of children,* ed. Rochelle Beck and Heather Bastow Weiss. Reprint Series no. 9. Cambridge: Harvard Education Review.

Henderson, A. M. 1949. The cost of children. Part I. *Population Studies* 3:130–50.

———. 1950. The cost of children. Part II. *Population Studies* 4:267–98.

Hill, C. Russell, and Frank P. Stafford. 1974. Allocation of time to pre-school children and educational opportunity. *Journal of Human Resources* 9 (Summer):323–43.

———. 1985. Parental care of children: Time diary estimates of quantity predictability and variety. In *Time, goods, and well-being,* ed. F. Thomas Juster and Frank P. Stafford, 415–37. Ann Arbor: University of Michigan Press.

Hollister, R. G., and J. L. Palmer. 1972. The impact of inflation on the poor. In *Redistribution to the rich and the poor,* ed. K. E. Boulding and M. Pfaff. Belmont, Calif.: Wadsworth.

Horney, Mary Jean, and Marjorie B. McElroy. 1980. A Nash-bargained linear expenditure system: The demand for leisure and goods. Working paper no. 8041. Center for Math Studies in Business and Economics, University of Chicago.

Johnson, Harry G. 1973. *The theory of income distribution*. London: Gray-Mills Publishing.

Kakwani, Nanak. 1980. *Income inequality and poverty*. New York: Oxford University Press for the World Bank.

Kravis, Irving B. 1960. International differences in the distribution of income. *Review of Economics and Statistics*, no. 4: 408–16.

Kuznets, Simon. 1955. Economic growth and income inequality. *American Economic Review* 45(1):1–28.

———. 1975. Demographic aspects of the distribution of income among families: Recent trends in the U.S. In *Econometrics and economic theory: Essays in honor of Jan Tinbergen*, ed. W. Sellekaerts, 223–45.

Kyn, Oldrich. 1978. Education, sex, and income inequality in Soviet-type socialism. In *Income distribution and economic inequality*, ed. Zvi Griliches et al., 274–89. New York: Halsted Press.

Lampman, Robert J. 1962. *The share of the top wealth-holders in national wealth 1922–56*. Princeton, N.J.: Princeton University Press.

Land, Hilary. 1977. Inequalities in large families: More of the same or different? In *Equalities and inequalities in family life*, ed. Robert Chester and Jogh Peel, 163–76. New York: Academic Press.

Layard, Richard, and Antoni Zabalza. 1979. Family income distribution: Explanation and policy evaluation. *Journal of Political Economy* 87 (5), part 2: S133–62.

Lazear, Edward P. 1978. Resource allocation within an organization unit: Theory and application to the family. Mimeo.

———. 1983. Intergenerational externalities. *Canadian Journal of Economics* 16(2):212–28.

Lazear, Edward P., and Robert T. Michael, 1980. Family size and the distribution of real per capita income. *American Economic Review* 70(1):91–107.

Leibowitz, Arleen. 1974. Home investments in children. In *Economics of the family*, ed. T. W. Schultz, 432–52. Chicago: University of Chicago Press.

———. 1975. Education and the allocation of women's time. In *Education, income and human behavior*, ed. F. Thomas Juster, 171–98. New York: McGraw-Hill for NBER.

Light, Richard J. 1973. Abused and neglected children in America: A study of alternative policies. *Harvard Education Review* 43(4):556–98. Reprinted in 1974 in *The rights of children*. HER Reprint Series no. 9, 198–240.

Lillard, Lee. 1977. Inequality: Earnings vs. human wealth. *American Economic Review* 67(2):42–53.

Lindert, Peter H. 1978. *Fertility and scarcity in America*. Princeton, N.J.: Princeton University Press.

Lydall, Harold F. 1959. The long-term trend in the size distribution of income. *Journal of the Royal Statistical Society* A, 122, part 1: 1–37.

———. 1968. *The structure of earnings*. Oxford: Oxford University Press.

McElroy, Marjorie B., and Mary Jean Horney. 1981. Nash-bargained household decisions: Towards a generalization of the theory of demand. *International Economic Review* 22(2):333–49.

Mahoney, B. S. 1976. *The measure of poverty*. Washington, D.C.: Poverty Studies Task Force, U.S. Department of Health, Education and Welfare.

Mandelbrot, Benoit. 1960. The Pareto-Levy law and the distribution of income. *International Economic Review* 1:79–105.

Manser, Marilyn, and Murray Brown. 1979. Bargaining analyses of household decisions. In *Women in the labor market,* ed. Cynthia B. Lloyd, Emily S. Andrews, and Curtis L. Gilroy, 3–26. New York: Columbia University Press.

———. 1980. Marriage and household decision making: A bargaining analysis. *International Economic Review* 21(1):31–43.

Metcalf, C. E. 1969. The size distribution of personal income during the business cycle. *American Economic Review* 59(4), part 1:657–68.

Michael, Robert T. 1972. *The effect of education on efficiency in consumption.* New York: Columbia University Press for NBER.

———. 1979. Variation across households in the rate of inflation. *Journal of Money, Credit, and Banking* 11(1):32–46.

Miller, Herman P. 1966. *Income distribution in the United States.* 1960 Census Monograph. Washington, D.C.: U.S. Government Printing Office.

Mincer, Jacob. 1970. The distribution of labor incomes: A survey with special reference to the human capital approach. *Journal of Economic Literature* 8(1):1–26.

———. 1974. *Schooling, experience and earnings.* New York: Columbia University Press.

Mirer, Thad W. 1973. The effects of macroeconomic fluctuations on the distribution of income. *Review of Income and Wealth,* series 10, no. 4:385–406.

Mirrlees, J. A. 1971. An exploration in the theory of optimal income taxation. *Review of Economic Studies* 38 (April): 175–208.

Mnookin, Robert H., and L. Kornhauser. 1979. Bargaining in the shadow of the law: The case of divorce. *Yale Law Review* 88(5):950–97.

Muellbauer, John. 1974. Household production theory, quality, and the "Hedonic technique." *American Economic Review* 64(6):977–94.

———. 1977. Testing the Barten model of household composition effects and the cost of children. *Economic Journal* 87 (September): 460–87.

———. 1980. The estimation of the Prais-Houthakker model of equivalence scales. *Econometrica* 48(1): 153–76.

National Institute for Socioeconomic Research. 1984a. Review of literature and statutory provisions relating to the establishment and updating of child support funds. Mimeo. Prepared for the U.S. Department of Health and Human Services, Office of Child Support Enforcement, Rockville, Maryland.

————. 1984b. Review of selected state practices in establishing and updating child support funds. Mimeo. Prepared for the U.S. Department of Health and Human Services, Office of Child Support Enforcement, Rockville, Maryland.

Paglin, M. 1975. The measurement and trend of inequality: A basic revision. *American Economic Review* 65(4):598–609.

Pahl, Jan. 1980. Patterns of money management within marriage. *Journal of Social Policy* (3):313–35.

Papanek, Gustav F. 1978. Economic growth, income distribution, and the political process in less developed countries. In *Income distribution and economic inequality*, ed. Zvi Griliches et al., 259–73. New York: Halsted Press.

Pareto, V. 1896. La courbe de la répartition de la richesse. In *Recueil publié par la Faculté de Droit a l'occasion de l'exposition Nationale Suisse*, 373–87. Lausanne: University of Lausanne. Reprinted in 1965 in V. Pareto, *Ecrits sur la courbe de la répartition de la richesse*, ed. G. Busino. Geneva: Droz.

Paukert, F. 1973. Income distribution: Survey of the evidence. *International Labor Review* 108 (August/September):97–125.

Pechman, Joseph A., and Benjamin A. Okner. 1974. *Who bears the tax burden?* Washington, D.C.: The Brookings Institution.

Peters, Elizabeth. 1983. The impact of regulation of marriage, divorce, and property settlements in a private contracting framework. Ph.D. diss., Department of Economics, University of Chicago.

Pfaff, Martin, and Wolfgang Asam. 1978. Distributive effects of real transfers via public infrastructure: Conceptual problems and some empirical results. In *Income distribution and economic inequality*, ed. Zvi Griliches et al., 66–96. New York: Halsted Press.

Plotnick, R. D., and R. Skidmore. 1975. *Progress against poverty: A review of the 1964–1974 decade*. Madison, Wis.: Institute for Research on Poverty.

Pollak, Robert A., and Terrence J. Wales. 1979. Welfare comparisons and equivalence scales. *American Economic Review* 69 (March):216–21.

Prais, S. J., and H. S. Houthakker. 1955. *The analysis of family budgets*. Cambridge: Cambridge University Press.

Reder, Melvin W. 1969. Theory of income size distribution. In *Six papers on the size distribution of wealth and income*, ed. Lee Soltow, 205–50. New York: Columbia University Press for NBER.

Reed, R. H., and S. McIntosh. 1972. Costs of children. In *Economic aspects of population change*, ed. E. R. Morss and R. H. Reed, vol. 2, 337–50. Washington, D.C.: U.S. Commission on Population Growth and the American Future.

Reynolds, M., and E. Smolensky, eds. 1977. *Public expenditures, taxes, and the distribution of income: The U.S. 1950, 1961, 1970*. Madison, Wis.: Institute for Research on Poverty.

Rosensweig, Mark R., and P. T. Schultz. 1982. Market opportunities, genetic endowments and intrafamily resource distribution: Child survival in rural India. *American Economic Review* 72(4):803–15.

Rothbarth, Erwin. 1943. Notes on a method of determining equivalent incomes for families of different composition. In *War-time pattern of savings and spending*, ed. Charles Madge, appendix 4. Cambridge: Cambridge University Press.

Roy, A. D. 1950. The distribution of earnings and of individual output. *Economic Journal* 60 (September):489–505.

San Mateo County. 1984. Uniform domestic relations, local rules, for Bay Area Superior Courts. Informal 1-page memo. February.

Santa Clara County. 1984. Guidelines for users of support schedules. Informal 11-page memo. February.

Schultz, T. Paul, 1964. *The distribution of personal income*. Washington, D.C.: U.S. Government Printing Office.

———. 1969. Secular trends and cyclical behavior of income distribution in the United States: 1944–1965. In *Six Papers on the size distribution of wealth and income*, ed. Lee Soltow, 75–100. New York: Columbia University Press for NBER.

Slama, Jiri. 1978. A cross-country regression model of social inequality. In *Income distribution and economic inequality*, ed. Zvi Griliches et al., 306–23. New York: Halsted Press.

Smith, James D., and Stephen D. Franklin. 1974. The concentration of personal wealth 1922–1969. *American Economic Review* 64 (May):162–67.

Smith, James P. 1979. The distribution of family earnings. *Journal of Political Economy* 87(5), part 2:S163–92.

Smith, James P., and Michael P. Ward. 1985. Time-series growth in the female labor force. *Journal of Labor Economics* 3(1), supplement:S59–S90.

Solow, Robert M. 1967. Income inequality since the war. In *Inequality and poverty*, ed. Edward C. Budd, 50–64. New York: W. W. Norton.

Soltow, Lee. 1960. The distribution of income related to changes in the distributions of education, age, and occupation. *Review of Economics and Statistics* 42(4):450–53.

Stiglitz J. E. 1969. Distribution of income and wealth among individuals. *Econometrica* 37(3):382–97.

Stone J. R. N. 1954. *The measurement of consumers' expenditure and behaviour in the United Kingdom, 1920–1938*. Vol. 1. Cambridge: Cambridge University Press.

Taubman, Paul J. 1975. *Sources of inequality in earnings*. Amsterdam: North-Holland.

———. 1976. The determinants of earnings: Genetics, family and other environments. *American Economic Review* 66(5):858–70.

———. 1978. *Income distribution and redistribution*. Reading, Mass.: Addison-Wesley.

Tout, H. 1938. *The standard of living in Bristol*. London: Arrowsmith.

Turchi, Boone A. 1983. *Estimating the cost of children in the United States*. Chapel Hill, N.C.: Carolina Population Center, University of North Carolina.

———. 1984. The monetary cost of a child. *Studies in Contemporary Economics* 8:258–76.

United Kingdom. Central Statistical Office. 1979. *Social Trends,* no. 10. London: Her Majesty's Stationery Office.

Weiss, Yoram, and Robert J. Willis. 1985. Children as collective goods and divorce settlements. *Journal of Labor Economics* 3(3):268–92.

Weitzman, Lenore J. 1981a. The economics of divorce: Social and economic consequences of property, alimony and child support awards. *UCLA Law Review* 28(6):1181–1268.

———. 1981b. *The marriage contract: Spouses, lovers and the law.* New York: The Free Press.

Wiles, P. 1975. Recent data on Soviet income distribution. In *Economic aspects of life in the USSR* (main findings of colloquium held January 19–31, 1975). Brussels: North Atlantic Treaty Organization, Directorate of Economic Affairs.

Willis, Robert J. 1981. The direction of intergenerational transfers and demographic transition: The Caldwell hypothesis re-examined. Discussion Paper no. 81–3. Economics Research Center/National Opinion Research Center, Chicago.

Young, Michael. 1952. Distribution of income within the family. *British Journal of Sociology* 3:305–21.

Young, Michael, and Peter Willmott. 1973. *The symmetrical family.* London: Routledge & Kegan Paul.

Index

Abuse of children, 14, 61
Accelerated payment for child support, 182
Accounting identity, 5–6
Adults: clothing expenditures, 41–43; defining expenditures of, 6, 25, 79, 108, 111, 119, 201; number of, vs. child expenditures, 8, 97; school expenditures for, 49–52
Age: alimony and, 183; child-adult expenditure ratios and, 71, 81–82, 137, 201; child expenditures and, 32, 90, 99–106; child support and, 180; demographic changes, 117; expenditure patterns and, 2; income equivalence scales and, 195; income utility and, 147; regression error and, 109; school expenditures and, 50–51
Alcohol expenditures: adult consumption and, 6, 79, 201; black households, 84, 108; female-headed households, 120
Alimony: divorce laws and, 24; guidelines for, 183–84; household unit for, 19; income distribution and, 150–51; money fungibility and, 10, 170; remarriage and, 169; taxable, 179
American Medical Association (AMA), 14
Assets, divorce and, 172, 177–78

Babies, clothing expenditures for, 41
Baby-sitting, 5, 88, 97
Bargaining, 22–23, 55
BEA. *See* Bureau of Economic Analysis

Birth control, 61
Black households: child-adult expenditure ratios and, 81, 90–92, 137; child expenditures and, 7, 9; clothing expenditures of, 41–42, 45; expenditure patterns of, 33, 35, 84, 108; household characteristics, 130; 1960 vs. 1972, 126; schooling expenditures and, 51; size of, 92, 144
BLS. *See* Bureau of Labor Statistics
Borrowing, child support and, 182
Britain, 14–15, 18, 140–41, 194
Budgets: constraints, 79; savings and, 64
Bureau of Economic Analysis (BEA), 16
Bureau of Labor Statistics (BLS), 26, 194
Bureau of the Census, 26
Business cycle, income distribution and, 17

CES. *See* Consumer Expenditure Survey
Childbirth, 198
Child care, 5, 88, 97, 202–3
Childless households, 71–72, 75, 77, 82–83, 119
Children: abuse of, 14, 61; additional, expenditures and, 112, 141; adult expenditures and, 6; age of, 82, 99–106, 113, 180–81; allocation decisions and, 23; in black households, 130; characteristics of vs. expenditures on, 2, 28–36, 113; clothing expenditures on, 41–48; cost of, 24, 63, 112–13, 195–202; demand for, 196; distribution of income assumptions and, 5; employment status of, 82; forbid-

215

den goods for, 62; gender of, 31, 113,
203; handicapped, 181; joint custody of,
165–69; legal rights of, 13; lifetime expenditures, 99–106; number of, 8, 96–
99, 107, 144; poverty level and, 9–10,
146–47; remarriage and, 169; savings
and, 87, 96; scale economies and, 105;
schooling expenditures for, 49–52; separability assumption and, 71, 115; time
spent with, 202–3; unrelated, 93; utility
of, 55–57, 62–63, 193; well-being distribution and, 4–5. *See also* Child support;
Expenditure ratios, child-adult
Child support: accelerated payment, 182;
assets and, 172, 177–78; child-adult expenditure ratios and, 158–65; child's age
and, 180; computer program for, 11, 152;
cost-of-living adjustments, 180; custody
and, 165–69; divorce laws and, 24;
household elasticities and, 163; household unit for, 19; income and, 172–77;
income distribution and, 150–51; in-kind
transfers and, 126, 151, 184–85; luck
and, 187; money fungibility and, 10,
170; remarriage and, 169; scale economies and, 157, 161; setting standards for,
152–65; taxes and, 178–80; unemploy-
ment and, 177; utility of, 179
Clothing expenditures: across households,
40–48; adult consumption and, 6, 79,
201; in black households, 84, 108; child-
adult expenditure ratios and, 81; child
characteristics and, 31–36; in female-
headed households, 120; household size
and, 4, 29; intrahousehold distributions,
3; regressions for, 47
Cobb-Douglas function, 67
COLA. *See* Cost-of-Living adjustments
Community property, 134
Competitiveness, 23
Consumer Expenditure Survey (CES), 2, 6,
26–27; Espenshade study and, 199;
1960–61, 115; 1972–73, 77–78; 1981–
82, 205; Turchi study and, 200–202
Consumer Price Index (CPI): computation
of, 26; Espenshade study and, 199; inflation conversions and, 3–4
Consumption: age and, 181; black households, 92; consumption bundle, 2, 31–36,

66; consumption good, 55; decision making, 24; disguised, 20; dollar worth of,
148; education and, 141, 203; estimating
equivalence of, 201; forbidden goods
and, 62; household size and, 27, 97; individual utility and, 60; nonindividual aspects of, 19; observable vs. nonobservable items, 111; private vs. public goods,
204; public good utility and, 72–73; remarriage and, 169–70; savings as, 64,
78, 96. *See also* Expenditure(s)
Contracts, enforcement of, 64
Cost, definition of, 196
Cost-of-living adjustments, 180
CPI. *See* Consumer Price Index
CPS. *See* Current Population Survey
Crime, marital status and, 169
Current Population Survey (CPS), 16, 135–
38
Custody of children, 165–69
Czechoslovakia, 17

Decision making: household as unit for,
151; rules for, 22–24; utility function for,
72
Demand equations, 3, 193
Demand systems, expenditure structure
and, 195, 202
Demographic characteristics: changes in,
115–18; child-adult expenditure ratios
and, 67, 71, 80–81; household size and,
28; intrahousehold distributions and, 14,
204. *See also specific characteristics*
Department of Commerce, 16
Dictatorial behavior, 23
Distribution of income, intrahousehold, 1,
12, 112–13, 131–32; adult expenditure
determination and, 108, 111; basic assumptions, 5; child-adult expenditure ratios and, 6, 82–98; clothing expenditures
and, 40–48; CPS data and, 136–47; decision models for, 22–23; divorce and,
10, 13, 24, 150–90; economic models
and, 3, 15–18; economic trends and, 14;
equivalence scales and, 191–95; expenditure patterns and, 65, 76; government intervention and, 13; household characteristics and, 76, 96–99, 125–30, 141–49,
204; human capital and, 16; income